AWAKE TO TRUTH

---◆---

Find Abundant Life
Through the Transforming Power
of the Word of God

A 31-Day Devotional

General Editor
Clyde Bender

Awake to Truth

All Scripture verses are taken from King James Version, except where noted that the New King James Version was used:

NKJV Prophecy Bible. Copyright © 1983 by Thomas Nelson, Inc. Used by permission of HarperCollins Christian Publishing. www.harpercollinschristian.com

Nelson Study Material
Copyright © 1983 by Thomas Nelson Inc.

Copyright © 2024
All rights reserved. This book or any portion thereof may not be reproduced or used in any manner without the express written permission of the author, except for the use of brief quotations in a book review.

ISBN #: 979-8-218-40694-3

Copy editing and graphic design by Susanna Allen.

Printed in the United States of America, through Amazon Books.

ACKNOWLEDGEMENTS

———◆———

I wish to thank Susanna Allen; her stunning front cover is very appealing. Also, her expertise and mastery of the computer was instrumental in producing this book, of which could have never been published otherwise by me. I will be forever grateful for her tireless and cheerful attitude.

And a thank-you to the King Street Church staff for selflessly sharing their skills in this accomplishment. Surprisingly, the publishing of this book, "The Abundant Life" corresponded exactly to the theme chosen by the pastors for this year's study: "Abundant Life in Christ." This is not by coincidence, having relied on the Holy Spirit's presence in this assignment.

Finally, an appreciation to the personnel at Harper Collins Publishing as permission was granted for the use of the study material. Thank you.

TABLE OF CONTENTS

Acknowledgements

Preface   1

Introduction   Transformation – The Abundant Life   3

Day 1
Placed into God's Family   I John 3:2, "Beloved, Now we are children of God; and it has not yet been revealed what we shall be, but we know that when he is revealed, we shall be like him, for we shall see him as he is."   14

Day 2
God the Father of Believers   Romans 8:15, "For you did not receive the spirit of bondage again to fear, but you received the Spirit of adoption by whom we cry out, "Abba, Father."   18

Table of Contents

Day 3 **The Person of the Son of God**	Isaiah 9:6, "For unto us a Child is born, unto us a Son is given; and the government will be upon His shoulder. And His name will be called Wonderful, Counselor, Mighty God, Everlasting Father, Prince of Peace.	23
Day 4 **New Nature**	II Corinthians 5:17, "Therefore, if anyone is in Christ, he is a new creation; old things have passed away; behold, all things have become new."	31
Day 5 **Christ's Righteousness**	Isaiah 61:10, "I will greatly rejoice in the Lord, my soul shall be joyful in my God; for He has clothed me with the garments of salvation, he has covered me with the robe of righteousness, as a bridegroom decks himself with ornaments, and as a bride adorns herself with her jewels."	38
Day 6 **Free Gift**	Ephesians 2:8, "For by grace you have been saved through faith, and that not of yourselves; it is the gift of God,"	47

Day 7 **New Life: A Free Gift**	Romans 6:23, "For the wages of sin is death, but the gift of God is eternal life in Christ Jesus our Lord."	66
Day 8 **New Life: Based on Christ's Death**	Colossians 1:22, "In the body of His flesh through death, to present you holy, and blameless, and above reproach in His sight—"	81
Day 9 **New Life: Received by Faith**	Acts 16:31, "So they said, "Believe on the Lord Jesus Christ, and you will be saved, you and your household	89
Day 10 **The Right-eousness of Faith**	Romans 10:6-8, "But the righteousness of faith speaks in this way, "Do not say in your heart, 'Who will ascend into heaven?'" (that is, to bring Christ down from above) or, "Who will descend into the abyss?'" (that is, to bring Christ up from the dead). But what does it say? "The word is near you, in your mouth and in your heart" (that is, the word of faith which we preach):"	100

Day 11
Work of the Holy Spirit in Salvation

Titus 3:5, "Not by works of righteousness which we have done, but according to His mercy He saved us, through the washing of regeneration and renewing of the Holy Spirit,"

113

Day 12
The Person of the Holy Spirit

Ephesians 4:3, "Endeavoring to keep the unity of the Spirit in the bond of peace."

127

Day 13
Empowered by God

Acts 1:8, "But you shall receive power when the Holy Spirit has come upon you; and you shall be witnesses to Me in Jerusalem, and in all Judea and Samaria, and to the end of the earth."

135

Day 14
Promise of God

Titus 1:2 "In hope of eternal life which God, who cannot lie, promised before time began,"

140

Day 15
Witness of Spirit

I John 3:24, "Now he who keeps His commandments abides in Him, and He in him. And by this we know that He abides in us, by the Spirit whom He has given us."

146

Day 16 **Changed Life**	I Corinthians 6:11, "And such were some of you. But you were washed, but you were sanctified, but you were justified in the name of the Lord Jesus and by the Spirit of our God."	150
Day 17 **The Work of the Holy Spirit in Christian Living**	I Corinthians 6:19, "Or do you not know that your body is the temple of the Holy Spirit who is in you, whom you have from God, and you are not your own?"	156
Day 18 **God's Word Cleanses**	Psalm 119:9, "How can a young man cleanse his way? By taking heed according to Your word."	167
Day 19 **God's Word Confirms**	John 8:31, "Then Jesus said to those Jews who believed Him, "If you abide in My word, you are My disciples indeed."	174
Day 20 **God's Word Equips**	Proverbs 22:21, "That I may make you know the certainty of the words of truth, that you may answer words of truth to those who send to you?"	182

Table of Contents

Day 21
Confession

I John 1:9, "If we confess our sins, He is faithful and just to forgive us our sins and to cleanse us from all unrighteousness." — 189

Day 22
Walking in the Spirit: Confession

Psalm 73:1, "Truly God is good to Israel, to such as are pure in heart." — 197

Day 23
Walking in the Spirit: Yielding

Romans 12:1, "I beseech you therefore, brethren, by the mercies of God, that you present your bodies a living sacrifice, holy, acceptable to God, which is your reasonable service." — 206

Day 24
Walking in the Spirit: Filling

Ephesians 5:18, "And do not be drunk with wine, in which is dissipation; but be filled with the Spirit," — 214

Day 25
Everlasting Life

John 5:24, "Most assuredly, I say to you, he who hears My word and believes in Him who sent Me has everlasting life, and shall not come into judgment, but has passed from death into life." — 219

Day 26 God the Father of All	Malachi 2:10, "Have we not all one Father? Has not one God created us? Why do we deal treacherously with one another by profaning the covenant of the fathers?"	225
Day 27 Temptation by the World	I John 2:15, "Do not love the world or the things in the world. If anyone loves the world, the love of the Father is not in him."	235
Day 28 Temptation by the Flesh	Mark 14:38, "Watch and pray, lest you enter into temptation. The spirit indeed is willing, but the flesh is weak."	242
Day 29 Temptation by Satan	I Chronicles 21:1, "Now Satan stood up against Israel, and moved David to number Israel."	249
Day 30 Meditating Upon God's Word	Joshua 1:8, "This Book of the Law shall not depart from your mouth, but you shall meditate in it day and night, that you may observe to do according to all that is written in it. For then you will make your way prosperous, and then you will have good success."	265

| Day 31 **Obedience to God's Word** | Deuteronomy 31:12, "Gather the people together, men and women and little ones, and the stranger who is within your gates, that they may hear and that they may learn to fear the Lord your God and carefully observe all the words of this law." | 268 |

PREFACE

―――◆―――

JESUS CHRIST

Luke 2:11
"For there is born to you this day in the city of David a Savior, who is Christ the Lord."

SAVIOR	and	LORD
Righteousness - Right standing with God		Holiness - Placed under the Lordship of Christ

Righteousness (salvation) begins the transformation in the spirit, thus, spilling over and affecting the soul and body (flesh) as maturing in God and His Word continues. Holiness (Christ's Lordship.)

Philippians 2:8-11

"And being found in appearance as a man, He (Jesus) humbled Himself and became obedient to the point of death, even the death of the cross. Therefore God also has highly exalted Him and given Him the name which is above every name, that at the name of Jesus every knee should bow, of those in heaven, and of those on earth, and of those under the earth, and that every tongue should confess that Jesus Christ is Lord, to the glory of God the Father."

FLESH vs. SPIRIT

SOUL
(The Mind, The Will, The Emotions)
~ The Deciding Factor ~

Psalm 119:25-32

"My soul (mind) clings to the dust (flesh);
Revive me according to Your word (spirit).
I have declared my ways, and You answered me;
Teach me Your statutes.
Make me understand the way of Your precepts;
So shall I meditate on Your wonderful works.
My soul melts from heaviness (fleshly nature);
Strengthen me according to Your word (spiritual nature).
Remove from me the way of lying,
And grant me Your law graciously.
I have chosen the way of truth;
Your judgments I have laid before me.
I cling to Your testimonies;
O Lord, do not put me to shame!
I will run the course of Your commandments,
For You shall enlarge my heart."

INTRODUCTION

———•◆•———

"In the beginning God created the heavens and the earth."
Genesis 1:1

"Then God said, 'Let Us make man in Our <u>image</u>, according to Our likeness; let them have dominion over the fish of the sea, over the birds of the air, and over the cattle, over all the earth and over every creeping thing that creeps on the earth.' So God created man in His own <u>image</u>; in the <u>image</u> of God He created him; male and female He created them. Then God blessed them, and God said to them, 'Be fruitful and multiply; fill the earth and subdue it; have dominion over the fish of the sea, over the birds of the air, and over every living thing that moves on the earth.'" Genesis 1:26-28

"And the Lord God formed man of the dust of the ground, and breathed into his nostrils the breath of life; and man became a living being (spirit)." Genesis 2:7

"And they were both naked, the man and his wife, and were not ashamed." Genesis 2:25

"God is Spirit, and those who worship Him must worship in spirit and truth." John 4:24

Since man was created in
the <u>image</u> of God, who is spirit,
then we are <u>spirit</u> at the
first sound of the heart beat
in our mother's womb.

"For You [God] have formed my inward parts; You have covered (woven) me in my mother's womb. I will praise You, for I am fearfully and wonderfully made; Marvelous are Your works, And that my <u>soul</u> knows very well." Psalm 139:13-14

The soul is made up of the mind,
the will, and the emotions.

"Then the Lord God took the man [Adam] and put him in the garden of Eden to tend [cultivate] and keep it. And the Lord God commanded the man, saying, "Of every tree of the garden you may freely eat; but of the tree of the knowledge of good and evil you shall not eat, for in the day that you eat of it you shall surely die." Genesis 2:15-17

"Then the serpent [Satan] said to the woman, 'You will not surely die. For God knows that in the day you eat of it your eyes will be opened, and you will be like God, knowing good and evil.' So when the woman saw that the tree was good for food, that it was pleasant to the eyes, and a tree desirable to make one wise, she took of its fruit and ate. She also gave to her husband with her, and he ate. Then the eyes of both of them were opened, and they knew that they were naked; and they sewed fig leaves together and made themselves coverings." Genesis 3:4-7

Introduction

"I say then: Walk in the Spirit, and you shall not fulfill the lust of the flesh. For the flesh lusts against the Spirit, and the Spirit against the flesh; and these are contrary to one another, so that you do not do the things that you wish." Galatians 5:16-17

"It is the Spirit who gives life; the flesh profits nothing. The <u>words</u> that I speak to you are <u>spirit</u>, and they are <u>life</u>." John 6:63

"For the word of God is living and powerful, and sharper than any two-edged sword, piercing even to the division of soul and spirit, and of joints and marrow, and is a discerner of the thoughts and intents of the heart." Hebrews 4:12

The words of life and of truth from the
Scripture, which are spirit,
are understood through the reborn spirit.
The <u>spirit</u> is the main part
of our being and the only part made new.
Our <u>bodies</u> and <u>souls</u> need some work
to be done on them as indicated
in Romans 12:2, which states,
"Do not be conformed to this world, but be
transformed by the renewing of your <u>mind</u>"
(by God's Words which are
spirit, and life, and truth.)

So then, the way to overcome the flesh, world, and Satan, is to walk in the spirit, and you shall not fulfill the lust of the flesh.

WE MIGHT ASK, BUT HOW?

So the journey begins: (walking it out).

We do not do this by our own efforts,
but with the help and guidance
of the Holy Spirit given at the new birth.
In other words, our born again
human spirit, now in fellowship
and cooperating with God, who is spirit.

Notice the order of importance of the following:
1st Spirit *(no death, everlasting)*
  We are spirit, the core, the heart, main part
2nd Soul *(changeable, unsteady, undecided)*
  We have a soul, the mind, the will and the emotions.
3rd Body *(flesh, return to dust)*
  We live in a body, this earth suit.

The soul can fluctuate between
the dictates of the spirit, or the body (flesh)
and will gravitate to one or the other.
When soul and spirit are aligned
in agreement with God's Word, which is spirit,
the Word of Truth of the Scriptures,
then this will allow the spiritual nature to dominate.
Thus, influencing and exercising control over
the body (flesh) bringing the body under subjection
as transformation takes place.
All of this as the mind is being renewed
by the Word of God.

"Since you have purified your souls in obeying the truth through the Spirit in sincere love of the brethren, love one another fervently with a pure heart, having been born again, not of corruptible seed but incorruptible, through the word of God which lives and abides forever," I Peter 1:22-23

Introduction

In contrast, when soul and body
are aligned in agreement with the
concerns and affairs of this world (secular),
then this will allow the fleshly nature
to dominate, thus hindering the working of
the spirit. Hearts being darkened
and becoming unprofitable,
fulfilling the lust of the flesh."

"But I <u>discipline</u> my <u>body</u> and bring it into <u>subjection</u>, lest, when I have preached to others, I myself should become disqualified." I Corinthians 9:27

"Now the just shall live by faith; But if anyone draws back, My soul has no pleasure in him. But we are not of those who draw back to perdition, but of those who believe to the saving of the soul." Hebrews 10:38-39

"Therefore, my beloved, as you have always obeyed, not as in my presence only, but now much more in my absence, work out your own salvation with fear and trembling; for it is God who works in you both to will and to do for His good pleasure." Philippians 2:12-13

"The thief (devil) does not come except to steal, and to kill, and to destroy. I [Jesus] have come that they may have life, and that they may have it more abundantly." John 10:10

Now in this lifetime,
the abundant life that is promised
and was provided by Jesus' redemptive work,
depends on our behavior concerning
which way our soul is being persuaded.
The mind, the will, the emotions
the deciding factor.

"Beloved, I pray that you may prosper in all things and be in health, just as your soul prospers. For I rejoiced greatly when brethren came and testified of the truth that is in you, just as you walk in the truth. I have no greater joy than to hear that my children walk in truth." 3 John 2-4

WALKING IN THE TRUTH:

This is walking in the truth of God's Word,
and walking in God's Word is walking
in the Spirit, and walking in the Spirit is
walking in the prospering of the soul,
and walking in the prosperous souls is a walk
in the Abundant Life.

In other words, our prospering in the
Abundant Life will correspond to the extent
that our soul prospers.

(All hinges on our thinking.)

FLESH VS SPIRIT

So then, we having been saved and made
righteous (God's part) and back into right
standing with God by way of the new birth and
bound for heaven eternally.
We, here and now, are growing (maturing) unto
holiness (our part) under Christ's Lordship.

"His <u>divine power</u> has given to us all things that pertain to <u>life</u> and <u>godliness</u>, through the knowledge of Him who called us by glory and virtue, by which have been given to us exceedingly great and precious promises, that through these you may be partakers of the divine nature, having escaped the corruption that is in the world through lust." 2 Peter 1:3-4

Being mindful of all of this,
let us seek restored fellowship with God,
which results in the rebirth from our fallen spirit.
Always attentive to the Holy Spirit's
presence in our lives at all times.
Now, recognize the journey well under
way as we continue walking in the Spirit.

"Now the Lord is the Spirit; and where the Spirit of the Lord is, there is liberty. But we all, with unveiled face, beholding as in a mirror the glory of the Lord, are being transformed into the same <u>image</u> from glory to glory, just as by the Spirit of the Lord." 2 Corinthians 3:17-18

"For whom He foreknew, He also predestined to be conformed to the <u>image</u> of His Son, that He might be the firstborn among many brethren." Romans 8:29

"Do not lie to one another, since you have put off the old man with his deeds, and have put on the new man who is renewed in knowledge according to the <u>image</u> of Him who created him." Colossians 3:9-10

"But we are bound to give thanks to God always for you, brethren beloved by the Lord, because God from the beginning chose you for salvation through sanctification by the Spirit and belief in the truth, to which He called you by our gospel, for the obtaining of the glory of our Lord Jesus Christ." 2 Thessalonians 2:13-14

"Now may the God of peace Himself sanctify you completely; and may your whole <u>spirit</u>, <u>soul</u>, and <u>body</u> be preserved blameless at the coming of our Lord Jesus Christ. He who calls you is faithful, who also will do it." I Thessalonians 5:23-24

"Then the Lord knows how to deliver the godly out of temptations and to reserve the unjust under punishment for the day of judgment," 2 Peter 2:9

Now, as we near our journey's end and
are well informed of the
spirit's forever existence, whether it
be joined with the fallen state (eternal death)
or joined with the reborn state (eternal life.)
We, continuing to walk in obedience
to the truth of God's Word (spirit)
staying ready to meet God as our gracious
heavenly father and not as our judge.

"Then the dust will return to the earth as it was, and the spirit will return to God who gave it." Ecclesiastes 12:7

"And I say to you, My friends, do not be afraid of those who kill the body, and after that have no more that they can do. But I will show you whom you should fear: Fear Him who, after He has killed, has power to cast into hell; yes, I say to you, fear Him!" Luke 12:4-5

"He who believes in the Son has everlasting life; and he who does not believe the Son shall not see life, but the wrath of God abides on him." John 3:36

DAY 1

———◆———

Placed Into God's Family

ACTS 17:24-27, 30-31 KJV and v. 28, 29 NKJV

[24] God that made the world and all things therein, seeing that he is Lord of heaven and earth, dwelleth not in temples made with hands;
[25] Neither is worshipped with men's hands, as though he needed any thing, seeing he giveth to all life, and breath, and all things;
[26] And hath made of one blood all nations of men for to dwell on all the face of the earth, and hath determined the times before appointed, and the bounds of their habitation;
[27] That they should seek the Lord, if haply they might feel after him, and find him, though he be not far from every one of us:
[28] for in Him we live and move and have our being, as also some of your own poets have said, 'For we are also His offspring.'
[29] Therefore, since we are the offspring of God, we ought not to think that the Divine Nature is like gold or silver or stone, something shaped by art and man's devising.
[30] And the times of this ignorance God winked at; but now commandeth all men every where to repent:
[31] Because he hath appointed a day, in the which he will judge the world in righteousness by that man [Jesus] whom he hath ordained; whereof he hath given assurance unto all men, in that he hath raised him from the dead.

Day 1: Placed Into God's Family

> In a general sense all men and women are the offspring of God in that He is the Creator. This relationship, however, is not sufficient to offset the penalty of sin, because all persons are sinners separated from God.

ROMANS 3:21, 22, 24-28 KJV, and v. 23 NKJV

[21] But now the righteousness of God without the law is manifested, being witnessed by the law and the prophets;

[22] Even the righteousness of God which is by faith of Jesus Christ unto all and upon all them that believe: for there is no difference:

[23] for all have sinned and fall short of the glory of God,

[24] being justified freely by his grace through the redemption that is in Christ Jesus:

[25] Whom God hath set forth to be a propitiation through faith in his blood, to declare his righteousness for the remission of sins that are past, through the forbearance of God;

[26] To declare, I say, at this time his righteousness: that he might be just, and the justifier of him which believeth in Jesus.

[27] Where is boasting then? It is excluded. By what law? of works? Nay: but by the law of faith.

[28] Therefore we conclude that a man is justified by faith without the deeds of the law.

> Therefore for a sinful person to become a child of God, a miraculous transformation must take place. The Bible refers to this change as being "born again."

JOHN 3:3 NKJV and v. 4-7 KJV

³ Jesus answered and said to him, "Most assuredly, I say to you, unless one is born again, he cannot see the kingdom of God."
⁴ Nicodemus saith unto him, How can a man be born when he is old? can he enter the second time into his mother's womb, and be born?
⁵ Jesus answered, Verily, verily, I say unto thee, Except a man be born of water and of the Spirit, he cannot enter into the kingdom of God.
⁶ That which is born of the flesh is flesh; and that which is born of the Spirit is spirit.
⁷ Marvel not that I said unto thee, Ye must be born again.

When an individual places his faith in Christ as Savior, he is born again into a new, spiritual, family relationship with God.

GALATIANS 3:26 NKJV, and v. 27-29 KJV

²⁶ For you are all sons of God through faith in Christ Jesus.
²⁷ For as many of you as have been baptized into Christ have put on Christ.
²⁸ There is neither Jew nor Greek, there is neither bond nor free, there is neither male nor female: for ye are all one in Christ Jesus.
²⁹ And if ye be Christ's, then are ye Abraham's seed, and heirs according to the promise.

One is no longer in bondage to the master
but becomes a free son possessing
all the rights and privileges of sonship.
One of these benefits is the right to call God
Abba, an affectionate term meaning "Father."

Day 1: Placed Into God's Family

> This marvelous relationship carries
> responsibilities with it, as well as privileges.
> Everyone who has the hope of having
> his sonship perfected someday
> is presently purifying his own life.
> Since he bears the family relationship to God,
> he must also exhibit the family character.

ROMANS 8:14 KJV and v. 15 NKJV

[14] For as many as are led by the Spirit of God, they are the sons of God.

[15] For you did not receive the spirit of bondage again to fear, but you received the Spirit of adoption by whom we cry out, "Abba, Father."

I JOHN 2:28-29 KJV

[28] And now, little children, abide in him; that, when he shall appear, we may have confidence, and not be ashamed before him at his coming.

[29] If ye know that he is righteous, ye know that every one that doeth righteousness is born of him.

I JOHN 3:1-3 KJV

[1] Behold, what manner of love the Father hath bestowed upon us, that we should be called the sons of God: therefore the world knoweth us not, because it knew him not.

[2] Beloved, now are we the sons of God, and it doth not yet appear what we shall be: but we know that, when he shall appear, we shall be like him; for we shall see him as he is.

[3] And every man that hath this hope in him purifieth himself, even as he is pure.

DAY 2

―――◆―――

God the Father of Believers

God is the Father of all who believe
in Christ in a special sense not
shared by unbelievers.
God is called their Father, first of all,
because they have a new standing before Him.
While unbelievers are the offspring of God,
because He created them, they do not
have the standing of sons.
Their standing is rather as condemned
sinners before God the judge.

JOHN 3:14-17, 19, 20 KJV and v. 18 NKJV

[14] And as Moses lifted up the serpent in the wilderness, even so must the Son of man be lifted up:

[15] That whosoever believeth in him should not perish, but have eternal life.

[16] For God so loved the world, that he gave his only begotten Son, that whosoever believeth in him should not perish, but have everlasting life.

[17] For God sent not his Son into the world to condemn the world; but that the world through him might be saved.

[18] He who believes in Him is not condemned; but he who does not believe is condemned already, because he has not believed in the name of the only begotten Son of God.

[19] And this is the condemnation, that light is come into the world, and men loved darkness rather than light, because their deeds were evil.

[20] For every one that doeth evil hateth the light, neither cometh to the light, lest his deeds should be reproved.

> When a person believes in Christ as Savior, his estate is wonderfully changed from grim condemnation to privileged sonship. This new standing grants to all believers the legal right and spiritual privileges of divine sonship: heirs of God and joint heirs with Christ.

ROMANS 8:14-16 KJV and v. 17 NKJV

[14] For as many as are led by the Spirit of God, they are the sons of God.

[15] For ye have not received the spirit of bondage again to fear; but ye have received the Spirit of adoption, whereby we cry, Abba, Father.

[16] The Spirit itself beareth witness with our spirit, that we are the children of God:

[17] and if children, then heirs—heirs of God and joint heirs with Christ, if indeed we suffer with Him, that we may also be glorified together.

> God is the Father of believers also in the sense that He gives them new life.

2 PETER 1:1-3 KJV and v. 4 NKJV

¹ Simon Peter, a servant and an apostle of Jesus Christ, to them that have obtained like precious faith with us through the righteousness of God and our Saviour Jesus Christ:
² Grace and peace be multiplied unto you through the knowledge of God, and of Jesus our Lord,
³ According as his divine power hath given unto us all things that pertain unto life and godliness, through the knowledge of him that hath called us to glory and virtue:
⁴ by which have been given to us exceedingly great and precious promises, that through these you may be partakers of the divine nature, having escaped the corruption that is in the world through lust.

> To obtain God as Father is not a result of one's own merit but a result of Christ's, the one who believes in Christ as Savior enters into the blessed Father-child relationship with God solely on the ground of Christ sonship.

HEBREWS 2:9-16, 18 KJV and v. 17 NKJV

⁹ But we see Jesus, who was made a little lower than the angels for the suffering of death, crowned with glory and honour; that he by the grace of God should taste death for every man.
¹⁰ For it became him, for whom are all things, and by whom are all things, in bringing many sons unto glory, to make the captain of their salvation perfect through sufferings.
¹¹ For both he that sanctifieth and they who are sanctified are all of one: for which cause he is not ashamed to call them brethren,
¹² Saying, I will declare thy name unto my brethren, in the midst of the church will I sing praise unto thee.

¹³ And again, I will put my trust in him. And again, Behold I and the children which God hath given me.

¹⁴ Forasmuch then as the children are partakers of flesh and blood, he also himself likewise took part of the same; that through death he might destroy him that had the power of death, that is, the devil;

¹⁵ And deliver them who through fear of death were all their lifetime subject to bondage.

¹⁶ For verily he took not on him the nature of angels; but he took on him the seed of Abraham.

¹⁷ Therefore, in all things He had to be made like His brethren, that He might be a merciful and faithful High Priest in things pertaining to God, to make propitiation for the sins of the people.

¹⁸ For in that he himself hath suffered being tempted, he is able to succour them that are tempted.

HEBREWS 3:1-2 KJV

¹ Wherefore, holy brethren, partakers of the heavenly calling, consider the Apostle and High Priest of our profession, Christ Jesus;

² Who was faithful to him that appointed him, as also Moses was faithful in all his house.

It is the grand privilege and calling of those who know God as Father to graciously invite unbelievers to meet God as Father and not as judge.

II TIMOTHY 3:10-17 KJV

¹⁰ But thou hast fully known my [Paul's] doctrine, manner of life, purpose, faith, longsuffering, charity, patience,

[11] Persecutions, afflictions, which came unto me at Antioch, at Iconium, at Lystra; what persecutions I endured: but out of them all the Lord delivered me.
[12] Yea, and all that will live godly in Christ Jesus shall suffer persecution.
[13] But evil men and seducers shall wax worse and worse, deceiving, and being deceived.
[14] But continue thou in the things which thou hast learned and hast been assured of, knowing of whom thou hast learned them;
[15] And that from a child thou hast known the holy scriptures, which are able to make thee wise unto salvation through faith which is in Christ Jesus.
[16] All scripture is given by inspiration of God, and is profitable for doctrine, for reproof, for correction, for instruction in righteousness:
[17] That the man of God may be perfect, thoroughly furnished unto all good works.

II TIMOTHY 4:1-2 KJV

[1] I charge thee therefore before God, and the Lord Jesus Christ, who shall judge the quick and the dead at his appearing and his kingdom;
[2] Preach the word; be instant in season, out of season; reprove, rebuke, exhort with all long suffering and doctrine.

DAY 3

The Person of the Son of God

ISAIAH 9:6 NKJV and 7 KJV

⁶ For unto us a Child is born,
Unto us a Son is given;
And the government will be upon His shoulder.
And His name will be called
Wonderful, Counselor, Mighty God,
Everlasting Father, Prince of Peace.
⁷ Of the increase of His government and peace
There will be no end,
Upon the throne of David and over His kingdom,
To order it and establish it with judgment and justice
From that time forward, even forever.
The zeal of the Lord of hosts will perform this.

It is crucial to remember that the existence
of the Son of God did not commence
with his birth in Bethlehem.
He is spoken of as the Son before
he became a man.

GALATIANS 4:4 NKJV, 5-7 KJV

⁴ But when the fullness of the time had come, God sent forth His Son, born of a woman, born under the law,
⁵ to redeem those who were under the law, that we might receive the adoption as sons.
⁶ And because you are sons, God has sent forth the Spirit of His Son into your hearts, crying out, "Abba, Father!"
⁷ Therefore you are no longer a slave but a son, and if a son, then an heir of God through Christ.

Micah prophesies of his birth, but yet states that his "going forth have been from of old, from everlasting."

MICAH 5:2, NKJV

"But you, Bethlehem Ephrathah,
Though you are little among the thousands of Judah,
Yet out of you shall come forth to Me
The One to be Ruler in Israel,
Whose goings forth are from of old,
From everlasting."

He existed "in the beginning" before anything was created.

JOHN 1:1-3, NKJV and 4-18 KJV

¹ In the beginning was the Word, and the Word was with God, and the Word was God.
² He was in the beginning with God.
³ All things were made through Him, and without Him nothing was made that was made.

Day 3: The Person of the Son of God

⁴ In him was life; and the life was the light of men.
⁵ And the light shineth in darkness; and the darkness comprehended it not.
⁶ There was a man sent from God, whose name was John.
⁷ The same came for a witness, to bear witness of the Light, that all men through him might believe.
⁸ He was not that Light, but was sent to bear witness of that Light.
⁹ That was the true Light, which lighteth every man that cometh into the world.
¹⁰ He was in the world, and the world was made by him, and the world knew him not.
¹¹ He came unto his own, and his own received him not.
¹² But as many as received him, to them gave he power to become the sons of God, even to them that believe on his name:
¹³ Which were born, not of blood, nor of the will of the flesh, nor of the will of man, but of God.
¹⁴ And the Word was made flesh, and dwelt among us, (and we beheld his glory, the glory as of the only begotten of the Father,) full of grace and truth.
¹⁵ John bare witness of him, and cried, saying, This was he of whom I spake, He that cometh after me is preferred before me: for he was before me.
¹⁶ And of his fulness have all we received, and grace for grace.
¹⁷ For the law was given by Moses, but grace and truth came by Jesus Christ.
¹⁸ No man hath seen God at any time, the only begotten Son, which is in the bosom of the Father, he hath declared him.

He [Jesus] took on a body permanently when He was conceived in Mary's womb. This incomparable event of God's becoming man in Jesus Christ is called the incarnation. This miracle was prophesied hundreds of years previously.

ISAIAH 7:14, NJKV

[14] Therefore the Lord Himself will give you a sign: Behold, the virgin shall conceive and bear a Son, and shall call His name Immanuel.

This was fulfilled historically in Mary in whose womb the Holy Spirit's power conceived a child.

LUKE 1:30-34, 36-38, KJV and 35 NKJV

[30] And the angel said unto her, Fear not, Mary: for thou hast found favour with God.
[31] And, behold, thou shalt conceive in thy womb, and bring forth a son, and shalt call his name Jesus.
[32] He shall be great, and shall be called the Son of the Highest: and the Lord God shall give unto him the throne of his father David:
[33] And he shall reign over the house of Jacob for ever; and of his kingdom there shall be no end.
[34] Then said Mary unto the angel, How shall this be, seeing I know not a man?
[35] And the angel answered and said to her, "The Holy Spirit will come upon you, and the power of the Highest will overshadow you; therefore, also, that Holy One who is to be born will be called the Son of God.
[36] And, behold, thy cousin Elisabeth, she hath also conceived a son in her old age: and this is the sixth month with her, who was called barren.
[37] For with God nothing shall be impossible.
[38] And Mary said, Behold the handmaid of the Lord; be it unto me according to thy word. And the angel departed from her.

> Thus Christ, the sinless God-man,
> was qualified to become our Redeemer.

HEBREWS 9:11-14, KJV

[11] But Christ being come an high priest of good things to come, by a greater and more perfect tabernacle, not made with hands, that is to say, not of this building;
[12] Neither by the blood of goats and calves, but by his own blood he entered in once into the holy place, having obtained eternal redemption for us.
[13] For if the blood of bulls and of goats, and the ashes of an heifer sprinkling the unclean, sanctifieth to the purifying of the flesh:
[14] How much more shall the blood of Christ, who through the eternal Spirit offered himself without spot to God, purge your conscience from dead works to serve the living God?

EPHESIANS 1:3-14, KJV

[3] Blessed be the God and Father of our Lord Jesus Christ, who hath blessed us with all spiritual blessings in heavenly places in Christ:
[4] According as he hath chosen us in him before the foundation of the world, that we should be holy and without blame before him in love:
[5] Having predestinated us unto the adoption of children by Jesus Christ to himself, according to the good pleasure of his will,
[6] To the praise of the glory of his grace, wherein he hath made us accepted in the beloved.
[7] In whom we have redemption through his blood, the forgiveness of sins, according to the riches of his grace;
8 Wherein he hath abounded toward us in all wisdom and prudence;
[9] Having made known unto us the mystery of his will, according to his good pleasure which he hath purposed in himself:

¹⁰ That in the dispensation of the fulness of times he might gather together in one all things in Christ, both which are in heaven, and which are on earth; even in him:
¹¹ In whom also we have obtained an inheritance, being predestinated according to the purpose of him who worketh all things after the counsel of his own will:
¹² That we should be to the praise of his glory, who first trusted in Christ.
¹³ In whom ye also trusted, after that ye heard the word of truth, the gospel of your salvation: in whom also after that ye believed, ye were sealed with that holy Spirit of promise,
¹⁴ Which is the earnest of our inheritance until the redemption of the purchased possession, unto the praise of his glory.

He was fully God and fully man united in one person forever. Even now, at the right hand of God, He is the God-man.

I TIMOTHY 2:1-4, 6-8 KJV, and 5 NKJV
¹ I [Paul] exhort therefore, that, first of all, supplications, prayers, intercessions, and giving of thanks, be made for all men;
² For kings, and for all that are in authority; that we may lead a quiet and peaceable life in all godliness and honesty.
³ For this is good and acceptable in the sight of God our Saviour;
⁴ Who will have all men to be saved, and to come unto the knowledge of the truth.
⁵ For there is one God and one Mediator between God and men, the Man Christ Jesus,
⁶ Who gave himself a ransom for all, to be testified in due time.
⁷ Whereunto I am ordained a preacher, and an apostle, (I speak the truth in Christ, and lie not;) a teacher of the Gentiles in faith and verity.

⁸ I will therefore that men pray every where, lifting up holy hands, without wrath and doubting.

> The great condescension of the Son of God's becoming a man serves eternally as a perfect model of humility and self-giving love.

PHILIPPIANS 2:1-4, 6-16 KJV, and v. 5 NKJV

¹ If there be therefore any consolation in Christ, if any comfort of love, if any fellowship of the Spirit, if any bowels and mercies,
² Fulfil ye my joy, that ye be likeminded, having the same love, being of one accord, of one mind.
³ Let nothing be done through strife or vainglory; but in lowliness of mind let each esteem other better than themselves.
⁴ Look not every man on his own things, but every man also on the things of others.
⁵ Let this mind be in you, which was also in Christ Jesus:
⁶ Who, being in the form of God, thought it not robbery to be equal with God:
⁷ But made himself of no reputation, and took upon him the form of a servant, and was made in the likeness of men:
⁸ And being found in fashion as a man, he humbled himself, and became obedient unto death, even the death of the cross.
⁹ Wherefore God also hath highly exalted him, and given him a name which is above every name:
¹⁰ That at the name of Jesus every knee should bow, of things in heaven, and things in earth, and things under the earth;
¹¹ And that every tongue should confess that Jesus Christ is Lord, to the glory of God the Father.
¹² Wherefore, my beloved, as ye have always obeyed, not as in my [Paul's] presence only, but now much more in my absence, work out your own salvation with fear and trembling.
¹³ For it is God which worketh in you both to will and to do of his good pleasure.

[14] Do all things without murmurings and disputings:
[15] That ye may be blameless and harmless, the sons of God, without rebuke, in the midst of a crooked and perverse nation, among whom ye shine as lights in the world;
[16] Holding forth the word of life; that I may rejoice in the day of Christ, that I have not run in vain, neither laboured in vain.

DAY 4

---◆---

New Nature

II CORINTHIANS 5:17 NKJV, and 18-21 KJV

[17] Therefore, if anyone is in Christ, he is a new creation; old things have passed away; behold, all things have become new.
[18] And all things are of God, who hath reconciled us to himself by Jesus Christ, and hath given to us the ministry of reconciliation;
[19] To wit, that God was in Christ, reconciling the world unto himself, not imputing their trespasses unto them; and hath committed unto us the word of reconciliation.
[20] Now then we are ambassadors for Christ, as though God did beseech you by us: we pray you in Christ's stead, be ye reconciled to God.
[21] For he hath made him to be sin for us, who knew no sin; that we might be made the righteousness of God in him.

> The term new nature refers to the spiritual transformation that occurs within the inner man when a person believes in Christ as Savior. The Christian is now a new man as opposed to the old man that he was before he became a Christian.

ROMANS 6:3-5, 7-14 KJV and v. 6 NKJV

³ Know ye not, that so many of us as were baptized into Jesus Christ were baptized into his death?

⁴ Therefore we are buried with him by baptism into death: that like as Christ was raised up from the dead by the glory of the Father, even so we also should walk in newness of life.

⁵ For if we have been planted together in the likeness of his death, we shall be also in the likeness of his resurrection:

⁶ Knowing this, that our old man was crucified with Him, that the body of sin might be done away with, that we should no longer be slaves of sin.

⁷ For he that is dead is freed from sin.

⁸ Now if we be dead with Christ, we believe that we shall also live with him:

⁹ Knowing that Christ being raised from the dead dieth no more; death hath no more dominion over him.

¹⁰ For in that he died, he died unto sin once: but in that he liveth, he liveth unto God.

¹¹ Likewise reckon ye also yourselves to be dead indeed unto sin, but alive unto God through Jesus Christ our Lord.

¹² Let not sin therefore reign in your mortal body, that ye should obey it in the lusts thereof.

¹³ Neither yield ye your members as instruments of unrighteousness unto sin: but yield yourselves unto God, as those that are alive from the dead, and your members as instruments of righteousness unto God.

¹⁴ For sin shall not have dominion over you: for ye are not under the law, but under grace.

EPHESIANS 2:1-14, 16-22 KJV, and v.15 NKJV

¹ And you hath he quickened, who were dead in trespasses and sins;

² Wherein in time past ye walked according to the course of this world, according to the prince of the power of the air, the spirit that now worketh in the children of disobedience:

Day 4: New Nature

³ Among whom also we all had our conversation in times past in the lusts of our flesh, fulfilling the desires of the flesh and of the mind; and were by nature the children of wrath, even as others.

⁴ But God, who is rich in mercy, for his great love wherewith he loved us,

⁵ Even when we were dead in sins, hath quickened us together with Christ, (by grace ye are saved;)

⁶ And hath raised us up together, and made us sit together in heavenly places in Christ Jesus:

⁷ That in the ages to come he might shew the exceeding riches of his grace in his kindness toward us through Christ Jesus.

⁸ For by grace are ye saved through faith; and that not of yourselves: it is the gift of God:

⁹ Not of works, lest any man should boast.

¹⁰ For we are his workmanship, created in Christ Jesus unto good works, which God hath before ordained that we should walk in them.

¹¹ Wherefore remember, that ye being in time past Gentiles in the flesh, who are called Uncircumcision by that which is called the Circumcision in the flesh made by hands;

¹² That at that time ye were without Christ, being aliens from the commonwealth of Israel, and strangers from the covenants of promise, having no hope, and without God in the world:

¹³ But now in Christ Jesus ye who sometimes were far off are made nigh by the blood of Christ.

¹⁴ For he is our peace, who hath made both one, and hath broken down the middle wall of partition between us;

¹⁵ Having abolished in his flesh the enmity, even the law of commandments contained in ordinances; for to make in himself of twain one new man, so making peace;

¹⁶ And that he might reconcile both unto God in one body by the cross, having slain the enmity thereby:

¹⁷ And came and preached peace to you which were afar off, and to them that were nigh.

¹⁸ For through him we both have access by one Spirit unto the Father.

¹⁹ Now therefore ye are no more strangers and foreigners, but fellow citizens with the saints, and of the household of God;
²⁰ And are built upon the foundation of the apostles and prophets, Jesus Christ himself being the chief corner stone;
²¹ In whom all the building fitly framed together groweth unto an holy temple in the Lord:
²² In whom ye also are builded together for an habitation of God through the Spirit.

The Christian, he is not the old man
renovated or refreshed; he is a brand-new man
with a new family, a new set of values,
new motivations, and new possessions.
The old man is still present in the new life and
expresses himself in corrupting deeds
such as lying. The new man, to be visible,
must be put on as one would put on a
new suit of clothes.

EPHESIANS 4:17-21, 25-32 KJV, and v. 22-24 NKJV

¹⁷ This I [Paul] say therefore, and testify in the Lord, that ye henceforth walk not as other Gentiles walk, in the vanity of their mind,
¹⁸ Having the understanding darkened, being alienated from the life of God through the ignorance that is in them, because of the blindness of their heart:
¹⁹ Who being past feeling have given themselves over unto lasciviousness, to work all uncleanness with greediness.
²⁰ But ye have not so learned Christ;
²¹ If so be that ye have heard him, and have been taught by him, as the truth is in Jesus:
²² that you put off, concerning your former conduct, the old man which grows corrupt according to the deceitful lusts,
²³ and be renewed in the spirit of your mind,

Day 4: New Nature

²⁴ and that you put on the new man which was created according to God, in true righteousness and holiness.
²⁵ Wherefore putting away lying, speak every man truth with his neighbour: for we are members one of another.
²⁶ Be ye angry, and sin not: let not the sun go down upon your wrath:
²⁷ Neither give place to the devil.
²⁸ Let him that stole steal no more: but rather let him labour, working with his hands the thing which is good, that he may have to give to him that needeth.
²⁹ Let no corrupt communication proceed out of your mouth, but that which is good to the use of edifying, that it may minister grace unto the hearers.
³⁰ And grieve not the holy Spirit of God, whereby ye are sealed unto the day of redemption.
³¹ Let all bitterness, and wrath, and anger, and clamour, and evil speaking, be put away from you, with all malice:
³² And be ye kind one to another, tenderhearted, forgiving one another, even as God for Christ's sake hath forgiven you.

COLOSSIANS 3:1-8, 11-17 KJV, and v. 9-10 NKJV

¹ If ye then be risen with Christ, seek those things which are above, where Christ sitteth on the right hand of God.
² Set your affection on things above, not on things on the earth.
³ For ye are dead, and your life is hid with Christ in God.
⁴ When Christ, who is our life, shall appear, then shall ye also appear with him in glory.
⁵ Mortify therefore your members which are upon the earth; fornication, uncleanness, inordinate affection, evil concupiscence, and covetousness, which is idolatry:
⁶ For which things' sake the wrath of God cometh on the children of disobedience:
⁷ In the which ye also walked some time, when ye lived in them.
⁸ But now ye also put off all these; anger, wrath, malice, blasphemy, filthy communication out of your mouth.
⁹ Do not lie to one another, since you have put off the old man with his deeds,

[10] and have put on the new man who is renewed in knowledge according to the image of Him who created him,

[11] Where there is neither Greek nor Jew, circumcision nor uncircumcision, Barbarian, Scythian, bond nor free: but Christ is all, and in all.

[12] Put on therefore, as the elect of God, holy and beloved, bowels of mercies, kindness, humbleness of mind, meekness, longsuffering;

[13] Forbearing one another, and forgiving one another, if any man have a quarrel against any: even as Christ forgave you, so also do ye.

[14] And above all these things put on charity, which is the bond of perfectness.

[15] And let the peace of God rule in your hearts, to the which also ye are called in one body; and be ye thankful.

[16] Let the word of Christ dwell in you richly in all wisdom; teaching and admonishing one another in psalms and hymns and spiritual songs, singing with grace in your hearts to the Lord.

[17] And whatsoever ye do in word or deed, do all in the name of the Lord Jesus, giving thanks to God and the Father by him.

In other words, the new nature must be cultivated or nurtured by spiritual decisiveness to grow in Christ. We must not revert to putting on the old suit of the former life: rather, we must continue to grow in this new life.

EPHESIANS 5:8 NKJV, and v. 9-21 KJV

[8] For you were once darkness, but now you are light in the Lord. Walk as children of light

[9] (For the fruit of the Spirit is in all goodness and righteousness and truth;)

[10] Proving what is acceptable unto the Lord.

[11] And have no fellowship with the unfruitful works of darkness, but rather reprove them.

¹² For it is a shame even to speak of those things which are done of them in secret.
¹³ But all things that are reproved are made manifest by the light: for whatsoever doth make manifest is light.
¹⁴ Wherefore he saith, Awake thou that sleepest, and arise from the dead, and Christ shall give thee light.
¹⁵ See then that ye walk circumspectly, not as fools, but as wise,
¹⁶ Redeeming the time, because the days are evil.
¹⁷ Wherefore be ye not unwise, but understanding what the will of the Lord is.
¹⁸ And be not drunk with wine, wherein is excess; but be filled with the Spirit;
¹⁹ Speaking to yourselves in psalms and hymns and spiritual songs, singing and making melody in your heart to the Lord;
²⁰ Giving thanks always for all things unto God and the Father in the name of our Lord Jesus Christ;
²¹ Submitting yourselves one to another in the fear of God.

The message of the new nature is a message of supreme hope: the Spirit of God can accomplish a life-changing transformation for all who will only believe in Christ.

DAY 5

Christ's Righteousness

ISAIAH 61:8-9, 11 KJV, and v. 10 NKJV

⁸ For I the Lord love judgment, I hate robbery for burnt offering; and I will direct their work in truth, and I will make an everlasting covenant with them.
⁹ And their seed shall be known among the Gentiles, and their offspring among the people: all that see them shall acknowledge them, that they are the seed which the Lord hath blessed.
¹⁰ I will greatly rejoice in the Lord,
My soul shall be joyful in my God;
For He has clothed me with the garments of salvation,
He has covered me with the robe of righteousness,
As a bridegroom decks himself with ornaments,
And as a bride adorns herself with her jewels.
¹¹ For as the earth bringeth forth her bud, and as the garden causeth the things that are sown in it to spring forth; so the Lord God will cause righteousness and praise to spring forth before all the nations.

Day 5: Christ's Righteousness

One of the most awesome requirement of God made upon men and women is that they be righteous, that is, conform to His ethical and moral standards.

PSALM 15:1, 3-5 KJV, and v. 2 NKJV

¹ Lord, who shall abide in thy tabernacle? who shall dwell in thy holy hill?
² He who walks uprightly,
And works righteousness,
And speaks the truth in his heart;
³ He that backbiteth not with his tongue, nor doeth evil to his neighbour, nor taketh up a reproach against his neighbour.
⁴ In whose eyes a vile person is contemned; but he honoureth them that fear the Lord. He that sweareth to his own hurt, and changeth not.
⁵ He that putteth not out his money to usury, nor taketh reward against the innocent. He that doeth these things shall never be moved.

PSALM 16:1-11 KJV

¹ Preserve me, O God: for in thee do I put my trust.
² O my soul, thou hast said unto the Lord, Thou art my Lord: my goodness extendeth not to thee;
³ But to the saints that are in the earth, and to the excellent, in whom is all my delight.
⁴ Their sorrows shall be multiplied that hasten after another god: their drink offerings of blood will I not offer, nor take up their names into my lips.
⁵ The Lord is the portion of mine inheritance and of my cup: thou maintainest my lot.
⁶ The lines are fallen unto me in pleasant places; yea, I have a goodly heritage.

⁷ I will bless the Lord, who hath given me counsel: my reins also instruct me in the night seasons.
⁸ I have set the Lord always before me: because he is at my right hand, I shall not be moved.
⁹ Therefore my heart is glad, and my glory rejoiceth: my flesh also shall rest in hope.
¹⁰ For thou wilt not leave my soul in hell; neither wilt thou suffer thine Holy One to see corruption.
¹¹ Thou wilt shew me the path of life: in thy presence is fulness of joy; at thy right hand there are pleasures for evermore.

MICAH 6:8 NKJV

He has shown you, O man, what is good;
And what does the Lord require of you
But to do justly,
To love mercy,
And to walk humbly with your God?

Since God is holy, He cannot allow sinners into His presence.

JEREMIAH 23:5-8 KJV

⁵ Behold, the days come, saith the Lord, that I will raise unto David a righteous Branch, and a King shall reign and prosper, and shall execute judgment and justice in the earth.
⁶ In his days Judah shall be saved, and Israel shall dwell safely: and this is his name whereby he shall be called, The Lord Our Righteousness.
⁷ Therefore, behold, the days come, saith the Lord, that they shall no more say, The Lord liveth, which brought up the children of Israel out of the land of Egypt;
⁸ But, The Lord liveth, which brought up and which led the seed of the house of Israel out of the north country, and from all countries whither I had driven them; and they shall dwell in their own land.

Day 5: Christ's Righteousness

I PETER 1:13-23 KJV

[13] Wherefore gird up the loins of your mind, be sober, and hope to the end for the grace that is to be brought unto you at the revelation of Jesus Christ;

[14] As obedient children, not fashioning yourselves according to the former lusts in your ignorance:

[15] But as he which hath called you is holy, so be ye holy in all manner of conversation;

[16] Because it is written, Be ye holy; for I am holy.

[17] And if ye call on the Father, who without respect of persons judgeth according to every man's work, pass the time of your sojourning here in fear:

[18] Forasmuch as ye know that ye were not redeemed with corruptible things, as silver and gold, from your vain conversation received by tradition from your fathers;

[19] But with the precious blood of Christ, as of a lamb without blemish and without spot:

[20] Who verily was foreordained before the foundation of the world, but was manifest in these last times for you,

[21] Who by him do believe in God, that raised him up from the dead, and gave him glory; that your faith and hope might be in God.

[22] Seeing ye have purified your souls in obeying the truth through the Spirit unto unfeigned love of the brethren, see that ye love one another with a pure heart fervently:

[23] Being born again, not of corruptible seed, but of incorruptible, by the word of God, which liveth and abideth for ever.

> Since all persons are sinners, they could not be saved apart from the super-natural intervention of God.

ROMANS 3:21-22, 24-26 KJV, and v. 23 NJKV

²¹ But now the righteousness of God without the law is manifested, being witnessed by the law and the prophets;
²² Even the righteousness of God which is by faith of Jesus Christ unto all and upon all them that believe: for there is no difference:
²³ For all have sinned and fall short of the glory of God,
²⁴ Being justified freely by his grace through the redemption that is in Christ Jesus:
²⁵ Whom God hath set forth to be a propitiation through faith in his blood, to declare his righteousness for the remission of sins that are past, through the forbearance of God;
²⁶ To declare, I say, at this time his righteousness: that he might be just, and the justifier of him which believeth in Jesus.

II TIMOTHY 1:6-10 KJV

⁶ Wherefore I put thee in remembrance that thou stir up the gift of God, which is in thee by the putting on of my [Paul's] hands.
⁷ For God hath not given us the spirit of fear; but of power, and of love, and of a sound mind.
⁸ Be not thou therefore ashamed of the testimony of our Lord, nor of me his prisoner: but be thou partaker of the afflictions of the gospel according to the power of God;
⁹ Who hath saved us, and called us with an holy calling, not according to our works, but according to his own purpose and grace, which was given us in Christ Jesus before the world began,
¹⁰ But is now made manifest by the appearing of our Saviour Jesus Christ, who hath abolished death, and hath brought life and immortality to light through the gospel:

> The righteous demands of God coupled
> with the inability of man might present an
> insoluble dilemma. God Himself, however,
> has graciously solved the problem.
> He sent Christ, who never sinned, to die for our
> sins and thus satisfy His own wrath toward us.
> Simply put, it means that God, at the cross, treated
> Christ as though He had committed our sins even
> though He was righteous.
> On the other hand, when we believe in Christ,
> He treats us as though we were
> as righteous as Christ.

II CORINTHIANS 5:17-20 KJV, and v. 21 NKJV

[17] Therefore if any man be in Christ, he is a new creature: old things are passed away; behold, all things are become new.
[18] And all things are of God, who hath reconciled us to himself by Jesus Christ, and hath given to us the ministry of reconciliation;
[19] To wit, that God was in Christ, reconciling the world unto himself, not imputing their trespasses unto them; and hath committed unto us the word of reconciliation.
[20] Now then we are ambassadors for Christ, as though God did beseech you by us: we pray you in Christ's stead, be ye reconciled to God.
[21] For He made Him who knew no sin to be sin for us, that we might become the righteousness of God in Him.

ISAIAH 53:10-12 KJV

[10] Yet it pleased the Lord to bruise him; he hath put him to grief: when thou shalt make his soul an offering for sin, he shall see his seed, he shall prolong his days, and the pleasure of the Lord shall prosper in his hand.

¹¹ He shall see of the travail of his soul, and shall be satisfied: by his knowledge shall my righteous servant justify many; for he shall bear their iniquities.
¹² Therefore will I divide him a portion with the great, and he shall divide the spoil with the strong; because he hath poured out his soul unto death: and he was numbered with the transgressors; and he bare the sin of many, and made intercession for the transgressors.

The Bible calls this type of righteousness
"imputed righteousness."
That simply means that God puts to
our spiritual account the very worth of Christ,
much as though he were a banker adding an
inexhaustible deposit to our bank account.

ROMANS 4:3-5 KJV, and v. 6 NKJV

³ For what saith the scripture? Abraham believed God, and it was counted unto him for righteousness.
⁴ Now to him that worketh is the reward not reckoned of grace, but of debt.
⁵ But to him that worketh not, but believeth on him that justifieth the ungodly, his faith is counted for righteousness.
⁶ Just as David also describes the blessedness of the man to whom God imputes righteousness apart from works:

There are, sadly, many people who still
refuse to believe that such an abundant blessing
can be theirs as a free gift.

Day 5: Christ's Righteousness

EPHESIANS 2:4-7, 10 KJV, and v. 8-9 NKJV

⁴ But God, who is rich in mercy, for his great love wherewith he loved us,

⁵ Even when we were dead in sins, hath quickened us together with Christ, (by grace ye are saved;)

⁶ And hath raised us up together, and made us sit together in heavenly places in Christ Jesus:

⁷ That in the ages to come he might shew the exceeding riches of his grace in his kindness toward us through Christ Jesus.

⁸ For by grace you have been saved through faith, and that not of yourselves; it is the gift of God,

⁹ Not of works, lest anyone should boast.

¹⁰ For we are his workmanship, created in Christ Jesus unto good works, which God hath before ordained that we should walk in them.

Nevertheless, the Bible clearly urges
all men to trust in Jesus Christ as Savior and
thus be reckoned as righteous by God.

ROMANS 4:16-23, 25 KJV, and v. 24 NKJV

¹⁶ Therefore it is of faith, that it might be by grace; to the end the promise might be sure to all the seed; not to that only which is of the law, but to that also which is of the faith of Abraham; who is the father of us all,

¹⁷ (As it is written, I have made thee a father of many nations,) before him whom he believed, even God, who quickeneth the dead, and calleth those things which be not as though they were.

¹⁸ Who against hope believed in hope, that he might become the father of many nations, according to that which was spoken, So shall thy seed be.

¹⁹ And being not weak in faith, he considered not his own body now dead, when he was about an hundred years old, neither yet the deadness of Sarah's womb:

[20] He staggered not at the promise of God through unbelief; but was strong in faith, giving glory to God;
[21] And being fully persuaded that, what he had promised, he was able also to perform.
[22] And therefore it was imputed to him for righteousness.
[23] Now it was not written for his sake alone, that it was imputed to him;
[24] But for us also, to whom it shall be imputed, if we believe on him that raised up Jesus our Lord from the dead;
[25] Who was delivered for our offences, and was raised again for our justification.

ROMANS 5:1-2 KJV

[1] Therefore being justified by faith, we have peace with God through our Lord Jesus Christ:
[2] By whom also we have access by faith into this grace wherein we stand, and rejoice in hope of the glory of God.

DAY 6

―――◆―――

Free Gift

EPHESIANS 2:8-10 KJV

[8] For by grace are ye saved through faith; and that not of yourselves: it is the gift of God:
[9] Not of works, lest any man should boast.
[10] For we are his workmanship, created in Christ Jesus unto good works, which God hath before ordained that we should walk in them.

ROMANS 5:8-21 KJV

[8] But God commendeth his love toward us, in that, while we were yet sinners, Christ died for us.
[9] Much more then, being now justified by his blood, we shall be saved from wrath through him.
[10] For if, when we were enemies, we were reconciled to God by the death of his Son, much more, being reconciled, we shall be saved by his life.
[11] And not only so, but we also joy in God through our Lord Jesus Christ, by whom we have now received the atonement.
[12] Wherefore, as by one man [Adam] sin entered into the world, and death by sin; and so death passed upon all men, for that all have sinned:

¹³ (For until the law sin was in the world: but sin is not imputed when there is no law.
¹⁴ Nevertheless death reigned from Adam to Moses, even over them that had not sinned after the similitude of Adam's transgression, who is the figure of him that was to come.
¹⁵ But not as the offence, so also is the free gift. For if through the offence of one many be dead, much more the grace of God, and the gift by grace, which is by one man, Jesus Christ, hath abounded unto many.
¹⁶ And not as it was by one that sinned, so is the gift: for the judgment was by one to condemnation, but the free gift is of many offences unto justification.
¹⁷ For if by one man's offence death reigned by one; much more they which receive abundance of grace and of the gift of righteousness shall reign in life by one, Jesus Christ.)
¹⁸ Therefore as by the offence of one judgment came upon all men to condemnation; even so by the righteousness of one the free gift came upon all men unto justification of life.
¹⁹ For as by one man's disobedience many were made sinners, so by the obedience of one shall many be made righteous.
²⁰ Moreover the law entered, that the offence might abound. But where sin abounded, grace did much more abound:
²¹ That as sin hath reigned unto death, even so might grace reign through righteousness unto eternal life by Jesus Christ our Lord.

⟫ SALVATION IN JESUS ⟪

JOHN 3:16 KJV

For God so loved the world, that he gave his only begotten Son, that whosoever believeth in him should not perish, but have everlasting life.

EPHESIANS 1:3-23 KJV

³ Blessed be the God and Father of our Lord Jesus Christ, who hath blessed us with all spiritual blessings in heavenly places in Christ:

Day 6: Free Gift

⁴ According as he hath chosen us in him before the foundation of the world, that we should be holy and without blame before him in love:

⁵ Having predestinated us unto the adoption of children by Jesus Christ to himself, according to the good pleasure of his will,

⁶ To the praise of the glory of his grace, wherein he hath made us accepted in the beloved.

⁷ In whom we have redemption through his blood, the forgiveness of sins, according to the riches of his grace;

⁸ Wherein he hath abounded toward us in all wisdom and prudence;

⁹ Having made known unto us the mystery of his will, according to his good pleasure which he hath purposed in himself:

¹⁰ That in the dispensation of the fulness of times he might gather together in one all things in Christ, both which are in heaven, and which are on earth; even in him:

¹¹ In whom also we have obtained an inheritance, being predestinated according to the purpose of him who worketh all things after the counsel of his own will:

¹² That we should be to the praise of his glory, who first trusted in Christ.

¹³ In whom ye also trusted, after that ye heard the word of truth, the gospel of your salvation: in whom also after that ye believed, ye were sealed with that holy Spirit of promise,

¹⁴ Which is the earnest of our inheritance until the redemption of the purchased possession, unto the praise of his glory.

¹⁵ Wherefore I [Paul] also, after I heard of your faith in the Lord Jesus, and love unto all the saints,

¹⁶ Cease not to give thanks for you, making mention of you in my prayers;

¹⁷ That the God of our Lord Jesus Christ, the Father of glory, may give unto you the spirit of wisdom and revelation in the knowledge of him:

¹⁸ The eyes of your understanding being enlightened; that ye may know what is the hope of his calling, and what the riches of the glory of his inheritance in the saints,

¹⁹ And what is the exceeding greatness of his power to us-ward who believe, according to the working of his mighty power,
²⁰ Which he wrought in Christ, when he raised him from the dead, and set him at his own right hand in the heavenly places,
²¹ Far above all principality, and power, and might, and dominion, and every name that is named, not only in this world, but also in that which is to come:
²² And hath put all things under his feet, and gave him to be the head over all things to the church,
²³ Which is his body, the fulness of him that filleth all in all.

EPHESIANS 3:14-21 KJV

¹⁴ For this cause I [Paul] bow my knees unto the Father of our Lord Jesus Christ,
¹⁵ Of whom the whole family in heaven and earth is named,
¹⁶ That he would grant you, according to the riches of his glory, to be strengthened with might by his Spirit in the inner man;
¹⁷ That Christ may dwell in your hearts by faith; that ye, being rooted and grounded in love,
¹⁸ May be able to comprehend with all saints what is the breadth, and length, and depth, and height;
¹⁹ And to know the love of Christ, which passeth knowledge, that ye might be filled with all the fulness of God.
²⁰ Now unto him that is able to do exceeding abundantly above all that we ask or think, according to the power that worketh in us,
²¹ Unto him be glory in the church by Christ Jesus throughout all ages, world without end. Amen.

⫸ WISDOM ⫷

JAMES 1:5-8 KJV

⁵ If any of you lack wisdom, let him ask of God, that giveth to all men liberally, and upbraideth not; and it shall be given him.
⁶ But let him ask in faith, nothing wavering. For he that wavereth is like a wave of the sea driven with the wind and tossed.

⁷ For let not that man think that he shall receive any thing of the Lord.
⁸ A double minded man is unstable in all his ways.

JAMES 3:13-18 KJV

¹³ Who is a wise man and endued with knowledge among you? let him shew out of a good conversation his works with meekness of wisdom.
¹⁴ But if ye have bitter envying and strife in your hearts, glory not, and lie not against the truth.
¹⁵ This wisdom descendeth not from above, but is earthly, sensual, devilish.
¹⁶ For where envying and strife is, there is confusion and every evil work.
¹⁷ But the wisdom that is from above is first pure, then peaceable, gentle, and easy to be intreated, full of mercy and good fruits, without partiality, and without hypocrisy.
¹⁸ And the fruit of righteousness is sown in peace of them that make peace.

⇛ HOLY SPIRIT ⇚

LUKE 11:13 KJV

If ye then, being evil, know how to give good gifts unto your children: how much more shall your heavenly Father give the Holy Spirit to them that ask him?

ACTS 8:18-23 KJV

¹⁸ And when Simon saw that through laying on of the apostles' hands the Holy Ghost was given, he offered them money,
¹⁹ Saying, Give me also this power, that on whomsoever I lay hands, he may receive the Holy Ghost.
²⁰ But Peter said unto him, Thy money perish with thee, because thou hast thought that the gift of God may be purchased with money.

²¹ Thou hast neither part nor lot in this matter: for thy heart is not right in the sight of God.
²² Repent therefore of this thy wickedness, and pray God, if perhaps the thought of thine heart may be forgiven thee.
²³ For I perceive that thou art in the gall of bitterness, and in the bond of iniquity.

❯❯❯ REPENTANCE ❮❮❮

ACTS 11:12-18 KJV

¹² Then the Spirit told me [Peter] to go with them, doubting nothing. Moreover these six brethren accompanied me, and we entered the man's house.
¹³ And he shewed us how he had seen an angel in his house, which stood and said unto him, Send men to Joppa, and call for Simon, whose surname is Peter;
¹⁴ Who shall tell thee words, whereby thou and all thy house shall be saved.
¹⁵ And as I began to speak, the Holy Ghost fell on them, as on us at the beginning.
¹⁶ Then remembered I the word of the Lord, how that he said, John indeed baptized with water; but ye shall be baptized with the Holy Ghost.
¹⁷ Forasmuch then as God gave them the like gift as he did unto us, who believed on the Lord Jesus Christ; what was I, that I could withstand God?
¹⁸ When they heard these things, they held their peace, and glorified God, saying, Then hath God also to the Gentiles granted repentance unto life.

II PETER 3:9 KJV

The Lord is not slack concerning his promise, as some men count slackness; but is longsuffering to us-ward, not willing that any should perish, but that all should come to repentance.

⇛ BY GRACE ⇚

I PETER 4:7-14 KJV

⁷ But the end of all things is at hand: be ye therefore sober, and watch unto prayer.

⁸ And above all things have fervent charity among yourselves: for charity shall cover the multitude of sins.

⁹ Use hospitality one to another without grudging.

¹⁰ As every man hath received the gift, even so minister the same one to another, as good stewards of the manifold grace of God.

¹¹ If any man speak, let him speak as the oracles of God; if any man minister, let him do it as of the ability which God giveth: that God in all things may be glorified through Jesus Christ, to whom be praise and dominion for ever and ever. Amen.

¹² Beloved, think it not strange concerning the fiery trial which is to try you, as though some strange thing happened unto you:

¹³ But rejoice, inasmuch as ye are partakers of Christ's sufferings; that, when his glory shall be revealed, ye may be glad also with exceeding joy.

¹⁴ If ye be reproached for the name of Christ, happy are ye; for the spirit of glory and of God resteth upon you: on their part he is evil spoken of, but on your part he is glorified.

JAMES 4:4-8 KJV

⁴ Ye adulterers and adulteresses, know ye not that the friendship of the world is enmity with God? whosoever therefore will be a friend of the world is the enemy of God.

⁵ Do ye think that the scripture saith in vain, The spirit that dwelleth in us lusteth to envy?

⁶ But he giveth more grace. Wherefore he saith, God resisteth the proud, but giveth grace unto the humble.

⁷ Submit yourselves therefore to God. Resist the devil, and he will flee from you.

⁸ Draw nigh to God, and he will draw nigh to you. Cleanse your hands, ye sinners; and purify your hearts, ye double minded.

ACTS 20:32 KJV

And now, brethren, I commend you to God, and to the word of his grace, which is able to build you up, and to give you an inheritance among all them which are sanctified.

II PETER 3:17-18 KJV

[17] Ye therefore, beloved, seeing ye know these things before, beware lest ye also, being led away with the error of the wicked, fall from your own steadfastness.
[18] But grow in grace, and in the knowledge of our Lord and Saviour Jesus Christ. To him be glory both now and for ever. Amen.

I CORINTHIANS 1:2-9 KJV

[2] Unto the church of God which is at Corinth, to them that are sanctified in Christ Jesus, called to be saints, with all that in every place call upon the name of Jesus Christ our Lord, both their's and our's:
[3] Grace be unto you, and peace, from God our Father, and from the Lord Jesus Christ.
[4] I [Paul] thank my God always on your behalf, for the grace of God which is given you by Jesus Christ;
[5] That in every thing ye are enriched by him, in all utterance, and in all knowledge;
[6] Even as the testimony of Christ was confirmed in you:
[7] So that ye come behind in no gift; waiting for the coming of our Lord Jesus Christ:
[8] Who shall also confirm you unto the end, that ye may be blameless in the day of our Lord Jesus Christ.
[9] God is faithful, by whom ye were called unto the fellowship of his Son Jesus Christ our Lord.

2 CORINTHIANS 1:2-11 KJV

[2] Grace be to you and peace from God our Father, and from the Lord Jesus Christ.
[3] Blessed be God, even the Father of our Lord Jesus Christ, the Father of mercies, and the God of all comfort;

⁴ Who comforteth us in all our tribulation, that we may be able to comfort them which are in any trouble, by the comfort wherewith we ourselves are comforted of God.

⁵ For as the sufferings of Christ abound in us, so our consolation also aboundeth by Christ.

⁶ And whether we be afflicted, it is for your consolation and salvation, which is effectual in the enduring of the same sufferings which we also suffer: or whether we be comforted, it is for your consolation and salvation.

⁷ And our hope of you is steadfast, knowing, that as ye are partakers of the sufferings, so shall ye be also of the consolation.

⁸ For we would not, brethren, have you ignorant of our trouble which came to us in Asia, that we were pressed out of measure, above strength, insomuch that we despaired even of life:

⁹ But we had the sentence of death in ourselves, that we should not trust in ourselves, but in God which raiseth the dead:

¹⁰ Who delivered us from so great a death, and doth deliver: in whom we trust that he will yet deliver us;

¹¹ Ye also helping together by prayer for us, that for the gift bestowed upon us by the means of many persons thanks may be given by many on our behalf.

⇉ THROUGH FAITH ⇇

ROMANS 4:1-6 KJV

¹ What shall we say then that Abraham our father, as pertaining to the flesh, hath found?

² For if Abraham were justified by works, he hath whereof to glory; but not before God.

³ For what saith the scripture? Abraham believed God, and it was counted unto him for righteousness.

⁴ Now to him that worketh is the reward not reckoned of grace, but of debt.

⁵ But to him that worketh not, but believeth on him that justifieth the ungodly, his faith is counted for righteousness.

⁶ Even as David also describeth the blessedness of the man, unto whom God imputeth righteousness without works,

ROMANS 11:6 KJV

And if by grace, then is it no more of works: otherwise grace is no more grace. But if it be of works, then it is no more grace: otherwise work is no more work.

II TIMOTHY 1:6-10 KJV

⁶ Wherefore I [Paul] put thee in remembrance that thou stir up the gift of God, which is in thee by the putting on of my hands.
⁷ For God hath not given us the spirit of fear; but of power, and of love, and of a sound mind.
⁸ Be not thou therefore ashamed of the testimony of our Lord, nor of me his prisoner: but be thou partaker of the afflictions of the gospel according to the power of God;
⁹ Who hath saved us, and called us with an holy calling, not according to our works, but according to his own purpose and grace, which was given us in Christ Jesus before the world began,
¹⁰ But is now made manifest by the appearing of our Saviour Jesus Christ, who hath abolished death, and hath brought life and immortality to light through the gospel:

EPHESIANS 2:8-10 KJV

⁸ For by grace are ye saved through faith; and that not of yourselves: it is the gift of God:
⁹ Not of works, lest any man should boast.
¹⁰ For we are his workmanship, created in Christ Jesus unto good works, which God hath before ordained that we should walk in them.

ROMANS 10:6-17 KJV

⁶ But the righteousness which is of faith speaketh on this wise, Say not in thine heart, Who shall ascend into heaven? (that is, to bring Christ down from above:)

⁷ Or, Who shall descend into the deep? (that is, to bring up Christ again from the dead.)
⁸ But what saith it? The word is nigh thee, even in thy mouth, and in thy heart: that is, the word of faith, which we preach;
⁹ That if thou shalt confess with thy mouth the Lord Jesus, and shalt believe in thine heart that God hath raised him from the dead, thou shalt be saved.
¹⁰ For with the heart man believeth unto righteousness; and with the mouth confession is made unto salvation.
¹¹ For the scripture saith, Whosoever believeth on him shall not be ashamed.
¹² For there is no difference between the Jew and the Greek: for the same Lord over all is rich unto all that call upon him.
¹³ For whosoever shall call upon the name of the Lord shall be saved.
¹⁴ How then shall they call on him in whom they have not believed? and how shall they believe in him of whom they have not heard? and how shall they hear without a preacher?
¹⁵ And how shall they preach, except they be sent? as it is written, How beautiful are the feet of them that preach the gospel of peace, and bring glad tidings of good things!
¹⁶ But they have not all obeyed the gospel. For Esaias saith, Lord, who hath believed our report?
¹⁷ So then faith cometh by hearing, and hearing by the word of God.

II CORINTHIANS 5:5-10 KJV

⁵ Now he that hath wrought us for the selfsame thing is God, who also hath given unto us the earnest of the Spirit.
⁶ Therefore we are always confident, knowing that, whilst we are at home in the body, we are absent from the Lord:
⁷ (For we walk by faith, not by sight:)
⁸ We are confident, I say, and willing rather to be absent from the body, and to be present with the Lord.
⁹ Wherefore we labour, that, whether present or absent, we may be accepted of him.

¹⁰ For we must all appear before the judgment seat of Christ; that every one may receive the things done in his body, according to that he hath done, whether it be good or bad.

HEBREWS 11:6 KJV

But without faith it is impossible to please him: for he that cometh to God must believe that he is, and that he is a rewarder of them that diligently seek him.

HEBREWS 12:1-11 KJV

¹ Wherefore seeing we also are compassed about with so great a cloud of witnesses, let us lay aside every weight, and the sin which doth so easily beset us, and let us run with patience the race that is set before us,
² Looking unto Jesus the author and finisher of our faith; who for the joy that was set before him endured the cross, despising the shame, and is set down at the right hand of the throne of God.
³ For consider him that endured such contradiction of sinners against himself, lest ye be wearied and faint in your minds.
⁴ Ye have not yet resisted unto blood, striving against sin.
⁵ And ye have forgotten the exhortation which speaketh unto you as unto children, My son, despise not thou the chastening of the Lord, nor faint when thou art rebuked of him:
⁶ For whom the Lord loveth he chasteneth, and scourgeth every son whom he receiveth.
⁷ If ye endure chastening, God dealeth with you as with sons; for what son is he whom the father chasteneth not?
⁸ But if ye be without chastisement, whereof all are partakers, then are ye bastards, and not sons.
⁹ Furthermore we have had fathers of our flesh which corrected us, and we gave them reverence: shall we not much rather be in subjection unto the Father of spirits, and live?
¹⁰ For they verily for a few days chastened us after their own pleasure; but he for our profit, that we might be partakers of his holiness.

[11] Now no chastening for the present seemeth to be joyous, but grievous: nevertheless afterward it yieldeth the peaceable fruit of righteousness unto them which are exercised thereby.

⇒ IN LOVE ⇐

ROMANS 5:1-5 KJV

[1] Therefore being justified by faith, we have peace with God through our Lord Jesus Christ:
[2] By whom also we have access by faith into this grace wherein we stand, and rejoice in hope of the glory of God.
[3] And not only so, but we glory in tribulations also: knowing that tribulation worketh patience;
[4] And patience, experience; and experience, hope:
[5] And hope maketh not ashamed; because the love of God is shed abroad in our hearts by the Holy Ghost which is given unto us.

GALATIANS 5:13-14 KJV

[13] For, brethren, ye have been called unto liberty; only use not liberty for an occasion to the flesh, but by love serve one another.
[14] For all the law is fulfilled in one word, even in this; Thou shalt love thy neighbour as thyself.

ROMANS 13:8-14 KJV

[8] Owe no man any thing, but to love one another: for he that loveth another hath fulfilled the law.
[9] For this, Thou shalt not commit adultery, Thou shalt not kill, Thou shalt not steal, Thou shalt not bear false witness, Thou shalt not covet; and if there be any other commandment, it is briefly comprehended in this saying, namely, Thou shalt love thy neighbour as thyself.
[10] Love worketh no ill to his neighbour: therefore love is the fulfilling of the law.
[11] And that, knowing the time, that now it is high time to awake out of sleep: for now is our salvation nearer than when we believed.

¹² The night is far spent, the day is at hand: let us therefore cast off the works of darkness, and let us put on the armour of light.
¹³ Let us walk honestly, as in the day; not in rioting and drunkenness, not in chambering and wantonness, not in strife and envying.
¹⁴ But put ye on the Lord Jesus Christ, and make not provision for the flesh, to fulfil the lusts thereof.

I TIMOTHY 1:12-17 KJV

¹²And I [Paul] thank Christ Jesus our Lord, who hath enabled me, for that he counted me faithful, putting me into the ministry;
¹³ Who was before a blasphemer, and a persecutor, and injurious: but I obtained mercy, because I did it ignorantly in unbelief.
¹⁴ And the grace of our Lord was exceeding abundant with faith and love which is in Christ Jesus.
¹⁵ This is a faithful saying, and worthy of all acceptation, that Christ Jesus came into the world to save sinners; of whom I am chief.
¹⁶ Howbeit for this cause I obtained mercy, that in me first Jesus Christ might shew forth all longsuffering, for a pattern to them which should hereafter believe on him to life everlasting.
¹⁷ Now unto the King eternal, immortal, invisible, the only wise God, be honour and glory for ever and ever. Amen.

⇛ PEACE ⇚

PHILIPPIANS 4:4-9 KJV

⁴ Rejoice in the Lord always: and again I say, Rejoice.
⁵ Let your moderation be known unto all men. The Lord is at hand.
⁶ Be careful for nothing; but in every thing by prayer and supplication with thanksgiving let your requests be made known unto God.
⁷ And the peace of God, which passeth all understanding, shall keep your hearts and minds through Christ Jesus.

⁸ Finally, brethren, whatsoever things are true, whatsoever things are honest, whatsoever things are just, whatsoever things are pure, whatsoever things are lovely, whatsoever things are of good report; if there be any virtue, and if there be any praise, think on these things.

⁹ Those things, which ye have both learned, and received, and heard, and seen in me, do: and the God of peace shall be with you.

⫸ HEART ⫷

ACTS 15:6-11 KJV

⁶ And the apostles and elders came together for to consider of this matter.

⁷ And when there had been much disputing, Peter rose up, and said unto them, Men and brethren, ye know how that a good while ago God made choice among us, that the Gentiles by my mouth should hear the word of the gospel, and believe.

⁸ And God, which knoweth the hearts, bare them witness, giving them the Holy Ghost, even as he did unto us;

⁹ And put no difference between us and them, purifying their hearts by faith.

¹⁰ Now therefore why tempt ye God, to put a yoke upon the neck of the disciples, which neither our fathers nor we were able to bear?

¹¹ But we believe that through the grace of the Lord Jesus Christ we shall be saved, even as they.

COLOSSIANS 3:12-17 KJV

¹² Put on therefore, as the elect of God, holy and beloved, bowels of mercies, kindness, humbleness of mind, meekness, longsuffering;

¹³ Forbearing one another, and forgiving one another, if any man have a quarrel against any: even as Christ forgave you, so also do ye.

¹⁴ And above all these things put on charity, which is the bond of perfectness.

¹⁵ And let the peace of God rule in your hearts, to the which also ye are called in one body; and be ye thankful.

¹⁶ Let the word of Christ dwell in you richly in all wisdom; teaching and admonishing one another in psalms and hymns and spiritual songs, singing with grace in your hearts to the Lord.
¹⁷ And whatsoever ye do in word or deed, do all in the name of the Lord Jesus, giving thanks to God and the Father by him.

⟫ REST ⟪

HEBREWS 3:12-19 KJV

¹² Take heed, brethren, lest there be in any of you an evil heart of unbelief, in departing from the living God.
¹³ But exhort one another daily, while it is called Today; lest any of you be hardened through the deceitfulness of sin.
¹⁴ For we are made partakers of Christ, if we hold the beginning of our confidence steadfast unto the end;
¹⁵ While it is said, To day if ye will hear his voice, harden not your hearts, as in the provocation.
¹⁶ For some, when they had heard, did provoke: howbeit not all that came out of Egypt by Moses.
¹⁷ But with whom was he grieved forty years? was it not with them that had sinned, whose carcases fell in the wilderness?
¹⁸ And to whom sware he that they should not enter into his rest, but to them that believed not?
¹⁹ So we see that they could not enter in because of unbelief.

HEBREWS 4:1-3 KJV

¹ Let us therefore fear, lest, a promise being left us of entering into his rest, any of you should seem to come short of it.
² For unto us was the gospel preached, as well as unto them: but the word preached did not profit them, not being mixed with faith in them that heard it.
³ For we which have believed do enter into rest, as he said, As I have sworn in my wrath, if they shall enter into my rest: although the works were finished from the foundation of the world.

Day 6: Free Gift

HEBREWS 4:9-16 KJV

⁹ There remaineth therefore a rest to the people of God.

¹⁰ For he that is entered into his rest, he also hath ceased from his own works, as God did from his.

¹¹ Let us labour therefore to enter into that rest, lest any man fall after the same example of unbelief.

¹² For the word of God is quick, and powerful, and sharper than any twoedged sword, piercing even to the dividing asunder of soul and spirit, and of the joints and marrow, and is a discerner of the thoughts and intents of the heart.

¹³ Neither is there any creature that is not manifest in his sight: but all things are naked and opened unto the eyes of him with whom we have to do.

¹⁴ Seeing then that we have a great high priest, that is passed into the heavens, Jesus the Son of God, let us hold fast our profession.

¹⁵ For we have not an high priest which cannot be touched with the feeling of our infirmities; but was in all points tempted like as we are, yet without sin.

¹⁶ Let us therefore come boldly unto the throne of grace, that we may obtain mercy, and find grace to help in time of need.

⫸ GLORY ⫷

I PETER 1:2-16 KJV

² Elect according to the foreknowledge of God the Father, through sanctification of the Spirit, unto obedience and sprinkling of the blood of Jesus Christ: Grace unto you, and peace, be multiplied.

³ Blessed be the God and Father of our Lord Jesus Christ, which according to his abundant mercy hath begotten us again unto a lively hope by the resurrection of Jesus Christ from the dead,

⁴ To an inheritance incorruptible, and undefiled, and that fadeth not away, reserved in heaven for you,

⁵ Who are kept by the power of God through faith unto salvation ready to be revealed in the last time.

⁶ Wherein ye greatly rejoice, though now for a season, if need be, ye are in heaviness through manifold temptations:

⁷ That the trial of your faith, being much more precious than of gold that perisheth, though it be tried with fire, might be found unto praise and honour and glory at the appearing of Jesus Christ:
⁸ Whom having not seen, ye love; in whom, though now ye see him not, yet believing, ye rejoice with joy unspeakable and full of glory:
⁹ Receiving the end of your faith, even the salvation of your souls.
¹⁰ Of which salvation the prophets have enquired and searched diligently, who prophesied of the grace that should come unto you:
¹¹ Searching what, or what manner of time the Spirit of Christ which was in them did signify, when it testified beforehand the sufferings of Christ, and the glory that should follow.
¹² Unto whom it was revealed, that not unto themselves, but unto us they did minister the things, which are now reported unto you by them that have preached the gospel unto you with the Holy Ghost sent down from heaven; which things the angels desire to look into.
¹³ Wherefore gird up the loins of your mind, be sober, and hope to the end for the grace that is to be brought unto you at the revelation of Jesus Christ;
¹⁴ As obedient children, not fashioning yourselves according to the former lusts in your ignorance:
¹⁵ But as he which hath called you is holy, so be ye holy in all manner of conversation;
¹⁶ Because it is written, Be ye holy; for I am holy.

I THESSALONIANS 2:12-13 KJV

¹² That ye would walk worthy of God, who hath called you unto his kingdom and glory.
¹³ For this cause also thank we God without ceasing, because, when ye received the word of God which ye heard of us, ye received it not as the word of men, but as it is in truth, the word of God, which effectually worketh also in you that believe.

II PETER 1:3-4 KJV

³ According as his divine power hath given unto us all things that pertain unto life and godliness, through the knowledge of him that hath called us to glory and virtue:

[4] Whereby are given unto us exceeding great and precious promises: that by these ye might be partakers of the divine nature, having escaped the corruption that is in the world through lust.

PHILIPPIANS 3:20-21 KJV

[20] For our conversation is in heaven; from whence also we look for the Saviour, the Lord Jesus Christ:
[21] Who shall change our vile body, that it may be fashioned like unto his glorious body, according to the working whereby he is able even to subdue all things unto himself.

EPHESIANS 5:26-27 KJV

[26] That he might sanctify and cleanse it with the washing of water by the word,
[27] That he might present it to himself a glorious church, not having spot, or wrinkle, or any such thing; but that it should be holy and without blemish.

⫸ ETERNAL LIFE ⫷

1 JOHN 5:11-13 KJV

[11] And this is the record, that God hath given to us eternal life, and this life is in his Son.
[12] He that hath the Son hath life; and he that hath not the Son of God hath not life.
[13] These things have I written unto you that believe on the name of the Son of God; that ye may know that ye have eternal life, and that ye may believe on the name of the Son of God.

DAY 7

New Life: Free Gift

ROMANS 6:17-22 KJV, and v. 23 NKJV

[17] But God be thanked, that ye were the servants of sin, but ye have obeyed from the heart that form of doctrine which was delivered you.
[18] Being then made free from sin, ye became the servants of righteousness.
[19] I speak after the manner of men because of the infirmity of your flesh: for as ye have yielded your members servants to uncleanness and to iniquity unto iniquity; even so now yield your members servants to righteousness unto holiness.
[20] For when ye were the servants of sin, ye were free from righteousness.
[21] What fruit had ye then in those things whereof ye are now ashamed? for the end of those things is death.
[22] But now being made free from sin, and become servants to God, ye have your fruit unto holiness, and the end everlasting life.
[23] For the wages of sin is death, but the gift of God is eternal life in Christ Jesus our Lord.

Day 7: New Life: Free Gift

You can work for sin but it is a cruel master.
When it pays you off, its wage is death –
separation from God forever, in stark contrast, God
does not pay wages,
He has a free gift to offer – eternal life.
There is nothing that one can do to earn this gift.
If one could earn it, it would not be a gift;
it would be wages. Eternal life is just that – eternal
– it never ceases.
The basic concept underlying life is union. There
are three kinds of life mentioned in the Bible: (1)
Physical life – union of the soul
with the body; (2) spiritual life –
union of the soul with God; and (3) eternal life –
eternal union of the soul with God.
– *Our soul includes our mind, our will,
and our emotions.* –

ROMANS 12:1-2 KJV

¹ I beseech you therefore, brethren, by the mercies of God, that ye present your bodies a living sacrifice, holy, acceptable unto God, which is your reasonable service.

² And be not conformed to this world: but be ye transformed by the renewing of your mind, that ye may prove what is that good, and acceptable, and perfect, will of God.

---

(1) Physical life – union of the soul with the body
(natural, fleshly) – naturally minded – non-
Christian.

I CORINTHIANS 2:14 KJV

But the natural man receiveth not the things of the Spirit of God: for they are foolishness unto him: neither can he know them, because they are spiritually discerned.

EPHESIANS 2:1-3 KJV

[1] And you hath he quickened, who were dead in trespasses and sins;
[2] Wherein in time past ye walked according to the course of this world, according to the prince of the power of the air, the spirit that now worketh in the children of disobedience:
[3] Among whom also we all had our conversation in times past in the lusts of our flesh, fulfilling the desires of the flesh and of the mind; and were by nature the children of wrath, even as others.

GALATIANS 5:16-21 KJV

[16] This I say then, Walk in the Spirit, and ye shall not fulfil the lust of the flesh.
[17] For the flesh lusteth against the Spirit, and the Spirit against the flesh: and these are contrary the one to the other: so that ye cannot do the things that ye would.
[18] But if ye be led of the Spirit, ye are not under the law.
[19] Now the works of the flesh are manifest, which are these; Adultery, fornication, uncleanness, lasciviousness,
[20] Idolatry, witchcraft, hatred, variance, emulations, wrath, strife, seditions, heresies,
[21] Envyings, murders, drunkenness, revellings, and such like: of the which I tell you before, as I have also told you in time past, that they which do such things shall not inherit the kingdom of God.

I CORINTHIANS 6:9-11 KJV

[9] Know ye not that the unrighteous shall not inherit the kingdom of God? Be not deceived: neither fornicators, nor idolaters, nor adulterers, nor effeminate, nor abusers of themselves with mankind,
[10] Nor thieves, nor covetous, nor drunkards, nor revilers, nor extortioners, shall inherit the kingdom of God.

Day 7: New Life: Free Gift

¹¹ And such were some of you: but ye are washed, but ye are sanctified, but ye are justified in the name of the Lord Jesus, and by the Spirit of our God.

TITUS 3:3-8 KJV

³ For we ourselves also were sometimes foolish, disobedient, deceived, serving divers lusts and pleasures, living in malice and envy, hateful, and hating one another.
⁴ But after that the kindness and love of God our Saviour toward man appeared,
⁵ Not by works of righteousness which we have done, but according to his mercy he saved us, by the washing of regeneration, and renewing of the Holy Ghost;
⁶ Which he shed on us abundantly through Jesus Christ our Saviour;
⁷ That being justified by his grace, we should be made heirs according to the hope of eternal life.
⁸ This is a faithful saying, and these things I will that thou affirm constantly, that they which have believed in God might be careful to maintain good works. These things are good and profitable unto men.

JOHN 6:63 KJV

It is the spirit that quickeneth; the flesh profiteth nothing: the words that I speak unto you, they are spirit, and they are life.

II TIMOTHY 3:12-17 KJV

¹² Yea, and all that will live godly in Christ Jesus shall suffer persecution.
¹³ But evil men and seducers shall wax worse and worse, deceiving, and being deceived.
¹⁴ But continue thou in the things which thou hast learned and hast been assured of, knowing of whom thou hast learned them;
¹⁵ And that from a child thou hast known the holy scriptures, which are able to make thee wise unto salvation through faith which is in Christ Jesus.

¹⁶ All scripture is given by inspiration of God, and is profitable for doctrine, for reproof, for correction, for instruction in righteousness:
¹⁷ That the man of God may be perfect, thoroughly furnished unto all good works.

PSALM 19:7 KJV

The law of the Lord is perfect, converting the soul: the testimony of the Lord is sure, making wise the simple.

PSALM 119:130 KJV

The entrance of thy words giveth light; it giveth understanding unto the simple.

---

(2) Spiritual life – union of the soul with God (who is Spirit) – Holy Spirit minded – Christian.

EPHESIANS 2:18-22 KJV

¹⁸ For through him [Jesus] we both have access by one Spirit unto the Father.
¹⁹ Now therefore ye are no more strangers and foreigners, but fellow citizens with the saints, and of the household of God;
²⁰ And are built upon the foundation of the apostles and prophets, Jesus Christ himself being the chief corner stone;
²¹ In whom all the building fitly framed together groweth unto an holy temple in the Lord:
²² In whom ye also are builded together for an habitation of God through the Spirit.

I CORINTHIANS 3:16-23 KJV

¹⁶ Know ye not that ye are the temple of God, and that the Spirit of God dwelleth in you?

¹⁷ If any man defile the temple of God, him shall God destroy; for the temple of God is holy, which temple ye are.
¹⁸ Let no man deceive himself. If any man among you seemeth to be wise in this world, let him become a fool, that he may be wise.
¹⁹ For the wisdom of this world is foolishness with God. For it is written, He taketh the wise in their own craftiness.
²⁰ And again, The Lord knoweth the thoughts of the wise, that they are vain.
²¹ Therefore let no man glory in men. For all things are your's;
²² Whether Paul, or Apollos, or Cephas, or the world, or life, or death, or things present, or things to come; all are your's;
²³ And ye are Christ's; and Christ is God's.

I CORINTHIANS 2:9-16 KJV
⁹ But as it is written, Eye hath not seen, nor ear heard, neither have entered into the heart of man, the things which God hath prepared for them that love him.
¹⁰ But God hath revealed them unto us by his Spirit: for the Spirit searcheth all things, yea, the deep things of God.
¹¹ For what man knoweth the things of a man, save the spirit of man which is in him? even so the things of God knoweth no man, but the Spirit of God.
¹² Now we have received, not the spirit of the world, but the spirit which is of God; that we might know the things that are freely given to us of God.
¹³ Which things also we speak, not in the words which man's wisdom teacheth, but which the Holy Ghost teacheth; comparing spiritual things with spiritual.
¹⁴ But the natural man receiveth not the things of the Spirit of God: for they are foolishness unto him: neither can he know them, because they are spiritually discerned.
¹⁵ But he that is spiritual judgeth all things, yet he himself is judged of no man.
¹⁶ For who hath known the mind of the Lord, that he may instruct him? but we have the mind of Christ.

JOHN 6:63 KJV

It is the spirit that quickeneth; the flesh profiteth nothing: the words that I speak unto you, they are spirit, and they are life.

II CORINTHIANS 3:4-6 KJV

[4] And such trust have we through Christ to God-ward:
[5] Not that we are sufficient of ourselves to think any thing as of ourselves; but our sufficiency is of God;
[6] Who also hath made us able ministers of the new testament; not of the letter, but of the spirit: for the letter killeth, but the spirit giveth life.

ROMANS 8:1-7 KJV

[1] There is therefore now no condemnation to them which are in Christ Jesus, who walk not after the flesh, but after the Spirit.
[2] For the law of the Spirit of life in Christ Jesus hath made me free from the law of sin and death.
[3] For what the law could not do, in that it was weak through the flesh, God sending his own Son in the likeness of sinful flesh, and for sin, condemned sin in the flesh:
[4] That the righteousness of the law might be fulfilled in us, who walk not after the flesh, but after the Spirit.
[5] For they that are after the flesh do mind the things of the flesh; but they that are after the Spirit the things of the Spirit.
[6] For to be carnally minded is death; but to be spiritually minded is life and peace.
[7] Because the carnal mind is enmity against God: for it is not subject to the law of God, neither indeed can be.

– Carnally minded – Babes in Christ –

Day 7: New Life: Free Gift

I CORINTHIANS 3:1-3 KJV

¹ And I [Paul], brethren, could not speak unto you as unto spiritual, but as unto carnal, even as unto babes in Christ.
² I have fed you with milk, and not with meat: for hitherto ye were not able to bear it, neither yet now are ye able.
³ For ye are yet carnal: for whereas there is among you envying, and strife, and divisions, are ye not carnal, and walk as men?

ROMANS 8:8-11 KJV

⁸ So then they that are in the flesh cannot please God.
⁹ But ye are not in the flesh, but in the Spirit, if so be that the Spirit of God dwell in you. Now if any man have not the Spirit of Christ, he is none of his.
¹⁰ And if Christ be in you, the body is dead because of sin; but the Spirit is life because of righteousness.
¹¹ But if the Spirit of him that raised up Jesus from the dead dwell in you, he that raised up Christ from the dead shall also quicken your mortal bodies by his Spirit that dwelleth in you.

GALATIANS 3:1-6 KJV

¹ O foolish Galatians, who hath bewitched you, that ye should not obey the truth, before whose eyes Jesus Christ hath been evidently set forth, crucified among you?
² This only would I [Paul] learn of you, Received ye the Spirit by the works of the law, or by the hearing of faith?
³ Are ye so foolish? having begun in the Spirit, are ye now made perfect by the flesh?
⁴ Have ye suffered so many things in vain? if it be yet in vain.
⁵ He therefore that ministereth to you the Spirit, and worketh miracles among you, doeth he it by the works of the law, or by the hearing of faith?
⁶ Even as Abraham believed God, and it was accounted to him for righteousness.

GALATIANS 6:7-10 KJV

⁷ Be not deceived; God is not mocked: for whatsoever a man soweth, that shall he also reap.
⁸ For he that soweth to his flesh shall of the flesh reap corruption; but he that soweth to the Spirit shall of the Spirit reap life everlasting.
⁹ And let us not be weary in well doing: for in due season we shall reap, if we faint not.
¹⁰ As we have therefore opportunity, let us do good unto all men, especially unto them who are of the household of faith.

EPHESIANS 3:7-12 KJV

⁷ Whereof I [Paul] was made a minister, according to the gift of the grace of God given unto me by the effectual working of his power.
⁸ Unto me, who am less than the least of all saints, is this grace given, that I should preach among the Gentiles the unsearchable riches of Christ;
⁹ And to make all men see what is the fellowship of the mystery, which from the beginning of the world hath been hid in God, who created all things by Jesus Christ:
¹⁰ To the intent that now unto the principalities and powers in heavenly places might be known by the church the manifold wisdom of God,
¹¹ According to the eternal purpose which he purposed in Christ Jesus our Lord:
¹² In whom we have boldness and access with confidence by the faith of him.

HEBREWS 10:19-25 KJV

¹⁹ Having therefore, brethren, boldness to enter into the holiest by the blood of Jesus,
²⁰ By a new and living way, which he hath consecrated for us, through the veil, that is to say, his flesh;
²¹ And having an high priest over the house of God;
²² Let us draw near with a true heart in full assurance of faith, having our hearts sprinkled from an evil conscience, and our bodies washed with pure water.

²³ Let us hold fast the profession of our faith without wavering; (for he is faithful that promised;)
²⁴ And let us consider one another to provoke unto love and to good works:
²⁵ Not forsaking the assembling of ourselves together, as the manner of some is; but exhorting one another: and so much the more, as ye see the day approaching.

HEBREWS 10:35-39 KJV

³⁵ Cast not away therefore your confidence, which hath great recompence of reward.
³⁶ For ye have need of patience, that, after ye have done the will of God, ye might receive the promise.
³⁷ For yet a little while, and he that shall come will come, and will not tarry.
³⁸ Now the just shall live by faith: but if any man draw back, my soul shall have no pleasure in him.
³⁹ But we are not of them who draw back unto perdition; but of them that believe to the saving of the soul.

PSALMS 23:1-6 KJV

¹ The Lord is my shepherd; I shall not want.
² He maketh me to lie down in green pastures: he leadeth me beside the still waters.
³ He restoreth my soul: he leadeth me in the paths of righteousness for his name's sake.
⁴ Yea, though I walk through the valley of the shadow of death, I will fear no evil: for thou art with me; thy rod and thy staff they comfort me.
⁵ Thou preparest a table before me in the presence of mine enemies: thou anointest my head with oil; my cup runneth over.
⁶ Surely goodness and mercy shall follow me all the days of my life: and I will dwell in the house of the Lord for ever.

---

(3) Eternal life – Eternal union of the soul with God (eternal spirit) – heavenly minded – Spirit-led –

HEBREWS 9:11-15 KJV

[11] But Christ being come an high priest of good things to come, by a greater and more perfect tabernacle, not made with hands, that is to say, not of this building;

[12] Neither by the blood of goats and calves, but by his own blood he entered in once into the holy place, having obtained eternal redemption for us.

[13] For if the blood of bulls and of goats, and the ashes of an heifer sprinkling the unclean, sanctifieth to the purifying of the flesh:

[14] How much more shall the blood of Christ, who through the eternal Spirit offered himself without spot to God, purge your conscience from dead works to serve the living God?

[15] And for this cause he is the mediator of the new testament, that by means of death, for the redemption of the transgressions that were under the first testament, they which are called might receive the promise of eternal inheritance.

JOHN 4:24 KJV

God is a Spirit: and they that worship him must worship him in spirit and in truth.

JOHN 17:1-5 KJV

[1] These words spake Jesus, and lifted up his eyes to heaven, and said, Father, the hour is come; glorify thy Son, that thy Son also may glorify thee:

[2] As thou hast given him power over all flesh, that he should give eternal life to as many as thou hast given him.

[3] And this is life eternal, that they might know thee the only true God, and Jesus Christ, whom thou hast sent.

[4] I have glorified thee on the earth: I have finished the work which thou gavest me to do.

[5] And now, O Father, glorify thou me with thine own self with the glory which I had with thee before the world was.

JOHN 17:18-26 KJV

¹⁸ As thou hast sent me into the world, even so have I also sent them into the world.

¹⁹ And for their sakes I sanctify myself, that they also might be sanctified through the truth.

²⁰ Neither pray I for these alone, but for them also which shall believe on me through their word;

²¹ That they all may be one; as thou, Father, art in me, and I in thee, that they also may be one in us: that the world may believe that thou hast sent me.

²² And the glory which thou gavest me I have given them; that they may be one, even as we are one:

²³ I in them, and thou in me, that they may be made perfect in one; and that the world may know that thou hast sent me, and hast loved them, as thou hast loved me.

²⁴ Father, I will that they also, whom thou hast given me, be with me where I am; that they may behold my glory, which thou hast given me: for thou lovedst me before the foundation of the world.

²⁵ O righteous Father, the world hath not known thee: but I have known thee, and these have known that thou hast sent me.

²⁶ And I have declared unto them thy name, and will declare it: that the love wherewith thou hast loved me may be in them, and I in them.

EPHESIANS 4:7-16 KJV

⁷ But unto every one of us is given grace according to the measure of the gift of Christ.

⁸ Wherefore he [Jesus] saith, When he ascended up on high, he led captivity captive, and gave gifts unto men.

⁹ (Now that he ascended, what is it but that he also descended first into the lower parts of the earth?

¹⁰ He that descended is the same also that ascended up far above all heavens, that he might fill all things.)

¹¹ And he gave some, apostles; and some, prophets; and some, evangelists; and some, pastors and teachers;

¹² For the perfecting of the saints, for the work of the ministry, for the edifying of the body of Christ:

[13] Till we all come in the unity of the faith, and of the knowledge of the Son of God, unto a perfect man, unto the measure of the stature of the fulness of Christ:
[14] That we henceforth be no more children, tossed to and fro, and carried about with every wind of doctrine, by the sleight of men, and cunning craftiness, whereby they lie in wait to deceive;
[15] But speaking the truth in love, may grow up into him in all things, which is the head, even Christ:
16 From whom the whole body fitly joined together and compacted by that which every joint supplieth, according to the effectual working in the measure of every part, maketh increase of the body unto the edifying of itself in love.

HEBREWS 12:1-3 KJV

[1] Wherefore seeing we also are compassed about with so great a cloud of witnesses, let us lay aside every weight, and the sin which doth so easily beset us, and let us run with patience the race that is set before us,
[2] Looking unto Jesus the author and finisher of our faith; who for the joy that was set before him endured the cross, despising the shame, and is set down at the right hand of the throne of God.
[3] For consider him that endured such contradiction of sinners against himself, lest ye be wearied and faint in your minds.

HEBREWS 6:10-15 KJV

[10] For God is not unrighteous to forget your work and labour of love, which ye have shewed toward his name, in that ye have ministered to the saints, and do minister.
[11] And we desire that every one of you do shew the same diligence to the full assurance of hope unto the end:
[12] That ye be not slothful, but followers of them who through faith and patience inherit the promises.
[13] For when God made promise to Abraham, because he could swear by no greater, he sware by himself,
[14] Saying, Surely blessing I will bless thee, and multiplying I will multiply thee.
[15] And so, after he had patiently endured, he obtained the promise.

Day 7: New Life: Free Gift

I JOHN 2:24-28 KJV

²⁴ Let that therefore abide in you, which ye have heard from the beginning. If that which ye have heard from the beginning shall remain in you, ye also shall continue in the Son, and in the Father.
²⁵ And this is the promise that he hath promised us, even eternal life.
²⁶ These things have I written unto you concerning them that seduce you.
²⁷ But the anointing which ye have received of him abideth in you, and ye need not that any man teach you: but as the same anointing teacheth you of all things, and is truth, and is no lie, and even as it hath taught you, ye shall abide in him.
²⁸ And now, little children, abide in him; that, when he shall appear, we may have confidence, and not be ashamed before him at his coming.

I PETER 1:3-9 KJV

³ Blessed be the God and Father of our Lord Jesus Christ, which according to his abundant mercy hath begotten us again unto a lively hope by the resurrection of Jesus Christ from the dead,
⁴ To an inheritance incorruptible, and undefiled, and that fadeth not away, reserved in heaven for you,
⁵ Who are kept by the power of God through faith unto salvation ready to be revealed in the last time.
⁶ Wherein ye greatly rejoice, though now for a season, if need be, ye are in heaviness through manifold temptations:
⁷ That the trial of your faith, being much more precious than of gold that perisheth, though it be tried with fire, might be found unto praise and honour and glory at the appearing of Jesus Christ:
⁸ Whom having not seen, ye love; in whom, though now ye see him not, yet believing, ye rejoice with joy unspeakable and full of glory:
⁹ Receiving the end of your faith, even the salvation of your souls.

III JOHN v. 2 KJV

Beloved, I wish above all things that thou mayest prosper and be in health, even as thy soul prospereth.

JUDE 17-25 KJV

[17] But, beloved, remember ye the words which were spoken before of the apostles of our Lord Jesus Christ;
[18] How that they told you there should be mockers in the last time, who should walk after their own ungodly lusts.
[19] These be they who separate themselves, sensual, having not the Spirit.
[20] But ye, beloved, building up yourselves on your most holy faith, praying in the Holy Ghost,
[21] Keep yourselves in the love of God, looking for the mercy of our Lord Jesus Christ unto eternal life.
[22] And of some have compassion, making a difference:
[23] And others save with fear, pulling them out of the fire; hating even the garment spotted by the flesh.
[24] Now unto him that is able to keep you from falling, and to present you faultless before the presence of his glory with exceeding joy,
[25] To the only wise God our Saviour, be glory and majesty, dominion and power, both now and ever. Amen.

The gift of God is eternal life.
One receives this gift when he believes
in Jesus as his own personal Savior.
Having eternal life, he will never perish.

I THESSALONIANS 5:23-24 KJV

[23] And the very God of peace sanctify you wholly; and I pray God your whole spirit and soul and body be preserved blameless unto the coming of our Lord Jesus Christ.
[24] Faithful is he that calleth you, who also will do it.

DAY 8

---·---

New Life: Based on Christ's Death

> Salvation is free, but it is not cheap.
> Salvation is a gift and costs me nothing,
> but it cost God everything – it cost Jesus His life.
> The wages of sin is death (separation from God.)
> God's gift is eternal life (eternal union of
> the soul with God). This is possible because of the
> death of Jesus on Calvary's cross.

COLOSSIANS 1:19-21, 23 KJV, and v. 22 NKJV

[19] For it pleased the Father that in him [Jesus] should all fulness dwell;
[20] And, having made peace through the blood of his cross, by him to reconcile all things unto himself; by him, I say, whether they be things in earth, or things in heaven.
[21] And you, that were sometime alienated and enemies in your mind by wicked works, yet now hath he reconciled
[22] In the body of His flesh through death, to present you holy, and blameless, and above reproach in His sight—

²³ If ye continue in the faith grounded and settled, and be not moved away from the hope of the gospel, which ye have heard, and which was preached to every creature which is under heaven; whereof I Paul am made a minister;

COLOSSIANS 1:9-14 KJV

⁹ For this cause we also, since the day we heard it, do not cease to pray for you, and to desire that ye might be filled with the knowledge of his will in all wisdom and spiritual understanding;
¹⁰ That ye might walk worthy of the Lord unto all pleasing, being fruitful in every good work, and increasing in the knowledge of God;
¹¹ Strengthened with all might, according to his glorious power, unto all patience and longsuffering with joyfulness;
¹² Giving thanks unto the Father, which hath made us meet to be partakers of the inheritance of the saints in light:
¹³ Who hath delivered us from the power of darkness, and hath translated us into the kingdom of his dear Son:
¹⁴ In whom we have redemption through his blood, even the forgiveness of sins:

> Jesus actually took sin's penalty for
> every man, woman, and child
> who ever has lived or ever will live.
> As he hung upon the cross he cried
> 'Eli, Eli, Lama Sabachthani?'
> Being interpreted, he cried,
> 'My God, My God, why have you forsaken me?'

ISAIAH 53:10-12 KJV

¹⁰ Yet it pleased the Lord to bruise him; he hath put him to grief: when thou shalt make his soul an offering for sin, he shall see his seed, he shall prolong his days, and the pleasure of the Lord shall prosper in his hand.

¹¹ He shall see of the travail of his soul, and shall be satisfied: by his knowledge shall my righteous servant justify many; for he shall bear their iniquities.
¹² Therefore will I divide him a portion with the great, and he shall divide the spoil with the strong; because he hath poured out his soul unto death: and he was numbered with the transgressors; and he bare the sin of many, and made intercession for the transgressors.

1 CORINTHIANS 15:1-4 KJV

¹ Moreover, brethren, I [Paul] declare unto you the gospel which I preached unto you, which also ye have received, and wherein ye stand;
² By which also ye are saved, if ye keep in memory what I preached unto you, unless ye have believed in vain.
³ For I delivered unto you first of all that which I also received, how that Christ died for our sins according to the scriptures;
⁴ And that he was buried, and that he rose again the third day according to the scriptures:

ROMANS 5:18-21 KJV

¹⁸ Therefore as by the offence of one [Adam] judgment came upon all men to condemnation; even so by the righteousness of one [Jesus] the free gift came upon all men unto justification of life.
¹⁹ For as by one man's disobedience many were made sinners, so by the obedience of one shall many be made righteous.
²⁰ Moreover the law entered, that the offence might abound. But where sin abounded, grace did much more abound:
²¹ That as sin hath reigned unto death, even so might grace reign through righteousness unto eternal life by Jesus Christ our Lord.

ROMANS 6:5-14 KJV

⁵ For if we have been planted together in the likeness of his death, we shall be also in the likeness of his resurrection:
⁶ Knowing this, that our old man is crucified with him, that the body of sin might be destroyed, that henceforth we should not serve sin.

⁷ For he that is dead is freed from sin.
⁸ Now if we be dead with Christ, we believe that we shall also live with him:
⁹ Knowing that Christ being raised from the dead dieth no more; death hath no more dominion over him.
¹⁰ For in that he died, he died unto sin once: but in that he liveth, he liveth unto God.
¹¹ Likewise reckon ye also yourselves to be dead indeed unto sin, but alive unto God through Jesus Christ our Lord.
¹² Let not sin therefore reign in your mortal body, that ye should obey it in the lusts thereof.
¹³ Neither yield ye your members as instruments of unrighteousness unto sin: but yield yourselves unto God, as those that are alive from the dead, and your members as instruments of righteousness unto God.
¹⁴ For sin shall not have dominion over you: for ye are not under the law, but under grace.

1 PETER 3:18 KJV

⁹ For Christ also hath once suffered for sins, the just for the unjust, that he might bring us to God, being put to death in the flesh, but quickened by the Spirit:

> Jesus was separated from God the Father
> so that you and I do not have to be.
> This is the heart of the atonement.
> The marvel of it all is that he did this while we
> were His enemies: but God demonstrates His own
> love toward us, in that while we
> were still sinners, Christ died for us.

ROMANS 5:1-7, 9-11 KJV, and v. 8 NKJV

¹ Therefore being justified by faith, we have peace with God through our Lord Jesus Christ:

Day 8: New Life: Based on Christ's Death

² By whom also we have access by faith into this grace wherein we stand, and rejoice in hope of the glory of God.

³ And not only so, but we glory in tribulations also: knowing that tribulation worketh patience;

⁴ And patience, experience; and experience, hope:

⁵ And hope maketh not ashamed; because the love of God is shed abroad in our hearts by the Holy Ghost which is given unto us.

⁶ For when we were yet without strength, in due time Christ died for the ungodly.

⁷ For scarcely for a righteous man will one die: yet peradventure for a good man some would even dare to die.

⁸ But God demonstrates His own love toward us, in that while we were still sinners, Christ died for us.

⁹ Much more then, being now justified by his blood, we shall be saved from wrath through him.

¹⁰ For if, when we were enemies, we were reconciled to God by the death of his Son, much more, being reconciled, we shall be saved by his life.

¹¹ And not only so, but we also joy in God through our Lord Jesus Christ, by whom we have now received the atonement.

JOHN 5:24-30 KJV

²⁴ Verily, verily, I [Jesus] say unto you, He that heareth my word, and believeth on him that sent me, hath everlasting life, and shall not come into condemnation; but is passed from death unto life.

²⁵ Verily, verily, I say unto you, The hour is coming, and now is, when the dead shall hear the voice of the Son of God: and they that hear shall live.

²⁶ For as the Father hath life in himself; so hath he given to the Son to have life in himself;

²⁷ And hath given him authority to execute judgment also, because he is the Son of man.

²⁸ Marvel not at this: for the hour is coming, in the which all that are in the graves shall hear his voice,

²⁹ And shall come forth; they that have done good, unto the resurrection of life; and they that have done evil, unto the resurrection of damnation.

³⁰ I can of mine own self do nothing: as I hear, I judge: and my judgment is just; because I seek not mine own will, but the will of the Father which hath sent me.

HEBREWS 2:5-18 KJV

⁵ For unto the angels hath he [God] not put in subjection the world to come, whereof we speak.
⁶ But one in a certain place testified, saying, What is man, that thou art mindful of him? or the son of man that thou visitest him?
⁷ Thou madest him a little lower than the angels; thou crownedst him with glory and honour, and didst set him over the works of thy hands:
⁸ Thou hast put all things in subjection under his feet. For in that he put all in subjection under him, he left nothing that is not put under him. But now we see not yet all things put under him.
⁹ But we see Jesus, who was made a little lower than the angels for the suffering of death, crowned with glory and honour; that he by the grace of God should taste death for every man.
¹⁰ For it became him, for whom are all things, and by whom are all things, in bringing many sons unto glory, to make the captain of their salvation perfect through sufferings.
¹¹ For both he that sanctifieth and they who are sanctified are all of one: for which cause he is not ashamed to call them brethren,
¹² Saying, I will declare thy name unto my brethren, in the midst of the church will I sing praise unto thee.
¹³ And again, I will put my trust in him. And again, Behold I and the children which God hath given me.
¹⁴ Forasmuch then as the children are partakers of flesh and blood, he also himself likewise took part of the same; that through death he might destroy him that had the power of death, that is, the devil;
¹⁵ And deliver them who through fear of death were all their lifetime subject to bondage.
¹⁶ For verily he took not on him the nature of angels; but he took on him the seed of Abraham.
¹⁷ Wherefore in all things it behoved him to be made like unto his brethren, that he might be a merciful and faithful high priest in

things pertaining to God, to make reconciliation for the sins of the people.

[18] For in that he himself hath suffered being tempted, he is able to succour them that are tempted.

ROMANS 8:18-39 KJV

[18] For I [Paul] reckon that the sufferings of this present time are not worthy to be compared with the glory which shall be revealed in us.

[19] For the earnest expectation of the creature waiteth for the manifestation of the sons of God.

[20] For the creature was made subject to vanity, not willingly, but by reason of him who hath subjected the same in hope,

[21] Because the creature itself also shall be delivered from the bondage of corruption into the glorious liberty of the children of God.

[22] For we know that the whole creation groaneth and travaileth in pain together until now.

[23] And not only they, but ourselves also, which have the firstfruits of the Spirit, even we ourselves groan within ourselves, waiting for the adoption, to wit, the redemption of our body.

[24] For we are saved by hope: but hope that is seen is not hope: for what a man seeth, why doth he yet hope for?

[25] But if we hope for that we see not, then do we with patience wait for it.

[26] Likewise the Spirit also helpeth our infirmities: for we know not what we should pray for as we ought: but the Spirit itself maketh intercession for us with groanings which cannot be uttered.

[27] And he that searcheth the hearts knoweth what is the mind of the Spirit, because he maketh intercession for the saints according to the will of God.

[28] And we know that all things work together for good to them that love God, to them who are the called according to his purpose.

[29] For whom he did foreknow, he also did predestinate to be conformed to the image of his Son, that he might be the firstborn among many brethren.

³⁰ Moreover whom he did predestinate, them he also called: and whom he called, them he also justified: and whom he justified, them he also glorified.

³¹ What shall we then say to these things? If God be for us, who can be against us?

³² He that spared not his own Son, but delivered him up for us all, how shall he not with him also freely give us all things?

³³ Who shall lay any thing to the charge of God's elect? It is God that justifieth.

³⁴ Who is he that condemneth? It is Christ that died, yea rather, that is risen again, who is even at the right hand of God, who also maketh intercession for us.

³⁵ Who shall separate us from the love of Christ? shall tribulation, or distress, or persecution, or famine, or nakedness, or peril, or sword?

³⁶ As it is written, For thy sake we are killed all the day long; we are accounted as sheep for the slaughter.

³⁷ Nay, in all these things we are more than conquerors through him that loved us.

³⁸ For I am persuaded, that neither death, nor life, nor angels, nor principalities, nor powers, nor things present, nor things to come,

³⁹ Nor height, nor depth, nor any other creature, shall be able to separate us from the love of God, which is in Christ Jesus our Lord.

TITUS 2:11-15 KJV

¹¹ For the grace of God that bringeth salvation hath appeared to all men,

¹² Teaching us that, denying ungodliness and worldly lusts, we should live soberly, righteously, and godly, in this present world;

¹³ Looking for that blessed hope, and the glorious appearing of the great God and our Saviour Jesus Christ;

¹⁴ Who gave himself for us, that he might redeem us from all iniquity, and purify unto himself a peculiar people, zealous of good works.

¹⁵ These things speak, and exhort, and rebuke with all authority. Let no man despise thee.

DAY 9

New Life: Received by Faith

ACTS 16:31 NKJV

³¹ And they said, Believe on the Lord Jesus Christ, and thou shalt be saved, and thy house.

The words spoken to the Philippian jailer are the best news human ears have ever heard, for they clearly tell how we receive God's gift of eternal life, when we receive God's gift of eternal life we are said to be "saved." The basic concept underlying "salvation" or "being saved" is deliverance.

COLOSSIANS 1:13-15 KJV

¹³ Who [God] hath delivered us from the power of darkness, and hath translated us into the kingdom of his dear Son:
¹⁴ In whom we have redemption through his blood, even the forgiveness of sins:
¹⁵ Who is the image of the invisible God, the firstborn of every creature:

JOHN 3:34-36 KJV

³⁴ For he whom God hath sent speaketh the words of God: for God giveth not the Spirit by measure unto him.
³⁵ The Father loveth the Son, and hath given all things into his hand.
³⁶ He that believeth on the Son hath everlasting life: and he that believeth not the Son shall not see life; but the wrath of God abideth on him.

ROMANS 10:17 KJV

¹⁷ So then faith cometh by hearing, and hearing by the word of God.

I THESSALONIANS 1:2-6 KJV

² We give thanks to God always for you all, making mention of you in our prayers;
³ Remembering without ceasing your work of faith, and labour of love, and patience of hope in our Lord Jesus Christ, in the sight of God and our Father;
⁴ Knowing, brethren beloved, your election of God.
⁵ For our gospel came not unto you in word only, but also in power, and in the Holy Ghost, and in much assurance; as ye know what manner of men we were among you for your sake.
⁶ And ye became followers of us, and of the Lord, having received the word in much affliction, with joy of the Holy Ghost.

EPHESIANS 1:13-23 KJV

¹³ In whom ye also trusted, after that ye heard the word of truth, the gospel of your salvation: in whom also after that ye believed, ye were sealed with that holy Spirit of promise,
¹⁴ Which is the earnest of our inheritance until the redemption of the purchased possession, unto the praise of his glory.
¹⁵ Wherefore I also, after I [Paul] heard of your faith in the Lord Jesus, and love unto all the saints,

¹⁶ Cease not to give thanks for you, making mention of you in my prayers;
¹⁷ That the God of our Lord Jesus Christ, the Father of glory, may give unto you the spirit of wisdom and revelation in the knowledge of him:
¹⁸ The eyes of your understanding being enlightened; that ye may know what is the hope of his calling, and what the riches of the glory of his inheritance in the saints,
¹⁹ And what is the exceeding greatness of his power to us-ward who believe, according to the working of his mighty power,
²⁰ Which he wrought in Christ, when he raised him from the dead, and set him at his own right hand in the heavenly places,
²¹ Far above all principality, and power, and might, and dominion, and every name that is named, not only in this world, but also in that which is to come:
²² And hath put all things under his feet, and gave him to be the head over all things to the church,
²³ Which is his body, the fulness of him that filleth all in all.

ROMANS 8:29-30 KJV

²⁹ For whom he [God] did foreknow, he also did predestinate to be conformed to the image of his Son, that he might be the firstborn among many brethren.
³⁰ Moreover whom he did predestinate, them he also called: and whom he called, them he also justified: and whom he justified, them he also glorified.

I PETER 2:9-10 KJV

⁹ But ye are a chosen generation, a royal priesthood, an holy nation, a peculiar people; that ye should shew forth the praises of him who hath called you out of darkness into his marvellous light;
¹⁰ Which in time past were not a people, but are now the people of God: which had not obtained mercy, but now have obtained mercy.

JUDE 3-5 KJV

³ Beloved, when I [Jude] gave all diligence to write unto you of the common salvation, it was needful for me to write unto you, and exhort you that ye should earnestly contend for the faith which was once delivered unto the saints.
⁴ For there are certain men crept in unawares, who were before of old ordained to this condemnation, ungodly men, turning the grace of our God into lasciviousness, and denying the only Lord God, and our Lord Jesus Christ.
⁵ I will therefore put you in remembrance, though ye once knew this, how that the Lord, having saved the people out of the land of Egypt, afterward destroyed them that believed not.

ROMANS 10:17 KJV

¹⁷ So then faith cometh by hearing, and hearing by the word of God.

COLOSSIANS 1:21-23 KJV

²¹ And you, that were sometime alienated and enemies in your mind by wicked works, yet now hath he reconciled
²² In the body of his flesh through death, to present you holy and unblameable and unreproveable in his sight:
²³ If ye continue in the faith grounded and settled, and be not moved away from the hope of the gospel, which ye have heard, and which was preached to every creature which is under heaven; whereof I Paul am made a minister;

COLOSSIANS 2:9-10 KJV

⁹ For in him [Jesus] dwelleth all the fulness of the Godhead bodily.
¹⁰ And ye are complete in him, which is the head of all principality and power:

PHILIPPIANS 1:6 KJV

⁶ Being confident of this very thing, that he which hath begun a good work in you will perform it until the day of Jesus Christ:

ROMANS 5:1-2 KJV

[1] Therefore being justified by faith, we have peace with God through our Lord Jesus Christ:
[2] By whom also we have access by faith into this grace wherein we stand, and rejoice in hope of the glory of God.

HEBREWS 13:20-21 KJV

[20] Now the God of peace, that brought again from the dead our Lord Jesus, that great shepherd of the sheep, through the blood of the everlasting covenant,
[21] Make you perfect in every good work to do his will, working in you that which is well pleasing in his sight, through Jesus Christ; to whom be glory for ever and ever. Amen.

COLOSSIANS 1:24-29 KJV

[24] Who [Paul] now rejoice in my sufferings for you, and fill up that which is behind of the afflictions of Christ in my flesh for his body's sake, which is the church:
[25] Whereof I am made a minister, according to the dispensation of God which is given to me for you, to fulfil the word of God;
[26] Even the mystery which hath been hid from ages and from generations, but now is made manifest to his saints:
[27] To whom God would make known what is the riches of the glory of this mystery among the Gentiles; which is Christ in you, the hope of glory:
[28] Whom we preach, warning every man, and teaching every man in all wisdom; that we may present every man perfect in Christ Jesus:
[29] Whereunto I also labour, striving according to his working, which worketh in me mightily.

I CORINTHIANS 1:26-31 KJV

[26] For ye see your calling, brethren, how that not many wise men after the flesh, not many mighty, not many noble, are called:

²⁷ But God hath chosen the foolish things of the world to confound the wise; and God hath chosen the weak things of the world to confound the things which are mighty;
²⁸ And base things of the world, and things which are despised, hath God chosen, yea, and things which are not, to bring to nought things that are:
²⁹ That no flesh should glory in his presence.
³⁰ But of him are ye in Christ Jesus, who of God is made unto us wisdom, and righteousness, and sanctification, and redemption:
³¹ That, according as it is written, He that glorieth, let him glory in the Lord.

II CORINTHIANS 5:20-21 KJV

²⁰ Now then we are ambassadors for Christ, as though God did beseech you by us: we pray you in Christ's stead, be ye reconciled to God.
²¹ For he hath made him to be sin for us, who knew no sin; that we might be made the righteousness of God in him.

II PETER 1:2-11 KJV

² Grace and peace be multiplied unto you through the knowledge of God, and of Jesus our Lord,
³ According as his divine power hath given unto us all things that pertain unto life and godliness, through the knowledge of him that hath called us to glory and virtue:
⁴ Whereby are given unto us exceeding great and precious promises: that by these ye might be partakers of the divine nature, having escaped the corruption that is in the world through lust.
⁵ And beside this, giving all diligence, add to your faith virtue; and to virtue knowledge;
⁶ And to knowledge temperance; and to temperance patience; and to patience godliness;
⁷ And to godliness brotherly kindness; and to brotherly kindness charity.

⁸ For if these things be in you, and abound, they make you that ye shall neither be barren nor unfruitful in the knowledge of our Lord Jesus Christ.
⁹ But he that lacketh these things is blind, and cannot see afar off, and hath forgotten that he was purged from his old sins.
¹⁰ Wherefore the rather, brethren, give diligence to make your calling and election sure: for if ye do these things, ye shall never fall:
¹¹ For so an entrance shall be ministered unto you abundantly into the everlasting kingdom of our Lord and Saviour Jesus Christ.

1 PETER 4:10-14 KJV

¹⁰ As every man hath received the gift, even so minister the same one to another, as good stewards of the manifold grace of God.
¹¹ If any man speak, let him speak as the oracles of God; if any man minister, let him do it as of the ability which God giveth: that God in all things may be glorified through Jesus Christ, to whom be praise and dominion for ever and ever. Amen.
¹² Beloved, think it not strange concerning the fiery trial which is to try you, as though some strange thing happened unto you:
¹³ But rejoice, inasmuch as ye are partakers of Christ's sufferings; that, when his glory shall be revealed, ye may be glad also with exceeding joy.
¹⁴ If ye be reproached for the name of Christ, happy are ye; for the spirit of glory and of God resteth upon you: on their part he is evil spoken of, but on your part he is glorified.

II CORINTHIANS 1:7-10 KJV

⁷ And our hope of you is steadfast, knowing, that as ye are partakers of the sufferings, so shall ye be also of the consolation.
⁸ For we [Paul] would not, brethren, have you ignorant of our trouble which came to us in Asia, that we were pressed out of measure, above strength, insomuch that we despaired even of life:
⁹ But we had the sentence of death in ourselves, that we should not trust in ourselves, but in God which raiseth the dead:
¹⁰ Who delivered us from so <u>great a death</u>, and <u>doth deliver</u>: in whom we trust that he <u>will yet deliver us</u>;

We are delivered from the PENALTY of sin (death, separation from God) and from the POWER of sin; ultimately we will be delivered from the very PRESENCE of sin and will be delivered into the very presence of God.

⇒ DELIVERED FROM THE PENALTY OF SIN ⇐

II CORINTHIANS 1:10 KJV

¹⁰ [God] Who delivered us from so <u>great a death</u>, and doth deliver: in whom we trust that he will yet deliver us;

ROMANS 6:23 KJV

²³ For the wages of sin is death; but the gift of God is eternal life through Jesus Christ our Lord.

II PETER 2:9 KJV

⁹ The Lord knoweth how to deliver the godly out of temptations, and to reserve the unjust unto the day of judgment to be punished:

⇒ DELIVERED FROM THE POWER OF SIN ⇐

II CORINTHIANS 1:10 KJV

¹⁰ [God] Who delivered us from so great a death, and <u>doth deliver</u>: in whom we trust that he will yet deliver us;

ROMANS 6:14 KJV

¹⁴ For sin shall not have dominion over you: for ye are not under the law, but under grace.

Day 9: New Life: Received by Faith

ROMANS 6:22 KJV

²² But now being made free from sin, and become servants to God, ye have your fruit unto holiness, and the end everlasting life.

COLOSSIANS 1:13 KJV

¹³ Who hath delivered us from the power of darkness, and hath translated us into the kingdom of his dear Son:

GALATIANS 1:3-4 KJV

³ Grace be to you and peace from God the Father, and from our Lord Jesus Christ,
⁴ Who gave himself for our sins, that he might deliver us from this present evil world, according to the will of God and our Father:

GALATIANS 2:19-20 KJV

¹⁹ For I [Paul] through the law am dead to the law, that I might live unto God.
²⁰ I am crucified with Christ: nevertheless I live; yet not I, but Christ liveth in me: and the life which I now live in the flesh I live by the faith of the Son of God, who loved me, and gave himself for me.

⇛ DELIVERED FROM THE PRESENCE OF SIN ⇚

II CORINTHIANS 1:10 KJV

¹⁰ [God] Who delivered us from so great a death, and doth deliver: in whom we trust that he <u>will yet deliver us</u>;

I JOHN 4:15-17 KJV

¹⁵ Whosoever shall confess that Jesus is the Son of God, God dwelleth in him, and he in God.
¹⁶ And we have known and believed the love that God hath to us. God is love; and he that dwelleth in love dwelleth in God, and God in him.

¹⁷ Herein is our love made perfect, that we may have boldness in the day of judgment: because as he is, so are we in this world.

II TIMOTHY 4:18 KJV

¹⁸ And the Lord shall deliver me from every evil work, and will preserve me unto his heavenly kingdom: to whom be glory for ever and ever. Amen.

PSALM 140:13 KJV

¹³ Surely the righteous shall give thanks unto thy name: the upright shall dwell in thy presence.

I JOHN 2:28-29 KJV

²⁸ And now, little children, abide in him; that, when he shall appear, we may have confidence, and not be ashamed before him at his coming.
²⁹ If ye know that he is righteous, ye know that every one that doeth righteousness is born of him.

I JOHN 3:1-3 KJV

¹ Behold, what manner of love the Father hath bestowed upon us, that we should be called the sons of God: therefore the world knoweth us not, because it knew him not.
² Beloved, now are we the sons of God, and it doth not yet appear what we shall be: but we know that, when he shall appear, we shall be like him; for we shall see him as he is.
³ And every man that hath this hope in him purifieth himself, even as he is pure.

> We receive new life by faith – believing that Jesus died for our sins, that his death was in our place and that his payment for sin is fully acceptable in God's sight. We are to forsake all—repent of our sins and to take him – by faith turn to God for our salvation.

Day 9: New Life: Received by Faith

ACTS 20:20 KJV and v. 21 NJKV

[20] And how I [Paul] kept back nothing that was profitable unto you, but have shewed you, and have taught you publicly, and from house to house,

[21] testifying to Jews, and also to Greeks, repentance toward God and faith toward our Lord Jesus Christ.

ROMANS 10:17 KJV

[17] So then faith comes by hearing, and hearing by the word of God.

DAY 10

―――•―――

The Righteousness of Faith

ROMANS 1:16-32 KJV

[16] For I [Paul] am not ashamed of the gospel of Christ: for it is the power of God unto salvation to every one that believeth; to the Jew first, and also to the Greek.
[17] For therein is the righteousness of God revealed from faith to faith: as it is written, The just shall live by faith.
[18] For the wrath of God is revealed from heaven against all ungodliness and unrighteousness of men, who hold the truth in unrighteousness;
[19] Because that which may be known of God is manifest in them; for God hath shewed it unto them.
[20] For the invisible things of him from the creation of the world are clearly seen, being understood by the things that are made, even his eternal power and Godhead; so that they are without excuse:
[21] Because that, when they knew God, they glorified him not as God, neither were thankful; but became vain in their imaginations, and their foolish heart was darkened.
[22] Professing themselves to be wise, they became fools,
[23] And changed the glory of the uncorruptible God into an image made like to corruptible man, and to birds, and four footed beasts, and creeping things.

Day 10: The Righteousness of Faith

²⁴ Wherefore God also gave them up to uncleanness through the lusts of their own hearts, to dishonour their own bodies between themselves:
²⁵ Who changed the truth of God into a lie, and worshipped and served the creature more than the Creator, who is blessed for ever. Amen.
²⁶ For this cause God gave them up unto vile affections: for even their women did change the natural use into that which is against nature:
²⁷ And likewise also the men, leaving the natural use of the woman, burned in their lust one toward another; men with men working that which is unseemly, and receiving in themselves that recompence of their error which was meet.
²⁸ And even as they did not like to retain God in their knowledge, God gave them over to a reprobate mind, to do those things which are not convenient;
²⁹ Being filled with all unrighteousness, fornication, wickedness, covetousness, maliciousness; full of envy, murder, debate, deceit, malignity; whisperers,
³⁰ Backbiters, haters of God, despiteful, proud, boasters, inventors of evil things, disobedient to parents,
³¹ Without understanding, covenant breakers, without natural affection, implacable, unmerciful:
³² Who knowing the judgment of God, that they which commit such things are worthy of death, not only do the same, but have pleasure in them that do them.

I CORINTHIANS 6:9-11 KJV

⁹ Know ye not that the unrighteous shall not inherit the kingdom of God? Be not deceived: neither fornicators, nor idolaters, nor adulterers, nor effeminate, nor abusers of themselves with mankind,
¹⁰ Nor thieves, nor covetous, nor drunkards, nor revilers, nor extortioners, shall inherit the kingdom of God.
¹¹ And such were some of you: but ye are washed, but ye are sanctified, but ye are justified in the name of the Lord Jesus, and by the Spirit of our God.

I CORINTHIANS 1:18 KJV

¹⁸ For the preaching of the cross is to them that perish foolishness; but unto us which are saved it is the power of God.

II CORINTHIANS 5:17-21 KJV

¹⁷ Therefore if any man be in Christ, he is a new creature: old things are passed away; behold, all things are become new
¹⁸ And all things are of God, who hath reconciled us to himself by Jesus Christ, and hath given to us the ministry of reconciliation;
¹⁹ To wit, that God was in Christ, reconciling the world unto himself, not imputing their trespasses unto them; and hath committed unto us the word of reconciliation.
²⁰ Now then we are ambassadors for Christ, as though God did beseech you by us: we pray you in Christ's stead, be ye reconciled to God.
²¹ For he hath made him to be sin for us, who knew no sin; that we might be made the righteousness of God in him.

EPHESIANS 4:21-24 KJV

²¹ If so be that ye have heard him, and have been taught by him, as the truth is in Jesus:
²² That ye put off concerning the former conversation the old man, which is corrupt according to the deceitful lusts;
²³ And be renewed in the spirit of your mind;
²⁴ And that ye put on the new man, which after God is created in righteousness and true holiness.

II CORINTHIANS 4:6-18 KJV

⁶ For God, who commanded the light to shine out of darkness, hath shined in our hearts, to give the light of the knowledge of the glory of God in the face of Jesus Christ.
⁷ But we have this treasure in earthen vessels, that the excellency of the power may be of God, and not of us.
⁸ We are troubled on every side, yet not distressed; we are perplexed, but not in despair;
⁹ Persecuted, but not forsaken; cast down, but not destroyed;

Day 10: The Righteousness of Faith

¹⁰ Always bearing about in the body the dying of the Lord Jesus, that the life also of Jesus might be made manifest in our body.
¹¹ For we which live are always delivered unto death for Jesus' sake, that the life also of Jesus might be made manifest in our mortal flesh.
¹² So then death worketh in us, but life in you.
¹³ We having the same spirit of faith, according as it is written, I believed, and therefore have I spoken; we also believe, and therefore speak;
¹⁴ Knowing that he which raised up the Lord Jesus shall raise up us also by Jesus, and shall present us with you.
¹⁵ For all things are for your sakes, that the abundant grace might through the thanksgiving of many redound to the glory of God.
¹⁶ For which cause we faint not; but though our outward man perish, yet the inward man is renewed day by day.
¹⁷ For our light affliction, which is but for a moment, worketh for us a far more exceeding and eternal weight of glory;
¹⁸ While we look not at the things which are seen, but at the things which are not seen: for the things which are seen are temporal; but the things which are not seen are eternal.

HEBREWS 11:1-7 KJV

¹ Now faith is the substance of things hoped for, the evidence of things not seen.
² For by it the elders obtained a good report.
³ Through faith we understand that the worlds were framed by the word of God, so that things which are seen were not made of things which do appear.
⁴ By faith Abel offered unto God a more excellent sacrifice than Cain, by which he obtained witness that he was righteous, God testifying of his gifts: and by it he being dead yet speaketh.
⁵ By faith Enoch was translated that he should not see death; and was not found, because God had translated him: for before his translation he had this testimony, that he pleased God.
⁶ But without faith it is impossible to please him: for he that cometh to God must believe that he is, and that he is a rewarder of them that diligently seek him.

⁷ By faith Noah, being warned of God of things not seen as yet, moved with fear, prepared an ark to the saving of his house; by the which he condemned the world, and became heir of the righteousness which is by faith.

ROMANS 4:13-25 KJV

¹³ For the promise, that he should be the heir of the world, was not to Abraham, or to his seed, through the law, but through the righteousness of faith.
¹⁴ For if they which are of the law be heirs, faith is made void, and the promise made of none effect:
¹⁵ Because the law worketh wrath: for where no law is, there is no transgression.
¹⁶ Therefore it is of faith, that it might be by grace; to the end the promise might be sure to all the seed; not to that only which is of the law, but to that also which is of the faith of Abraham; who is the father of us all,
¹⁷ (As it is written, I have made thee a father of many nations,) before him whom he believed, even God, who quickeneth the dead, and calleth those things which be not as though they were.
¹⁸ Who against hope believed in hope, that he might become the father of many nations, according to that which was spoken, So shall thy seed be.
¹⁹ And being not weak in faith, he considered not his own body now dead, when he was about an hundred years old, neither yet the deadness of Sarah's womb:
²⁰ He staggered not at the promise of God through unbelief; but was strong in faith, giving glory to God;
²¹ And being fully persuaded that, what he had promised, he was able also to perform.
²² And therefore it was imputed to him for righteousness.
²³ Now it was not written for his sake alone, that it was imputed to him;
²⁴ But for us also, to whom it shall be imputed, if we believe on him that raised up Jesus our Lord from the dead;
²⁵ Who was delivered for our offences, and was raised again for our justification.

Day 10: The Righteousness of Faith

ISAIAH 53:3-12 KJV

³ He [Jesus] is despised and rejected of men; a man of sorrows, and acquainted with grief: and we hid as it were our faces from him; he was despised, and we esteemed him not.
⁴ Surely he hath borne our griefs, and carried our sorrows: yet we did esteem him stricken, smitten of God, and afflicted.
⁵ But he was wounded for our transgressions, he was bruised for our iniquities: the chastisement of our peace was upon him; and with his stripes we are healed.
⁶ All we like sheep have gone astray; we have turned every one to his own way; and the Lord hath laid on him the iniquity of us all.
⁷ He was oppressed, and he was afflicted, yet he opened not his mouth: he is brought as a lamb to the slaughter, and as a sheep before her shearers is dumb, so he openeth not his mouth.
⁸ He was taken from prison and from judgment: and who shall declare his generation? for he was cut off out of the land of the living: for the transgression of my people was he stricken.
⁹ And he made his grave with the wicked, and with the rich in his death; because he had done no violence, neither was any deceit in his mouth.
¹⁰ Yet it pleased the Lord to bruise him; he hath put him to grief: when thou shalt make his soul an offering for sin, he shall see his seed, he shall prolong his days, and the pleasure of the Lord shall prosper in his hand.
¹¹ He shall see of the travail of his soul, and shall be satisfied: by his knowledge shall my righteous servant justify many; for he shall bear their iniquities.
¹² Therefore will I divide him a portion with the great, and he shall divide the spoil with the strong; because he hath poured out his soul unto death: and he was numbered with the transgressors; and he bare the sin of many, and made intercession for the transgressors.

II CORINTHIANS 5:21 KJV

²¹ For he [God] hath made him to be sin for us, who knew no sin; that we might be made the righteousness of God in him.

ROMANS 10:1-17 KJV

[1] Brethren, my heart's desire and prayer to God for Israel is, that they might be saved.

[2] For I [Paul] bear them record that they have a zeal of God, but not according to knowledge.

[3] For they being ignorant of God's righteousness, and going about to establish their own righteousness, have not submitted themselves unto the righteousness of God.

[4] For Christ is the end of the law for righteousness to every one that believeth.

[5] For Moses describeth the righteousness which is of the law, That the man which doeth those things shall live by them.

[6] But the righteousness which is of faith speaketh on this wise, Say not in thine heart, Who shall ascend into heaven? (that is, to bring Christ down from above:)

[7] Or, Who shall descend into the deep? (that is, to bring up Christ again from the dead.)

[8] But what saith it? The word is nigh thee, even in thy mouth, and in thy heart: that is, the word of faith, which we preach;

[9] That if thou shalt confess with thy mouth the Lord Jesus, and shalt believe in thine heart that God hath raised him from the dead, thou shalt be saved.

[10] For with the heart man believeth unto righteousness; and with the mouth confession is made unto salvation.

[11] For the scripture saith, Whosoever believeth on him shall not be ashamed.

[12] For there is no difference between the Jew and the Greek: for the same Lord over all is rich unto all that call upon him.

[13] For whosoever shall call upon the name of the Lord shall be saved.

[14] How then shall they call on him in whom they have not believed? and how shall they believe in him of whom they have not heard? and how shall they hear without a preacher?

[15] And how shall they preach, except they be sent? as it is written, How beautiful are the feet of them that preach the gospel of peace, and bring glad tidings of good things!

¹⁶ But they have not all obeyed the gospel. For Esaias saith, Lord, who hath believed our report?
¹⁷ So then faith cometh by hearing, and hearing by the word of God.

II CORINTHIANS 4:13-14 KJV

¹³ We having the same spirit of faith, according as it is written, I believed, and therefore have I spoken; we also believe, and therefore speak;
¹⁴ Knowing that he which raised up the Lord Jesus shall raise up us also by Jesus, and shall present us with you.

ROMANS 8:10-14 KJV

¹⁰ And if Christ be in you, the body is dead because of sin; but the Spirit is life because of righteousness.
¹¹ But if the Spirit of him that raised up Jesus from the dead dwell in you, he that raised up Christ from the dead shall also quicken your mortal bodies by his Spirit that dwelleth in you.
¹² Therefore, brethren, we are debtors, not to the flesh, to live after the flesh.
¹³ For if ye live after the flesh, ye shall die: but if ye through the Spirit do mortify the deeds of the body, ye shall live.
¹⁴ For as many as are led by the Spirit of God, they are the sons of God.

PSALM 1:1-6 KJV

¹ Blessed is the man that walketh not in the counsel of the ungodly, nor standeth in the way of sinners, nor sitteth in the seat of the scornful.
² But his delight is in the law of the Lord; and in his law doth he meditate day and night.
³ And he shall be like a tree planted by the rivers of water, that bringeth forth his fruit in his season; his leaf also shall not wither; and whatsoever he doeth shall prosper.
⁴ The ungodly are not so: but are like the chaff which the wind driveth away.

⁵ Therefore the ungodly shall not stand in the judgment, nor sinners in the congregation of the righteous.
⁶ For the Lord knoweth the way of the righteous: but the way of the ungodly shall perish.

HEBREWS 4:12-16 KJV

¹² For the word of God is quick, and powerful, and sharper than any two-edged sword, piercing even to the dividing asunder of soul and spirit, and of the joints and marrow, and is a discerner of the thoughts and intents of the heart.
¹³ Neither is there any creature that is not manifest in his sight: but all things are naked and opened unto the eyes of him with whom we have to do.
¹⁴ Seeing then that we have a great high priest, that is passed into the heavens, Jesus the Son of God, let us hold fast our profession.
¹⁵ For we have not an high priest which cannot be touched with the feeling of our infirmities; but was in all points tempted like as we are, yet without sin.
¹⁶ Let us therefore come boldly unto the throne of grace, that we may obtain mercy, and find grace to help in time of need.

I PETER 1:20-23 KJV

²⁰ Who [Jesus] verily was foreordained before the foundation of the world, but was manifest in these last times for you,
²¹ Who by him do believe in God, that raised him up from the dead, and gave him glory; that your faith and hope might be in God.
²² Seeing ye have purified your souls in obeying the truth through the Spirit unto unfeigned love of the brethren, see that ye love one another with a pure heart fervently:
²³ Being born again, not of corruptible seed, but of incorruptible, by the word of God, which liveth and abideth for ever.

Day 10: The Righteousness of Faith

II PETER 1:1-11 KJV

¹ Simon Peter, a servant and an apostle of Jesus Christ, to them that have obtained like precious faith with us through the righteousness of God and our Saviour Jesus Christ:
² Grace and peace be multiplied unto you through the knowledge of God, and of Jesus our Lord,
³ According as his divine power hath given unto us all things that pertain unto life and godliness, through the knowledge of him that hath called us to glory and virtue:
⁴ Whereby are given unto us exceeding great and precious promises: that by these ye might be partakers of the divine nature, having escaped the corruption that is in the world through lust.
⁵ And beside this, giving all diligence, add to your faith virtue; and to virtue knowledge;
⁶ And to knowledge temperance; and to temperance patience; and to patience godliness;
⁷ And to godliness brotherly kindness; and to brotherly kindness charity.
⁸ For if these things be in you, and abound, they make you that ye shall neither be barren nor unfruitful in the knowledge of our Lord Jesus Christ.
⁹ But he that lacketh these things is blind, and cannot see afar off, and hath forgotten that he was purged from his old sins.
¹⁰ Wherefore the rather, brethren, give diligence to make your calling and election sure: for if ye do these things, ye shall never fall:
¹¹ For so an entrance shall be ministered unto you abundantly into the everlasting kingdom of our Lord and Saviour Jesus Christ.

I THESSALONIANS 1:1-6 KJV

¹ Paul, and Silvanus, and Timotheus, unto the church of the Thessalonians which is in God the Father and in the Lord Jesus Christ: Grace be unto you, and peace, from God our Father, and the Lord Jesus Christ.
² We give thanks to God always for you all, making mention of you in our prayers;

³ Remembering without ceasing your work of faith, and labour of love, and patience of hope in our Lord Jesus Christ, in the sight of God and our Father;
⁴ Knowing, brethren beloved, your election of God.
⁵ For our gospel came not unto you in word only, but also in power, and in the Holy Ghost, and in much assurance; as ye know what manner of men we were among you for your sake.
⁶ And ye became followers of us, and of the Lord, having received the word in much affliction, with joy of the Holy Ghost.

GALATIANS 5:5 KJV

⁵ For we through the Spirit wait for the hope of righteousness by faith.

HEBREWS 10:35-39 KJV

³⁵ Cast not away therefore your confidence, which hath great recompence of reward.
³⁶ For ye have need of patience, that, after ye have done the will of God, ye might receive the promise.
³⁷ For yet a little while, and he that shall come will come, and will not tarry.
³⁸ Now the just shall live by faith: but if any man draw back, my soul shall have no pleasure in him.
³⁹ But we are not of them who draw back unto perdition; but of them that believe to the saving of the soul.

II THESSALONIANS 1:1-12 KJV

¹ Paul, and Silvanus, and Timotheus, unto the church of the Thessalonians in God our Father and the Lord Jesus Christ:
² Grace unto you, and peace, from God our Father and the Lord Jesus Christ.
³ We are bound to thank God always for you, brethren, as it is meet, because that your faith groweth exceedingly, and the charity of every one of you all toward each other aboundeth;

Day 10: The Righteousness of Faith

⁴ So that we ourselves glory in you in the churches of God for your patience and faith in all your persecutions and tribulations that ye endure:
⁵ Which is a manifest token of the righteous judgment of God, that ye may be counted worthy of the kingdom of God, for which ye also suffer:
⁶ Seeing it is a righteous thing with God to recompense tribulation to them that trouble you;
⁷ And to you who are troubled rest with us, when the Lord Jesus shall be revealed from heaven with his mighty angels,
⁸ In flaming fire taking vengeance on them that know not God, and that obey not the gospel of our Lord Jesus Christ:
⁹ Who shall be punished with everlasting destruction from the presence of the Lord, and from the glory of his power;
¹⁰ When he shall come to be glorified in his saints, and to be admired in all them that believe (because our testimony among you was believed) in that day.
¹¹ Wherefore also we pray always for you, that our God would count you worthy of this calling, and fulfil all the good pleasure of his goodness, and the work of faith with power:
¹² That the name of our Lord Jesus Christ may be glorified in you, and ye in him, according to the grace of our God and the Lord Jesus Christ.

LUKE 18:7-8 KJV

⁷ And shall not God avenge his own elect, which cry day and night unto him, though he bear long with them?
⁸ I [Jesus] tell you that he will avenge them speedily. Nevertheless when the Son of man cometh, shall he find faith on the earth?

MARK 11:22-26 KJV

²² And Jesus answering saith unto them, Have faith in God.
²³ For verily I say unto you, That whosoever shall say unto this mountain, Be thou removed, and be thou cast into the sea; and shall not doubt in his heart, but shall believe that those things which he saith shall come to pass; he shall have whatsoever he saith.

²⁴ Therefore I say unto you, What things soever ye desire, when ye pray, believe that ye receive them, and ye shall have them.
²⁵ And when ye stand praying, forgive, if ye have ought against any: that your Father also which is in heaven may forgive you your trespasses.
²⁶ But if ye do not forgive, neither will your Father which is in heaven forgive your trespasses.

II CORINTHIANS 4:13 KJV

¹³ We having the same spirit of faith, according as it is written, I believed, and therefore have I spoken; we also believe, and therefore speak;

GALATIANS 3:5-6 KJV

⁵ He therefore that ministereth to you the Spirit, and worketh miracles among you, doeth he it by the works of the law, or by the hearing of faith?
⁶ Even as Abraham believed God, and it was accounted to him for righteousness.

HEBREWS 4:1-3 KJV

¹ Let us therefore fear, lest, a promise being left us of entering into his rest, any of you should seem to come short of it.
² For unto us was the gospel preached, as well as unto them: but the word preached did not profit them, not being mixed with faith in them that heard it.
³ For we which have believed do enter into rest, as he said, As I have sworn in my wrath, if they shall enter into my rest: although the works were finished from the foundation of the world.

DAY 11

---◆---

Work of the Holy Spirit in Salvation

TITUS 2:11-15 KJV

[11] For the grace of God that bringeth salvation hath appeared to all men,
[12] Teaching us that, denying ungodliness and worldly lusts, we should live soberly, righteously, and godly, in this present world;
[13] Looking for that blessed hope, and the glorious appearing of the great God and our Saviour Jesus Christ;
[14] Who gave himself for us, that he might redeem us from all iniquity, and purify unto himself a peculiar people, zealous of good works.
[15] These things speak, and exhort, and rebuke with all authority. Let no man despise thee.

TITUS 3:1-4, 6-8 KJV and v. 5 NKJV

[1] Put them in mind to be subject to principalities and powers, to obey magistrates, to be ready to every good work,
[2] To speak evil of no man, to be no brawlers, but gentle, shewing all meekness unto all men.
[3] For we ourselves also were sometimes foolish, disobedient, deceived, serving divers lusts and pleasures, living in malice and envy, hateful, and hating one another.

⁴ But after that the kindness and love of God our Saviour toward man appeared,

⁵ Not by works of righteousness which we have done, but according to His mercy He saved us, through the washing of regeneration and renewing of the Holy Spirit,

⁶ Which he shed on us abundantly through Jesus Christ our Saviour;

⁷ That being justified by his grace, we should be made heirs according to the hope of eternal life.

⁸ This is a faithful saying, and these things I will that thou affirm constantly, that they which have believed in God might be careful to maintain good works. These things are good and profitable unto men.

JOHN 14:12-21 KJV

¹² Verily, verily, I [Jesus] say unto you, He that believeth on me, the works that I do shall he do also; and greater works than these shall he do; because I go unto my Father.

¹³ And whatsoever ye shall ask in my name, that will I do, that the Father may be glorified in the Son.

¹⁴ If ye shall ask any thing in my name, I will do it.

¹⁵ If ye love me, keep my commandments.

¹⁶ And I will pray the Father, and he shall give you another Comforter, that he may abide with you for ever;

¹⁷ Even the Spirit of truth; whom the world cannot receive, because it seeth him not, neither knoweth him: but ye know him; for he dwelleth with you, and shall be in you.

¹⁸ I will not leave you comfortless: I will come to you.

¹⁹ Yet a little while, and the world seeth me no more; but ye see me: because I live, ye shall live also.

²⁰ At that day ye shall know that I am in my Father, and ye in me, and I in you.

²¹ He that hath my commandments, and keepeth them, he it is that loveth me: and he that loveth me shall be loved of my Father, and I will love him, and will manifest myself to him.

Day 11: Work of the Holy Spirit in Salvation

There are three wonderful works performed by the Holy Spirit in preparing unsaved people to become Christians. Satan would enjoy nothing more than to destroy people before they make their decision to accept Christ as Savior. But the Holy Spirit prevents this from occurring.

---

1. The work of the Holy Spirit in restraining.

ISAIAH 59:19 NKJV and v. 20-21 KJV

[19] So shall they fear the name of the Lord from the west, and His glory from the rising of the sun; when the enemy comes in like a flood, the Spirit of the Lord will lift up a standard against him.
[20] "And the Redeemer shall come to Zion, and unto them that turn from transgression in Jacob, saith the Lord.
[21] As for me, this is my covenant with them, saith the Lord; My spirit that is upon thee, and my words which I have put in thy mouth, shall not depart out of thy mouth, nor out of the mouth of thy seed, nor out of the mouth of thy seed's seed, saith the Lord, from henceforth and for ever.

LUKE 10:17-20 KJV

[17] And the seventy returned again with joy, saying, Lord, even the devils are subject unto us through thy name.
[18] And he [Jesus] said unto them, I beheld Satan as lightning fall from heaven.
[19] Behold, I give unto you power to tread on serpents and scorpions, and over all the power of the enemy: and nothing shall by any means hurt you.
[20] Notwithstanding in this rejoice not, that the spirits are subject unto you; but rather rejoice, because your names are written in heaven.

JOHN 12:31-32 KJV

³¹ Now is the judgment of this world: now shall the prince of this world be cast out.
³² And I, if I be lifted up from the earth, will draw all men unto me.

COLOSSIANS 2:12-15 KJV

¹² Buried with him [Jesus] in baptism, wherein also ye are risen with him through the faith of the operation of God, who hath raised him from the dead.
¹³ And you, being dead in your sins and the uncircumcision of your flesh, hath he quickened together with him, having forgiven you all trespasses;
¹⁴ Blotting out the handwriting of ordinances that was against us, which was contrary to us, and took it out of the way, nailing it to his cross;
¹⁵ And having spoiled principalities and powers, he made a shew of them openly, triumphing over them in it.

JOHN 16:5-7, 9-11 KJV and v. 8 NKJV

⁵ But now I [Jesus] go my way to him that sent me; and none of you asketh me, Whither goest thou?
⁶ But because I have said these things unto you, sorrow hath filled your heart.
⁷ Nevertheless I tell you the truth; It is expedient for you that I go away: for if I go not away, the Comforter will not come unto you; but if I depart, I will send him unto you.
⁸ And when He has come, He [Holy Spirit] will <u>convict</u> the world of <u>sin</u>, and of <u>righteousness</u>, and of <u>judgment</u>:
⁹ Of sin, because they believe not on me;
¹⁰ Of righteousness, because I go to my Father, and ye see me no more;
¹¹ Of <u>judgment, because the prince of this world [Satan] is judged</u>. [Holy Spirit in restraining.]

2. The work of the Holy Spirit in convicting.

ACTS 2:32-41 KJV

[32] This Jesus hath God raised up, whereof we all are witnesses.
[33] Therefore being by the right hand of God exalted, and having received of the Father the promise of the Holy Ghost, he hath shed forth this, which ye now see and hear.
[34] For David is not ascended into the heavens: but he saith himself, The Lord said unto my Lord, Sit thou on my right hand,
[35] Until I make thy foes thy footstool.
[36] Therefore let all the house of Israel know assuredly, that God hath made the same Jesus, whom ye have crucified, both Lord and Christ.
[37] Now when they heard this, they were pricked in their heart, and said unto Peter and to the rest of the apostles, Men and brethren, what shall we do?
[38] Then Peter said unto them, Repent, and be baptized every one of you in the name of Jesus Christ for the remission of sins, and ye shall receive the gift of the Holy Ghost.
[39] For the promise is unto you, and to your children, and to all that are afar off, even as many as the Lord our God shall call.
[40] And with many other words did he testify and exhort, saying, Save yourselves from this untoward generation.
[41] Then they that gladly received his word were baptized: and the same day there were added unto them about three thousand souls.

JOHN 12:42-50 KJV

[42] Nevertheless among the chief rulers also many believed on him; but because of the Pharisees they did not confess him, lest they should be put out of the synagogue:
[43] For they loved the praise of men more than the praise of God.

Mankind's sin and righteousness are exposed by the Holy Spirit.

---

⁴⁴ Jesus cried and said, He that believeth on me, believeth not on me, but on him that sent me.
⁴⁵ And he that seeth me seeth him that sent me.
⁴⁶ I am come a light into the world, that whosoever believeth on me should not abide in darkness.
⁴⁷ And if any man hear my words, and believe not, I judge him not: for I came not to judge the world, but to save the world.
⁴⁸ He that rejecteth me, and receiveth not my words, hath one that judgeth him: the word that I have spoken, the same shall judge him in the last day.
⁴⁹ For I have not spoken of myself; but the Father which sent me, he gave me a commandment, what I should say, and what I should speak.
⁵⁰ And I know that his commandment is life everlasting: whatsoever I speak therefore, even as the Father said unto me, so I speak.

JOHN 3:34-36 KJV

³⁴ For he whom God hath sent speaketh the words of God: for God giveth not the Spirit by measure unto him.
³⁵ The Father loveth the Son, and hath given all things into his hand.
³⁶ He that believeth on the Son hath everlasting life: and he that believeth not the Son shall not see life; but the wrath of God abideth on him.

JOHN 14:26-29 KJV

²⁶ But the Comforter, which is the Holy Ghost, whom the Father will send in my name, he shall teach you all things, and bring all things to your remembrance, whatsoever I have said unto you.

²⁷ Peace I leave with you, my peace I give unto you: not as the world giveth, give I unto you. Let not your heart be troubled, neither let it be afraid.
²⁸ Ye have heard how I said unto you, I go away, and come again unto you. If ye loved me, ye would rejoice, because I said, I go unto the Father: for my Father is greater than I.
²⁹ And now I have told you before it come to pass, that, when it is come to pass, ye might believe.

JOHN 20:21-31 KJV

²¹ Then said Jesus to them again, Peace be unto you: as my Father hath sent me, even so send I you.
²² And when he had said this, he breathed on them, and saith unto them, Receive ye the Holy Ghost:
²³ Whose soever sins ye remit, they are remitted unto them; and whose soever sins ye retain, they are retained.
²⁴ But Thomas, one of the twelve, called Didymus, was not with them when Jesus came.
²⁵ The other disciples therefore said unto him, We have seen the Lord. But he said unto them, Except I shall see in his hands the print of the nails, and put my finger into the print of the nails, and thrust my hand into his side, I will not believe.
²⁶ And after eight days again his disciples were within, and Thomas with them: then came Jesus, the doors being shut, and stood in the midst, and said, Peace be unto you.
²⁷ Then saith he to Thomas, Reach hither thy finger, and behold my hands; and reach hither thy hand, and thrust it into my side: and be not faithless, but believing.
²⁸ And Thomas answered and said unto him, My Lord and my God.
²⁹ Jesus saith unto him, Thomas, because thou hast seen me, thou hast believed: blessed are they that have not seen, and yet have believed.
³⁰ And many other signs truly did Jesus in the presence of his disciples, which are not written in this book:

³¹ But these are written, that ye might believe that Jesus is the Christ, the Son of God; and that believing ye might have life through his name.

JOHN 16:5-7, 9-11 KJV, and v. 8 NKJV

⁵ But now I [Jesus] go my way to him that sent me; and none of you asketh me, Whither goest thou?
⁶ But because I have said these things unto you, sorrow hath filled your heart.
⁷ Nevertheless I tell you the truth; It is expedient for you that I go away: for if I go not away, the Comforter will not come unto you; but if I depart, I will send him unto you.
⁸ And when He has come, He will <u>convict</u> the world of <u>sin</u>, and of <u>righteousness</u>, and of <u>judgment</u>:
⁹ <u>Of sin, because they believe not on me</u>; [Holy Spirit in convicting]
¹⁰ Of righteousness, because I go to my Father, and ye see me no more;
¹¹ Of judgment, because the prince of this world is judged.

There are two well-known examples of sinners being convicted by the Holy Spirit in the book of Acts. Felix and King Agrippa.

➤ KING AGRIPPA ➤

ACTS 26:9-27, 29 KJV, and v. 28 NKJV

⁹ I [Paul] verily thought with myself, that I ought to do many things contrary to the name of Jesus of Nazareth.
¹⁰ Which thing I also did in Jerusalem: and many of the saints did I shut up in prison, having received authority from the chief priests; and when they were put to death, I gave my voice against them.

¹¹ And I punished them oft in every synagogue, and compelled them to blaspheme; and being exceedingly mad against them, I persecuted them even unto strange cities.

¹² Whereupon as I went to Damascus with authority and commission from the chief priests,

¹³ At midday, O king, I saw in the way a light from heaven, above the brightness of the sun, shining round about me and them which journeyed with me.

¹⁴ And when we were all fallen to the earth, I heard a voice speaking unto me, and saying in the Hebrew tongue, Saul, Saul, why persecutest thou me? it is hard for thee to kick against the pricks.

¹⁵ And I said, Who art thou, Lord? And he said, I am Jesus whom thou persecutest.

¹⁶ But rise, and stand upon thy feet: for I have appeared unto thee for this purpose, to make thee a minister and a witness both of these things which thou hast seen, and of those things in the which I will appear unto thee;

¹⁷ Delivering thee from the people, and from the Gentiles, unto whom now I send thee,

¹⁸ To open their eyes, and to turn them from darkness to light, and from the power of Satan unto God, that they may receive forgiveness of sins, and inheritance among them which are sanctified by faith that is in me.

¹⁹ Whereupon, O king Agrippa, I was not disobedient unto the heavenly vision:

²⁰ But shewed first unto them of Damascus, and at Jerusalem, and throughout all the coasts of Judaea, and then to the Gentiles, that they should repent and turn to God, and do works meet for repentance.

²¹ For these causes the Jews caught me in the temple, and went about to kill me.

²² Having therefore obtained help of God, I continue unto this day, witnessing both to small and great, saying none other things than those which the prophets and Moses did say should come:

²³ That Christ should suffer, and that he should be the first that should rise from the dead, and should shew light unto the people, and to the Gentiles.

²⁴ And as he thus spake for himself, Festus said with a loud voice, Paul, thou art beside thyself; much learning doth make thee mad.

²⁵ But he said, I am not mad, most noble Festus; but speak forth the words of truth and soberness.

²⁶ For the king knoweth of these things, before whom also I speak freely: for I am persuaded that none of these things are hidden from him; for this thing was not done in a corner.

²⁷ King Agrippa, believest thou the prophets? I know that thou believest.

²⁸ <u>Then</u> <u>Agrippa</u> <u>said</u> <u>to</u> <u>Paul</u>, "<u>You</u> <u>almost</u> <u>persuade</u> <u>me</u> <u>to</u> <u>become</u> <u>a</u> <u>Christian</u>."

²⁹ And Paul said, I would to God, that not only thou, but also all that hear me this day, were both almost, and altogether such as I am, except these bonds.

⋙ FELIX ⋘

ACTS 24:14-24 KJV and v. 25 NKJV

¹⁴ But this I [Paul] confess unto thee, that after the way which they call heresy, so worship I the God of my fathers, believing all things which are written in the law and in the prophets:

¹⁵ And have hope toward God, which they themselves also allow, that there shall be a resurrection of the dead, both of the just and unjust.

¹⁶ And herein do I exercise myself, to have always a conscience void to offence toward God, and toward men.

¹⁷ Now after many years I came to bring alms to my nation, and offerings.

¹⁸ Whereupon certain Jews from Asia found me purified in the temple, neither with multitude, nor with tumult.

¹⁹ Who ought to have been here before thee, and object, if they had ought against me.

²⁰ Or else let these same here say, if they have found any evil doing in me, while I stood before the council,
²¹ Except it be for this one voice, that I cried standing among them, Touching the resurrection of the dead I am called in question by you this day.
²² And when Felix heard these things, having more perfect knowledge of that way, he deferred them, and said, When Lysias the chief captain shall come down, I will know the uttermost of your matter.
²³ And he commanded a centurion to keep Paul, and to let him have liberty, and that he should forbid none of his acquaintance to minister or come unto him.
²⁴ And after certain days, when Felix came with his wife Drusilla, which was a Jewess, he sent for Paul, and heard him concerning the faith in Christ.
²⁵ Now as he reasoned about righteousness, self-control, and the judgment to come, <u>Felix was afraid and answered, "Go away for now; when I have a convenient time I will call for you</u>."

3. The work of the Holy Spirit in regenerating.

ACTS 10:34-43 KJV

³⁴ Then Peter opened his mouth, and said, Of a truth I perceive that God is no respecter of persons:
³⁵ But in every nation he that feareth him, and worketh righteousness, is accepted with him.
³⁶ The word which God sent unto the children of Israel, preaching peace by Jesus Christ: (he is Lord of all:)
³⁷ That word, I say, ye know, which was published throughout all Judaea, and began from Galilee, after the baptism which John preached;

⁸⁸ How God anointed Jesus of Nazareth with the Holy Ghost and with power: who went about doing good, and healing all that were oppressed of the devil; for God was with him.

³⁹ And we are witnesses of all things which he did both in the land of the Jews, and in Jerusalem; whom they slew and hanged on a tree:

⁴⁰ Him God raised up the third day, and shewed him openly;

⁴¹ Not to all the people, but unto witnesses chosen before God, even to us, who did eat and drink with him after he rose from the dead.

⁴² And he commanded us to preach unto the people, and to testify that it is he which was ordained of God to be the Judge of quick and dead.

⁴³ To him give all the prophets witness, that through his name whosoever believeth in him shall receive remission of sins.

When a repenting sinner accepts Christ as Savior he is given a new nature by the Holy Spirit.

II CORINTHIANS 5:17 NKJV

¹⁷ Therefore, if anyone is in Christ, he is a new creation; old things have passed away; behold, all things have become new.

TITUS 3:4-7 KJV

⁴ But after that the kindness and love of God our Saviour toward man appeared,

⁵ Not by works of righteousness which we have done, but according to his mercy he saved us, by the washing of regeneration, and renewing of the Holy Ghost;

⁶ Which he shed on us abundantly through Jesus Christ our Saviour;

⁷ That being justified by his grace, we should be made heirs according to the hope of eternal life.

Day 11: Work of the Holy Spirit in Salvation

II PETER 1:3-4 KJV

³ According as his divine power hath given unto us all things that pertain unto life and godliness, through the knowledge of him that hath called us to glory and virtue:
⁴ Whereby are given unto us exceeding great and precious promises: that by these ye might be partakers of the divine nature, having escaped the corruption that is in the world through lust.

II CORINTHIANS 7:1 KJV

¹ Having therefore these promises, dearly beloved, let us cleanse ourselves from all filthiness of the flesh and spirit, perfecting holiness in the fear of God.

ROMANS 12:1-2 KJV

¹ I beseech you therefore, brethren, by the mercies of God, that ye present your bodies a living sacrifice, holy, acceptable unto God, which is your reasonable service.
² And be not conformed to this world: but be ye transformed by the renewing of your mind, that ye may prove what is that good, and acceptable, and perfect, will of God.

Jesus carefully explained this ministry of the Holy Spirit to Nicodemus.

JOHN 3:3-7 NKJV, and v. 8 KJV

³ Jesus answered and said to him, "Most assuredly, I say to you, unless one is born again, he cannot see the kingdom of God."
⁴ Nicodemus said to Him, "How can a man be born when he is old? Can he enter a second time into his mother's womb and be born?"
⁵ Jesus answered, "Most assuredly, I say to you, unless one is born of water and the Spirit, he cannot enter the kingdom of God.

⁶ That which is born of the flesh is flesh, and that which is born of the Spirit is spirit.
⁷ Do not marvel that I said to you, 'You must be born again.'
⁸ The wind bloweth where it listeth, and thou hearest the sound thereof, but canst not tell whence it cometh, and whither it goeth: so is every one that is born of the Spirit.

JOHN 16:5-7, 9-11 KJV and v. 8 NKJV

⁵ But now I [Jesus] go my way to him that sent me; and none of you asketh me, Whither goest thou?
⁶ But because I have said these things unto you, sorrow hath filled your heart.
⁷ Nevertheless I tell you the truth; It is expedient for you that I go away: for if I go not away, the Comforter will not come unto you; but if I depart, I will send him unto you.
⁸ And when He has come, He will <u>convict</u> the world of <u>sin</u>, and of <u>righteousness</u>, and of <u>judgment</u>:
⁹ Of sin, because they believe not on me;
¹⁰ Of <u>righteousness, because I go to my Father, and ye see me no more</u>; [Holy Spirit in regenerating]
¹¹ Of judgment, because the prince of this world is judged.

DAY 12

The Person of the Holy Spirit

EPHESIANS 4:1-2, 4-6 KJV, and v. 3 NJKV

¹ I [Paul] therefore, the prisoner of the Lord, beseech you that ye walk worthy of the vocation wherewith ye are called,
² With all lowliness and meekness, with longsuffering, forbearing one another in love;
³ Endeavoring to keep the unity of the Spirit in the bond of peace.
⁴ There is one body, and one Spirit, even as ye are called in one hope of your calling;
⁵ One Lord, one faith, one baptism,
⁶ One God and Father of all, who is above all, and through all, and in you all.

> One of the most serious errors in the minds of many people concerning the Holy Spirit is that He is simply a principle or an influence. On the contrary, the Holy Spirit is as much a person (individual existence of a conscious being) as the Father and the Son.

ROMANS 8:26, 28-39 KJV, and verse 27 NKJV

²⁶Likewise the Spirit also helpeth our infirmities: for we know not what we should pray for as we ought: but the Spirit itself maketh intercession for us with groanings which cannot be uttered.

²⁷ Now He who searches the hearts knows what the mind of the Spirit is, because He makes intercession for the saints according to the will of God..

²⁸ And we know that all things work together for good to them that love God, to them who are the called according to his purpose.

²⁹ For whom he did foreknow, he also did predestinate to be conformed to the image of his Son, that he might be the firstborn among many brethren.

³⁰ Moreover whom he did predestinate, them he also called: and whom he called, them he also justified: and whom he justified, them he also glorified.

³¹ What shall we then say to these things? If God be for us, who can be against us?

³² He that spared not his own Son, but delivered him up for us all, how shall he not with him also freely give us all things?

³³ Who shall lay any thing to the charge of God's elect? It is God that justifieth.

³⁴ Who is he that condemneth? It is Christ that died, yea rather, that is risen again, who is even at the right hand of God, who also maketh intercession for us.

³⁵ Who shall separate us from the love of Christ? shall tribulation, or distress, or persecution, or famine, or nakedness, or peril, or sword?

³⁶ As it is written, For thy sake we are killed all the day long; we are accounted as sheep for the slaughter.

³⁷ Nay, in all these things we are more than conquerors through him that loved us.

³⁸ For I am persuaded, that neither death, nor life, nor angels, nor principalities, nor powers, nor things present, nor things to come,

³⁹ Nor height, nor depth, nor any other creature, shall be able to separate us from the love of God, which is in Christ Jesus our Lord.

Day 12: The Person of the Holy Spirit

1. The personality of the Holy Spirit
The Bible speaks of the mind and will of the Holy Spirit.

I CORINTHIANS 12:4-10 KJV, and v. 11 NKJV

⁴ Now there are diversities of gifts, but the same Spirit.
⁵ And there are differences of administrations, but the same Lord.
⁶ And there are diversities of operations, but it is the same God which worketh all in all.
⁷ But the manifestation of the Spirit is given to every man to profit withal.
⁸ For to one is given by the Spirit the word of wisdom; to another the word of knowledge by the same Spirit;
⁹ To another faith by the same Spirit; to another the gifts of healing by the same Spirit;
¹⁰ To another the working of miracles; to another prophecy; to another discerning of spirits; to another divers kinds of tongues; to another the interpretation of tongues:
¹¹ But one and the same Spirit works all these things, distributing to each one individually as He wills.

> He is often described as speaking directly to men in the book of Acts. During Paul's Second Missionary Journey the Apostle was forbidden by the Spirit to visit a certain mission field and then was instructed to proceed toward another field of service.

ACTS 16:6, 7, 10 NKJV and v. 8-9 KJV

⁶ Now when they had gone through Phrygia and the region of Galatia, they were forbidden by the Holy Spirit to preach the word in Asia.
⁷ After they had come to Mysia, they tried to go into Bithynia, but the Spirit did not permit them.

⁸ And they passing by Mysia came down to Troas.
⁹ And a vision appeared to Paul in the night; There stood a man of Macedonia, and prayed him, saying, Come over into Macedonia, and help us.
¹⁰ Now after he had seen the vision, immediately we sought to go to Macedonia, concluding that the Lord had called us to preach the gospel to them.

It was God's Spirit who spoke directly to
Christian leaders in the Antioch church,
commanding them to send Paul and Barnabas
on their first missionary journey.

ACTS 13:2 NKJV, and 13:3-4 KJV

² As they ministered to the Lord, and fasted, the Holy Ghost said, Separate me Barnabas and Saul for the work whereunto I have called them.
³ Then, having fasted and prayed, and laid hands on them, they sent them away.
⁴ So, being sent out by the Holy Spirit, they went down to Seleucia, and from there they sailed to Cyprus.

2. The Deity of the Holy Spirit
He is not only a real person, but He is also God, as is God the Father, He too is everywhere at once.

PSALM 139:1-6, 8-14 KJV, and v. 7 NKJV

¹ O lord, thou hast searched me, and known me.
² Thou knowest my downsitting and mine uprising, thou understandest my thought afar off.

³ Thou compassest my path and my lying down, and art acquainted with all my ways.

⁴ For there is not a word in my tongue, but, lo, O Lord, thou knowest it altogether.

⁵ Thou hast beset me behind and before, and laid thine hand upon me.

⁶ Such knowledge is too wonderful for me; it is high, I cannot attain unto it.

⁷ Where can I go from Your Spirit? Or where can I flee from Your presence?

⁸ If I ascend up into heaven, thou art there: if I make my bed in hell, behold, thou art there.

⁹ If I take the wings of the morning, and dwell in the uttermost parts of the sea;

¹⁰ Even there shall thy hand lead me, and thy right hand shall hold me.

¹¹ If I say, Surely the darkness shall cover me; even the night shall be light about me.

¹² Yea, the darkness hideth not from thee; but the night shineth as the day: the darkness and the light are both alike to thee.

¹³ For thou hast possessed my reins: thou hast covered me in my mother's womb.

¹⁴ I will praise thee; for I am fearfully and wonderfully made: marvellous are thy works; and that my soul knoweth right well.

As the Son is eternal, the Holy Spirit has also existed forever.

HEBREWS 9:11-13, 15-17 KJV, and v. 14 NKJV

¹¹ But Christ being come an high priest of good things to come, by a greater and more perfect tabernacle, not made with hands, that is to say, not of this building;

¹² Neither by the blood of goats and calves, but by his own blood he entered in once into the holy place, having obtained eternal redemption for us.
¹³ For if the blood of bulls and of goats, and the ashes of an heifer sprinkling the unclean, sanctifieth to the purifying of the flesh:
¹⁴ How much more shall the blood of Christ, who through the eternal Spirit offered Himself without spot to God, cleanse your conscience from dead works to serve the living God?
¹⁵ And for this cause he is the mediator of the new testament, that by means of death, for the redemption of the transgressions that were under the first testament, they which are called might receive the promise of eternal inheritance.
¹⁶ For where a testament is, there must also of necessity be the death of the testator.
¹⁷ For a testament is of force after men are dead: otherwise it is of no strength at all while the testator liveth.

He is often referred to as God in the Bible.

ACTS 5:3-4 NKJV

³ But Peter said, "Ananias, why has Satan filled your heart to lie to the Holy Spirit and keep back part of the price of the land for yourself?
4 While it remained, was it not your own? And after it was sold, was it not in your own control? Why have you conceived this thing in your heart? You have not lied to men but to God."

Finally, the Holy Spirit is equal with the Father and Son. This is seen during the baptism of Christ and is mentioned by Jesus Himself just prior to His ascension from the Mount of Olives.

Day 12: The Person of the Holy Spirit

MATTHEW 3:13-15 KJV and v. 16-17 NKJV

[13] Then cometh Jesus from Galilee to Jordan unto John, to be baptized of him.
[14] But John forbad him, saying, I have need to be baptized of thee, and comest thou to me?
[15] And Jesus answering said unto him, Suffer it to be so now: for thus it becometh us to fulfil all righteousness. Then he suffered him.
[16] When He had been baptized, Jesus came up immediately from the water; and behold, the heavens were opened to Him, and He saw the Spirit of God descending like a dove and alighting upon Him.
[17] And suddenly a voice came from heaven, saying, "This is My beloved Son, in whom I am well pleased."

ISAIAH 11:1-5 KJV

[1] And there shall come forth a rod out of the stem of Jesse, and a Branch shall grow out of his roots:
[2] And the spirit of the Lord shall rest upon him, the spirit of wisdom and understanding, the spirit of counsel and might, the spirit of knowledge and of the fear of the Lord;
[3] And shall make him of quick understanding in the fear of the Lord: and he shall not judge after the sight of his eyes, neither reprove after the hearing of his ears:
[4] But with righteousness shall he judge the poor, and reprove with equity for the meek of the earth: and he shall smite the earth: with the rod of his mouth, and with the breath of his lips shall he slay the wicked.
[5] And righteousness shall be the girdle of his loins, and faithfulness the girdle of his reins.

MATTHEW 28:18 KJV and v. 19-20 NKJV

[18] And Jesus came and spake unto them, saying, All power is given unto me in heaven and in earth.

[19] Go therefore and make disciples of all the nations, baptizing them in the name of the Father and of the Son and of the Holy Spirit,
[20] teaching them to observe all things that I have commanded you; and lo, I am with you always, even to the end of the age." Amen.

DAY 13

Empowered by God

ACTS 1:8-11 KJV

[8] But ye shall receive power, after that the Holy Ghost is come upon you: and ye shall be witnesses unto me both in Jerusalem, and in all Judaea, and in Samaria, and unto the uttermost part of the earth.
[9] And when he [Jesus] had spoken these things, while they beheld, he was taken up; and a cloud received him out of their sight.
[10] And while they looked steadfastly toward heaven as he went up, behold, two men stood by them in white apparel;
[11] Which also said, Ye men of Galilee, why stand ye gazing up into heaven? this same Jesus, which is taken up from you into heaven, shall so come in like manner as ye have seen him go into heaven.

One of the most common excuses for not becoming a Christian is the fear of failure to live the Christian life. Besides overlooking the fact that men cannot be saved on the basis of good works, this objection neglects the truth that God provides the power to live the Christian life.

TITUS 3:4, 6 KJV and v. 5 NKJV

⁴ But after that the kindness and love of God our Saviour toward man appeared,
⁵ not by works of righteousness which we have done, but according to His mercy He saved us, through the washing of regeneration and renewing of the Holy Spirit,
⁶ Which he shed on us abundantly through Jesus Christ our Saviour;

Before Christ was crucified He promised the coming of the Holy Spirit to help believers.

JOHN 16:13-14 NKJV

¹³ However, when He, the Spirit of truth, has come, He will guide you into all truth; for He will not speak on His own authority, but whatever He hears He will speak; and He will tell you things to come.
¹⁴ He will glorify Me, for He will take of what is Mine and declare it to you.

The subsequent events of the Book of Acts supply ample evidence of the fulfillment of this prophecy.

ACTS 4:7 NKJV and 8-10 KJV

⁷ And when they had set them in the midst, they asked, "By what power or by what name have you done this?"
⁸ Then Peter, filled with the Holy Ghost, said unto them, Ye rulers of the people, and elders of Israel,
⁹ If we this day be examined of the good deed done to the impotent man, by what means he is made whole;

Day 13: Empowered by God

¹⁰ Be it known unto you all, and to all the people of Israel, that by the name of Jesus Christ of Nazareth, whom ye crucified, whom God raised from the dead, even by him doth this man stand here before you whole.

ACTS 4:32, 34-35 KJV and v. 33 NKJV

³² And the multitude of them that believed were of one heart and of one soul: neither said any of them that ought of the things which he possessed was his own; but they had all things common.
³³ And with great power the apostles gave witness to the resurrection of the Lord Jesus. And great grace was upon them all.
³⁴ Neither was there any among them that lacked: for as many as were possessors of lands or houses sold them, and brought the prices of the things that were sold,
³⁵ And laid them down at the apostles' feet: and distribution was made unto every man according as he had need.

ACTS 6:7 KJV and v. 8 NKJV

⁷ And the word of God increased; and the number of the disciples multiplied in Jerusalem greatly; and a great company of the priests were obedient to the faith.
⁸ And Stephen, full of faith and power, did great wonders and signs among the people.

> The power of the Holy Spirit was not designed solely for the first-century. Rather, all Christians are indwelt by the Spirit and thus have His power available.

I CORINTHIANS 6:19 NKJV and v. 20 KJV

¹⁹ What? know ye not that your body is the temple of the Holy Ghost which is in you, which ye have of God, and ye are not your own?

²⁰ For ye are bought with a price: therefore glorify God in your body, and in your spirit, which are God's.

> However, living the Christian life under the Spirit's power must not be thought of as simply allowing the Spirit to take control while the believer does nothing. The believer still must live the Christian life, though he does it through the Spirit's power.

ROMANS 8:10-12, 14 KJV and v. 13 NKJV

¹⁰ And if Christ be in you, the body is dead because of sin; but the Spirit is life because of righteousness.
¹¹ But if the Spirit of him that raised up Jesus from the dead dwell in you, he that raised up Christ from the dead shall also quicken your mortal bodies by his Spirit that dwelleth in you.
¹² Therefore, brethren, we are debtors, not to the flesh, to live after the flesh.
¹³ For if you live according to the flesh you will die; but if by the Spirit you put to death the deeds of the body, you will live.
¹⁴ For as many as are led by the Spirit of God, they are the sons of God.

> It is you who are to put to death the sinful deeds of the body, but you are to do it through the Spirit's power. The Christian who struggles in his own strength to live the Christian life will fail. He must by faith appropriate daily the power of the Holy Spirit.

Day 13: Empowered by God

ROMANS 8:1-3, 6-9 KJV and 4-5 NKJV

[1] There is therefore now no condemnation to them which are in Christ Jesus, who walk not after the flesh, but after the Spirit.

[2] For the law of the Spirit of life in Christ Jesus hath made me free from the law of sin and death.

[3] For what the law could not do, in that it was weak through the flesh, God sending his own Son in the likeness of sinful flesh, and for sin, condemned sin in the flesh:

[4] that the righteous requirement of the law might be fulfilled in us who do not walk according to the flesh but according to the Spirit.

[5] For those who live according to the flesh set their minds on the things of the flesh, but those who live according to the Spirit, the things of the Spirit.

[6] For to be carnally minded is death; but to be spiritually minded is life and peace.

[7] Because the carnal mind is enmity against God: for it is not subject to the law of God, neither indeed can be.

[8] So then they that are in the flesh cannot please God.

[9] But ye are not in the flesh, but in the Spirit, if so be that the Spirit of God dwell in you. Now if any man have not the Spirit of Christ, he is none of his.

Described practically, this means that the believer trusts the Spirit to empower him in specific instances such as sharing his faith with others, resisting temptation, being faithful, etc. There is no secret formula that makes the Spirit's power available. It is simply a reliance on the Spirit to help

---

DAY 14

Promise of God

TITUS 1:1,3 KJV and v. 2 NKJV

[1] Paul, a servant of God, and an apostle of Jesus Christ, according to the faith of God's elect, and the acknowledging of the truth which is after godliness;
[2] In hope of eternal life which God, who cannot lie, promised before time began,
[3] But hath in due times manifested his word through preaching, which is committed unto me according to the commandment of God our Saviour;

Often the Christian will doubt his salvation simply because he doesn't feel saved, not understanding that the basis for that salvation is the promise of God and not emotional feelings. In fact, the entire Trinity is involved in this.

Day 14: Promise of God

1. **The promise and work of the Father in our salvation. He has promised to graciously accept in Christ all repenting sinners.**

EPHESIANS 1:3-5, 7-14 KJV and v. 6 NKJV

3 Blessed be the God and Father of our Lord Jesus Christ, who hath blessed us with all spiritual blessings in heavenly places in Christ:
4 According as he hath chosen us in him before the foundation of the world, that we should be holy and without blame before him in love:
5 Having predestinated us unto the adoption of children by Jesus Christ to himself, according to the good pleasure of his will,
6 To the praise of the glory of His grace, by which He made us accepted in the Beloved.
7 In whom we have redemption through his blood, the forgiveness of sins, according to the riches of his grace;
8 Wherein he hath abounded toward us in all wisdom and prudence;
9 Having made known unto us the mystery of his will, according to his good pleasure which he hath purposed in himself:
10 That in the dispensation of the fulness of times he might gather together in one all things in Christ, both which are in heaven, and which are on earth; even in him:
11 In whom also we have obtained an inheritance, being predestinated according to the purpose of him who worketh all things after the counsel of his own will:
12 That we should be to the praise of his glory, who first trusted in Christ.
13 In whom ye also trusted, after that ye heard the word of truth, the gospel of your salvation: in whom also after that ye believed, ye were sealed with that holy Spirit of promise,
14 Which is the earnest of our inheritance until the redemption of the purchased possession, unto the praise of his glory.

COLOSSIANS 3:1-2, 4 KJV and v. 3 NKJV

¹ If ye then be risen with Christ, seek those things which are above, where Christ sitteth on the right hand of God.
² Set your affection on things above, not on things on the earth.
³ For you died, and your life is hidden with Christ in God.
⁴ When Christ, who is our life, shall appear, then shall ye also appear with him in glory.

> This means a Christian has the right to be in heaven someday, for he is in Christ.
> God guarantees to us that He will work out all things for our good.

ROMANS 8:24-27, 29-30 KJV and v. 28 NKJV

²⁴ For we are saved by hope: but hope that is seen is not hope: for what a man seeth, why doth he yet hope for?
²⁵ But if we hope for that we see not, then do we with patience wait for it.
²⁶ Likewise the Spirit also helpeth our infirmities: for we know not what we should pray for as we ought: but the Spirit itself maketh intercession for us with groanings which cannot be uttered.
²⁷ And he that searcheth the hearts knoweth what is the mind of the Spirit, because he maketh intercession for the saints according to the will of God.
²⁸ And we know that all things work together for good to those who love God, to those who are the called according to His purpose.
²⁹ For whom he did foreknow, he also did predestinate to be conformed to the image of his Son, that he might be the firstborn among many brethren.
³⁰ Moreover whom he did predestinate, them he also called: and whom he called, them he also justified: and whom he justified, them he also glorified.

2. The promise and work of the Son. He has promised us eternal life and abundant life.

JOHN 5:21-23 KJV and v. 24 NKJV

²¹ For as the Father raiseth up the dead, and quickeneth them; even so the Son quickeneth whom he will.
²² For the Father judgeth no man, but hath committed all judgment unto the Son:
²³ That all men should honour the Son, even as they honour the Father. He that honoureth not the Son honoureth not the Father which hath sent him.
²⁴ "Most assuredly, I say to you, he who hears My word and believes in Him who sent Me has everlasting life, and shall not come into judgment, but has passed from death into life.

JOHN 10:9, 11 KJV and v. 10 NKJV

⁹ I [Jesus] am the door: by me if any man enter in, he shall be saved, and shall go in and out, and find pasture.
¹⁰ The thief does not come except to steal, and to kill, and to destroy. I have come that they may have life, and that they may have it more abundantly.
¹¹ I am the good shepherd: the good shepherd giveth his life for the sheep.

> This covers not only our final destiny in heaven, but also our present Christian service here on earth. He is, in fact, right now praying for us and ministering to us at His Father's right hand.

HEBREWS 8:1 NKJV and v. 2-3 KJV

¹ Now this is the main point of the things we are saying: We have such a High Priest, who is seated at the right hand of the throne of the Majesty in the heavens,
² A minister of the sanctuary, and of the true tabernacle, which the Lord pitched, and not man.
³ For every high priest is ordained to offer gifts and sacrifices: wherefore it is of necessity that this man have somewhat also to offer.

HEBREWS 9:18-23, 25-28 KJV and v. 24 NKJV

¹⁸ Whereupon neither the first testament was dedicated without blood.
¹⁹ For when Moses had spoken every precept to all the people according to the law, he took the blood of calves and of goats, with water, and scarlet wool, and hyssop, and sprinkled both the book, and all the people,
²⁰ Saying, This is the blood of the testament which God hath enjoined unto you.
²¹ Moreover he sprinkled with blood both the tabernacle, and all the vessels of the ministry.
²² And almost all things are by the law purged with blood; and without shedding of blood is no remission.
²³ It was therefore necessary that the patterns of things in the heavens should be purified with these; but the heavenly things themselves with better sacrifices than these.
²⁴ For Christ has not entered the holy places made with hands, which are copies of the true, but into heaven itself, now to appear in the presence of God for us;
²⁵ Nor yet that he should offer himself often, as the high priest entereth into the holy place every year with blood of others;
²⁶ For then must he often have suffered since the foundation of the world: but now once in the end of the world hath he appeared to put away sin by the sacrifice of himself.
²⁷ And as it is appointed unto men once to die, but after this the judgment:

^{28} So Christ was once offered to bear the sins of many; and unto them that look for him shall he appear the second time without sin unto salvation.

3. The promise and work of the Holy Spirit. The Holy Spirit is said to indwell the believer.

JOHN 14:15, 17 KJV and v. 16 NKJV

^{15} If ye love me, keep my commandments.
^{16} And I [Jesus] will pray the Father, and He will give you another Helper, that He may abide with you forever—
^{17} Even the Spirit of truth; whom the world cannot receive, because it seeth him not, neither knoweth him: but ye know him; for he dwelleth with you, and shall be in you.

ACTS 2:32-33 KJV

^{32} This Jesus hath God raised up, whereof we all are witnesses.
^{33} Therefore being by the right hand of God exalted, and having received of the Father the promise of the Holy Ghost, he hath shed forth this, which ye now see and hear.

In addition, He places all believing sinners into the body of Christ, thus assuring us of union with God Himself.

I CORINTHIANS 12:13 NKJV

^{13} For by one Spirit we were all baptized into one body—whether Jews or Greeks, whether slaves or free—and have all been made to drink into one Spirit.

DAY 15

Witness of the Spirit

ROMANS 8:16 NKJV and v. 17 KJV
¹⁶ The Spirit Himself bears witness with our spirit that we are children of God,
¹⁷ And if children, then heirs; heirs of God, and joint-heirs with Christ; if so be that we suffer with him, that we may be also glorified together.

While it is true that one need not always
feel spiritual to have new life in Christ,
nevertheless, feelings and emotions do play a vital
role in our salvation. Both Paul and John inform
us we can experience that inner
witness of the Holy Spirit to our Spirit.

I JOHN 3:22-23 KJV and v. 24 NKJV
²² And whatsoever we ask, we receive of him, because we keep his commandments, and do those things that are pleasing in his sight.

Day 15: Witness of the Spirit

²³ And this is his commandment, That we should believe on the name of his Son Jesus Christ, and love one another, as he gave us commandment.
²⁴ Now he who keeps His commandments abides in Him, and He in him. And by this we know that He abides in us, by the Spirit whom He has given us.

What does this mean? It means we can enjoy the quiet confidence given by the Spirit that we have indeed passed from death into life. It means we can now approach the mighty Creator of the vast universe and refer to Him as Abba, Father.

ROMANS 8:15 NKJV

¹ For you did not receive the spirit of bondage again to fear, but you received the Spirit of adoption by whom we cry out, "Abba, Father."

Abba is a very personal and intimate term for one's Father. Prior to Pentecost only Christ had used the title for God.

MARK 14:32-35 KJV and v. 36 NKJV

³² And they came to a place which was named Gethsemane: and he [Jesus] saith to his disciples, Sit ye here, while I shall pray.
³³ And he taketh with him Peter and James and John, and began to be sore amazed, and to be very heavy;
³⁴ And saith unto them, My soul is exceeding sorrowful unto death: tarry ye here, and watch.
³⁵ And he went forward a little, and fell on the ground, and prayed that, if it were possible, the hour might pass from him.

³⁶ And He said, "Abba, Father, all things are possible for You. Take this cup away from Me; nevertheless, not what I will, but what You will."

> It is almost akin to our modern title Daddy, or Papa. It not only means we can approach the Throne of Grace with a holy boldness, but we can also experience the blessing of knowing that the Father will hear and answer our prayers.

HEBREWS 10:14-25 KJV

¹⁴ For by one offering he [Jesus] hath perfected for ever them that are sanctified.

¹⁵ Whereof the Holy Ghost also is a witness to us: for after that he had said before,

¹⁶ This is the covenant that I will make with them after those days, saith the Lord, I will put my laws into their hearts, and in their minds will I write them;

¹⁷ And their sins and iniquities will I remember no more.

¹⁸ Now where remission of these is, there is no more offering for sin.

¹⁹ Having therefore, brethren, boldness to enter into the holiest by the blood of Jesus,

²⁰ By a new and living way, which he hath consecrated for us, through the veil, that is to say, his flesh;

²¹ And having an high priest over the house of God;

²² Let us draw near with a true heart in full assurance of faith, having our hearts sprinkled from an evil conscience, and our bodies washed with pure water.

²³ Let us hold fast the profession of our faith without wavering; (for he is faithful that promised;)

²⁴ And let us consider one another to provoke unto love and to good works:

²⁵ Not forsaking the assembling of ourselves together, as the manner of some is; but exhorting one another: and so much the more, as ye see the day approaching.

Day 15: Witness of the Spirit

HEBREWS 4:14-15 KJV, and v. 16 NKJV

[14] Seeing then that we have a great high priest, that is passed into the heavens, Jesus the Son of God, let us hold fast our profession.

[15] For we have not an high priest which cannot be touched with the feeling of our infirmities; but was in all points tempted like as we are, yet without sin.

[16] Let us therefore come boldly to the throne of grace, that we may obtain mercy and find grace to help in time of need.

I JOHN 3:18-21, 23-24 KJV, and v. 22 NKJV

[18] My little children, let us not love in word, neither in tongue; but in deed and in truth.

[19] And hereby we know that we are of the truth, and shall assure our hearts before him.

[20] For if our heart condemn us, God is greater than our heart, and knoweth all things.

[21] Beloved, if our heart condemn us not, then have we confidence toward God.

[22] And whatever we ask we receive from Him, because we keep His commandments and do those things that are pleasing in His sight.

[23] And this is his commandment, That we should believe on the name of his Son Jesus Christ, and love one another, as he gave us commandment.

[24] And he that keepeth his commandments dwelleth in him, and he in him. And hereby we know that he abideth in us, by the Spirit which he hath given us.

The Apostle Paul experiences this witness during a crisis in his life while preaching in Corinth.

ACTS 18:9-10 NKJV

[9] Now the Lord spoke to Paul in the night by a vision, "Do not be afraid, but speak, and do not keep silent;

[10] for I am with you, and no one will attack you to hurt you; for I have many people in this city."

DAY 16

―――◆―――

Changed Life

I CORINTHIANS 6:9-10 KJV and v. 11 NKJV

⁹ Know ye not that the unrighteous shall not inherit the kingdom of God? Be not deceived: neither fornicators, nor idolaters, nor adulterers, nor effeminate, nor abusers of themselves with mankind,
¹⁰ Nor thieves, nor covetous, nor drunkards, nor revilers, nor extortioners, shall inherit the kingdom of God.
¹¹ And such were some of you. But you were washed, but you were sanctified, but you were justified in the name of the Lord Jesus and by the Spirit of our God.

The first stanza of a famous
Christian song begins:
*What a wonderful change in my life has been
wrought since Jesus came into my heart.*
Without doubt the greatest proof of the
new birth is a changed life. The child of God now
suddenly loves the following:

Day 16: Changed Life

1. **He loves Jesus. Before conversion the sinner might hold Christ in high esteem, but after conversion he loves the Savior.**

I JOHN 5:1-2 NKJV and v. 3-5 KJV

[1] Whoever believes that Jesus is the Christ is born of God, and everyone who loves Him who begot also loves him who is begotten of Him.
[2] By this we know that we love the children of God, when we love God and keep His commandments.
[3] For this is the love of God, that we keep his commandments: and his commandments are not grievous.
[4] For whatsoever is born of God overcometh the world: and this is the victory that overcometh the world, even our faith.
[5] Who is he that overcometh the world, but he that believeth that Jesus is the Son of God?

2. **He loves the Bible. We should love God's Word as the Psalmist did in Psalm 119. He expresses His great love for God's Word.**

PSALM 119:47-48 NKJV

[47] And I will delight myself in Your commandments,
Which I love.
[48] My hands also I will lift up to Your commandments,
Which I love,
And I will meditate on Your statutes.

PSALM 119:97, 103 NKJV, and vs. 98-102, 104 KJV

⁹⁷ O how I love thy law! it is my meditation all the day.
⁹⁸ Thou through thy commandments hast made me wiser than mine enemies: for they are ever with me.
⁹⁹ I have more understanding than all my teachers: for thy testimonies are my meditation.
¹⁰⁰ I understand more than the ancients, because I keep thy precepts.
¹⁰¹ I have refrained my feet from every evil way, that I might keep thy word.
¹⁰² I have not departed from thy judgments: for thou hast taught me.
¹⁰³ How sweet are Your words to my taste, sweeter than honey to my mouth!
¹⁰⁴ Through thy precepts I get understanding: therefore I hate every false way.

PSALM 119:129 NKJV and v. 130 KJV

¹²⁹ Your testimonies are wonderful; therefore my soul keeps them.
¹³⁰ The entrance of thy words giveth light; it giveth understanding unto the simple.

3. He loves other Christians. We know that we have passed from death to life, because we love the brethren.

I JOHN 3:11-13, 15-16 KJV and v. 14 NKJV

¹¹ For this is the message that ye heard from the beginning, that we should love one another.
¹² Not as Cain, who was of that wicked one, and slew his brother. And wherefore slew he him? Because his own works were evil, and his brother's righteous.
¹³ Marvel not, my brethren, if the world hate you.
¹⁴ We know that we have passed from death to life, because we love the brethren. He who does not love his brother abides in death.

¹⁵ Whosoever hateth his brother is a murderer: and ye know that no murderer hath eternal life abiding in him.

¹⁶ Hereby perceive we the love of God, because he laid down his life for us: and we ought to lay down our lives for the brethren.

4. He loves his enemies.

MATTHEW 5:43-45 NKJV

⁴³ "You have heard that it was said, 'You shall love your neighbor and hate your enemy.'

⁴⁴ But I say to you, love your enemies, bless those who curse you, do good to those who hate you, and pray for those who spitefully use you and persecute you,

⁴⁵ that you may be sons of your Father in heaven; for He makes His sun rise on the evil and on the good, and sends rain on the just and on the unjust.

5. He loves the souls of all people.

ROMANS 10:1 NKJV and v. 2-4 KJV

¹ Brethren, my heart's desire and prayer to God for Israel is that they may be saved.

² For I bear them record that they have a zeal of God, but not according to knowledge.

³ For they being ignorant of God's righteousness, and going about to establish their own righteousness, have not submitted themselves unto the righteousness of God.

⁴ For Christ is the end of the law for righteousness to every one that believeth.

II CORINTHIANS 5:14 NKJV and v. 15-17 KJV

¹⁴ For the love of Christ compels us, because we judge thus: that if One died for all, then all died;

[15] And that he died for all, that they which live should not henceforth live unto themselves, but unto him which died for them, and rose again.
[16] Wherefore henceforth know we no man after the flesh: yea, though we have known Christ after the flesh, yet now henceforth know we him no more.
[17] Therefore if any man be in Christ, he is a new creature: old things are passed away; behold, all things are become new.

Like Paul, he too can cry out for the conversion of loved ones, "Brethren, my heart's desire and prayer to God for Israel is that they may be saved."

---

6. He loves the pure life.

I JOHN 2:15-17 NKJV

[15] Do not love the world or the things in the world. If anyone loves the world, the love of the Father is not in him.
[16] For all that is in the world—the lust of the flesh, the lust of the eyes, and the pride of life—is not of the Father but is of the world.
[17] And the world is passing away, and the lust of it; but he who does the will of God abides forever.

I JOHN 5:4 NKJV and v. 5 KJV

[4] For whatsoever is born of God overcometh the world: and this is the victory that overcometh the world, even our faith.
[5] Who is he who overcomes the world, but he who believes that Jesus is the Son of God?

7. He loves to talk to God.

Day 16: Changed Life

EPHESIANS 5:11-18, 20 KJV and v. 19 NKJV

[11] And have no fellowship with the unfruitful works of darkness, but rather reprove them.

[12] For it is a shame even to speak of those things which are done of them in secret.

[13] But all things that are reproved are made manifest by the light: for whatsoever doth make manifest is light.

[14] Wherefore he saith, Awake thou that sleepest, and arise from the dead, and Christ shall give thee light.

[15] See then that ye walk circumspectly, not as fools, but as wise,

[16] Redeeming the time, because the days are evil.

[17] Wherefore be ye not unwise, but understanding what the will of the Lord is.

[18] And be not drunk with wine, wherein is excess; but be filled with the Spirit;

[19] Speaking to one another in psalms and hymns and spiritual songs, singing and making melody in your heart to the Lord,

[20] Giving thanks always for all things unto God and the Father in the name of our Lord Jesus Christ;

DAY 17

The Work of the Holy Spirit in Christian Living

JOHN 7:37-39 KJV

37 In the last day, that great day of the feast, Jesus stood and cried, saying, If any man thirst, let him come unto me, and drink.
38 He that believeth on me, as the scripture hath said, out of his belly shall flow rivers of living water.
39 (But this spake he of the Spirit, which they that believe on him should receive: for the Holy Ghost was not yet given; because that Jesus was not yet glorified.)

JOHN 20:13-23 KJV

13 And they [angels] say unto her [Mary], Woman, why weepest thou? She saith unto them, Because they have taken away my Lord, and I know not where they have laid him.
14 And when she had thus said, she turned herself back, and saw Jesus standing, and knew not that it was Jesus.
15 Jesus saith unto her, Woman, why weepest thou? whom seekest thou? She, supposing him to be the gardener, saith unto him, Sir, if thou have borne him hence, tell me where thou hast laid him, and I will take him away.

Day 17: The Work of the Holy Spirit in Christian Living

¹⁶ Jesus saith unto her, Mary. She turned herself, and saith unto him, Rabboni; which is to say, Master.

¹⁷ Jesus saith unto her, Touch me not; for I am not yet ascended to my Father: but go to my brethren, and say unto them, I ascend unto my Father, and your Father; and to my God, and your God.

¹⁸ Mary Magdalene came and told the disciples that she had seen the Lord, and that he had spoken these things unto her.

¹⁹ Then the same day at evening, being the first day of the week, when the doors were shut where the disciples were assembled for fear of the Jews, came Jesus and stood in the midst, and saith unto them, Peace be unto you.

²⁰ And when he had so said, he shewed unto them his hands and his side. Then were the disciples glad, when they saw the Lord.

²¹ Then said Jesus to them again, Peace be unto you: as my Father hath sent me, even so send I you.

²² And when he had said this, he breathed on them, and saith unto them, Receive ye the Holy Ghost:

²³ Whose soever sins ye remit, they are remitted unto them; and whose soever sins ye retain, they are retained.

ACTS 1:1-14 KJV

¹ The former treatise have I made, O Theophilus, of all that Jesus began both to do and teach,

² Until the day in which he was taken up, after that he through the Holy Ghost had given commandments unto the apostles whom he had chosen:

³ To whom also he shewed himself alive after his passion by many infallible proofs, being seen of them forty days, and speaking of the things pertaining to the kingdom of God:

⁴ And, being assembled together with them, commanded them that they should not depart from Jerusalem, but wait for the promise of the Father, which, saith he, ye have heard of me.

⁵ For John truly baptized with water; but ye shall be baptized with the Holy Ghost not many days hence.

⁶ When they therefore were come together, they asked of him, saying, Lord, wilt thou at this time restore again the kingdom to Israel?

⁷ And he said unto them, It is not for you to know the times or the seasons, which the Father hath put in his own power.
⁸ But ye shall receive power, after that the Holy Ghost is come upon you: and ye shall be witnesses unto me both in Jerusalem, and in all Judaea, and in Samaria, and unto the uttermost part of the earth.
⁹ And when he had spoken these things, while they beheld, he was taken up; and a cloud received him out of their sight.
¹⁰ And while they looked steadfastly toward heaven as he went up, behold, two men stood by them in white apparel;
¹¹ Which also said, Ye men of Galilee, why stand ye gazing up into heaven? this same Jesus, which is taken up from you into heaven, shall so come in like manner as ye have seen him go into heaven.
¹² Then returned they unto Jerusalem from the mount called Olivet, which is from Jerusalem a sabbath day's journey.
¹³ And when they were come in, they went up into an upper room, where abode both Peter, and James, and John, and Andrew, Philip, and Thomas, Bartholomew, and Matthew, James the son of Alphaeus, and Simon Zelotes, and Judas the brother of James.
¹⁴ These all continued with one accord in prayer and supplication, with the women, and Mary the mother of Jesus, and with his brethren.

ACTS 2:1-4 KJV

¹ And when the day of Pentecost was fully come, they were all with one accord in one place.
² And suddenly there came a sound from heaven as of a rushing mighty wind, and it filled all the house where they were sitting.
³ And there appeared unto them cloven tongues like as of fire, and it sat upon each of them.
⁴ And they were all filled with the Holy Ghost, and began to speak with other tongues, as the Spirit gave them utterance.

Day 17: The Work of the Holy Spirit in Christian Living

ACTS 2:22-24 KJV

²² Ye men of Israel, hear these words; Jesus of Nazareth, a man approved of God among you by miracles and wonders and signs, which God did by him in the midst of you, as ye yourselves also know:
²³ Him, being delivered by the determinate counsel and foreknowledge of God, ye have taken, and by wicked hands have crucified and slain:
²⁴ Whom God hath raised up, having loosed the pains of death: because it was not possible that he should be holden of it.

ACTS 2:32-33 KJV

³² This Jesus hath God raised up, whereof we all are witnesses.
³³ Therefore being by the right hand of God exalted, and having received of the Father the promise of the Holy Ghost, he hath shed forth this, which ye now see and hear.

As a loving and wise mother tenderly watches over her child, so the Holy Spirit cares for the children of God.

---

1. **The Holy Spirit indwells Christians. The Bible teaches that all believers are indwelt by the Holy Spirit.**

I CORINTHIANS 6:19 NKJV and v. 20 KJV

¹⁹ Or do you not know that your body is the temple of the Holy Spirit who is in you, whom you have from God, and you are not your own?
²⁰ For ye are bought with a price: therefore glorify God in your body, and in your spirit, which are God's.

> The purpose of this indwelling ministry is to control the newly created nature given at conversion.

II CORINTHIANS 5:17 NKJV and v. 18-21 KJV

¹⁷ Therefore, if anyone is in Christ, he is a new creation; old things have passed away; behold, all things have become new.
¹⁸ And all things are of God, who hath reconciled us to himself by Jesus Christ, and hath given to us the ministry of reconciliation;
¹⁹ To wit, that God was in Christ, reconciling the world unto himself, not imputing their trespasses unto them; and hath committed unto us the word of reconciliation.
²⁰ Now then we are ambassadors for Christ, as though God did beseech you by us: we pray you in Christ's stead, be ye reconciled to God.
²¹ For he hath made him to be sin for us, who knew no sin; that we might be made the righteousness of God in him.

ROMANS 6:3-6 KJV

³ Know ye not, that so many of us as were baptized into Jesus Christ were baptized into his death?
⁴ Therefore we are buried with him by baptism into death: that like as Christ was raised up from the dead by the glory of the Father, even so we also should walk in newness of life.
⁵ For if we have been planted together in the likeness of his death, we shall be also in the likeness of his resurrection:
⁶ Knowing this, that our old man is crucified with him, that the body of sin might be destroyed, that henceforth we should not serve sin.

EPHESIANS 3:14-15, 17-21 KJV and v. 16 NKJV

¹⁴ For this cause I [Paul] bow my knees unto the Father of our Lord Jesus Christ,
¹⁵ Of whom the whole family in heaven and earth is named,

16 that He would grant you, according to the riches of His glory, to be strengthened with might through His Spirit in the inner man,
17 That Christ may dwell in your hearts by faith; that ye, being rooted and grounded in love,
18 May be able to comprehend with all saints what is the breadth, and length, and depth, and height;
19 And to know the love of Christ, which passeth knowledge, that ye might be filled with all the fulness of God.
20 Now unto him that is able to do exceeding abundantly above all that we ask or think, according to the power that worketh in us,
21 Unto him be glory in the church by Christ Jesus throughout all ages, world without end. Amen.

2. The Holy Spirit fills believers. We are admonished to "be filled with the Spirit."

EPHESIANS 5:18 NKJV

18 And do not be drunk with wine, in which is dissipation; but be filled with the Spirit,

---
The word "fill" means to be controlled.
The filling does not mean that
the Christian gets more of the Holy Spirit, but
rather, He gets more of us.

---

3. The Holy Spirit sanctifies the believer.

ROMANS 15:14-15 KJV and v. 16 NKJV

[14] And I [Paul] myself also am persuaded of you, my brethren, that ye also are full of goodness, filled with all knowledge, able also to admonish one another.
[15] Nevertheless, brethren, I have written the more boldly unto you in some sort, as putting you in mind, because of the grace that is given to me of God,
[16] That I might be a minister of Jesus Christ to the Gentiles, ministering the gospel of God, that the offering of the Gentiles might be acceptable, sanctified by the Holy Spirit.

II THESSALONIANS 2:13 NKJV and v. 14-17 KJV

[13] But we are bound to give thanks to God always for you, brethren beloved by the Lord, because God from the beginning chose you for salvation through sanctification by the Spirit and belief in the truth,
[14] Whereunto he called you by our gospel, to the obtaining of the glory of our Lord Jesus Christ.
[15] Therefore, brethren, stand fast, and hold the traditions which ye have been taught, whether by word, or our epistle.
[16] Now our Lord Jesus Christ himself, and God, even our Father, which hath loved us, and hath given us everlasting consolation and good hope through grace,
[17] Comfort your hearts, and stablish you in every good word and work.

4. The Holy Spirit produces fruit in the life of the believer. This fruit is described by Paul.

GALATIANS 5:22-23 NKJV and v. 24-26 KJV

[22] But the fruit of the Spirit is love, joy, peace, longsuffering, kindness, goodness, faithfulness,
[23] gentleness, self-control. Against such there is no law.

²⁴ And those who are Christ's have crucified the flesh with its affections and lusts.
²⁵ If we live in the Spirit, let us also walk in the Spirit.
²⁶ Let us not be desirous of vainglory, provoking one another and envying one another.

5. The Holy Spirit imparts gifts to Christians.

ROMANS 12:6-8 NKJV

⁶ Having then gifts differing according to the grace that is given to us, let us use them: if prophecy, let us prophesy in proportion to our faith;

⁷ or ministry, let us use it in our ministering; he who teaches, in teaching;

⁸ he who exhorts, in exhortation; he who gives, with liberality; he who leads, with diligence; he who shows mercy, with cheerfulness.

EPHESIANS 4:7-11 NKJV

⁷ But to each one of us grace was given according to the measure of Christ's gift.
⁸ Therefore He says:
"When He ascended on high,
He led captivity captive,
And gave gifts to men."
⁹ (Now this, "He ascended"—what does it mean but that He also first descended into the lower parts of the earth?
¹⁰ He who descended is also the One who ascended far above all the heavens, that He might fill all things.)
¹¹ And He Himself gave some to be apostles, some prophets, some evangelists, and some pastors and teachers,

---

A spiritual gift is an ability imparted to every Christian.

I PETER 4:7-9, 11 KJV and v. 10 NKJV

[7] But the end of all things is at hand: be ye therefore sober and watch unto prayer.

[8] And above all things, have fervent charity among yourselves, for charity shall cover the multitude of sins.

[9] Use hospitality one to another without grudging.

[10] As each one has received a gift, minister it to one another, as good stewards of the manifold grace of God.

[11] If any man speak, let him speak according to the oracles of God. If any man minister, let him do it according to the ability which God giveth, that God in all things may be glorified through Jesus Christ, to whom be praise and dominion for ever and ever. Amen.

The purpose of these gifts is twofold, namely, to glorify God and to edify the body of Christ.

EPHESIANS 4:12-13 NKJV, and v. 14-16 KJV

[12] for the equipping of the saints for the work of ministry, for the edifying of the body of Christ,

[13] till we all come to the unity of the faith and of the knowledge of the Son of God, to a perfect man, to the measure of the stature of the fullness of Christ;

[14] That we henceforth be no longer children, tossed to and fro and carried about with every wind of doctrine by the sleight of men and their cunning and craftiness, whereby they lie in wait to deceive;

[15] But speaking the truth in love, may grow up into Him in all things, who is the Head, even Christ,

¹⁶ From whom the whole body, fitly joined together and compacted by that which every joint supplieth, according to the effectual working in the measure of every part, maketh increase of the body unto the edifying of itself in love.

REVELATION 4:11 NKJV

¹¹ "You are worthy, O Lord,
To receive glory and honor and power;
For You created all things,
And by Your will they exist and were created."

6. The Holy Spirit teaches believers. He will instruct us in all spiritual things as we read the Word of God and abide in the Son of God.

JOHN 14:26 NKJV and v. 27-29 KJV

²⁶ But the Helper, the Holy Spirit, whom the Father will send in My name, He will teach you all things, and bring to your remembrance all things that I said to you.
²⁷ Peace I leave with you, my peace I give unto you: not as the world giveth, give I unto you. Let not your heart be troubled, neither let it be afraid.
²⁸ Ye have heard how I said unto you, I go away, and come again unto you. If ye loved me, ye would rejoice, because I said, I go unto the Father: for my Father is greater than I.
²⁹ And now I have told you before it come to pass, that, when it is come to pass, ye might believe.

I JOHN 2:24-27 NKJV, and v. 28-29 KJV

²⁴ Therefore let that abide in you which you heard from the beginning. If what you heard from the beginning abides in you, you also will abide in the Son and in the Father.

²⁵ And this is the promise that He has promised us—eternal life.
²⁶ These things I have written to you concerning those who try to deceive you.
²⁷ But the anointing which you have received from Him abides in you, and you do not need that anyone teach you; but as the same anointing teaches you concerning all things, and is true, and is not a lie, and just as it has taught you, you will abide in Him.
²⁸ And now, little children, abide in him; that, when he shall appear, we may have confidence, and not be ashamed before him at his coming.
²⁹ If ye know that he is righteous, ye know that every one that doeth righteousness is born of him.

DAY 18

---◆---

God's Word Cleanses

PSALM 51:7-13 KJV

[7] Purge me with hyssop, and I shall be clean: wash me, and I shall be whiter than snow.
[8] Make me to hear joy and gladness; that the bones which thou hast broken may rejoice.
[9] Hide thy face from my sins, and blot out all mine iniquities.
[10] Create in me a clean heart, O God; and renew a right spirit within me.
[11] Cast me not away from thy presence; and take not thy holy spirit from me.
[12] Restore unto me the joy of thy salvation; and uphold me with thy free spirit.
[13] Then will I teach transgressors thy ways; and sinners shall be converted unto thee.

PSALM 119:9 NKJV and v. 10-16 KJV

[9] How can a young man cleanse his way?
By taking heed according to Your word.
[10] With my whole heart have I sought thee: O let me not wander from thy commandments.

[11] Thy word have I hid in mine heart, that I might not sin against thee.
[12] Blessed art thou, O Lord: teach me thy statutes.
[13] With my lips have I declared all the judgments of thy mouth.
[14] I have rejoiced in the way of thy testimonies, as much as in all riches.
[15] I will meditate in thy precepts, and have respect unto thy ways.
[16] I will delight myself in thy statutes: I will not forget thy word.

One of the pieces of furniture in the Old Testament tabernacle was called the bronze laver. It consisted of a huge upright bronze bowl filled with water, resting upon a pedestal. The priests would often stop at this for it too has the power to cleanse. The Old Testament laver could only remove the physical dirt from human hands, but the Scriptures possess the ability to take away our moral filth.

I PETER 1:18-21, 23-25 KJV and v. 22 NKJV

[18] Forasmuch as ye know that ye were not redeemed with corruptible things, as silver and gold, from your vain conversation received by tradition from your fathers;
[19] But with the precious blood of Christ, as of a lamb without blemish and without spot:
[20] Who verily was foreordained before the foundation of the world, but was manifest in these last times for you,
[21] Who by him do believe in God, that raised him up from the dead, and gave him glory; that your faith and hope might be in God.
[22] Since you have purified your souls in obeying the truth through the Spirit in sincere love of the brethren, love one another fervently with a pure heart,

Day 18: God's Word Cleanses

²³ Being born again, not of corruptible seed, but of incorruptible, by the word of God, which liveth and abideth for ever.
²⁴ For all flesh is as grass, and all the glory of man as the flower of grass. The grass withereth, and the flower thereof falleth away:
²⁵ But the word of the Lord endureth for ever. And this is the word which by the gospel is preached unto you.

I JOHN 1:5-8, 10 KJV and v. 9 NKJV

⁵ This then is the message which we have heard of him, and declare unto you, that God is light, and in him is no darkness at all.
⁶ If we say that we have fellowship with him, and walk in darkness, we lie, and do not the truth:
⁷ But if we walk in the light, as he is in the light, we have fellowship one with another, and the blood of Jesus Christ his Son cleanseth us from all sin.
⁸ If we say that we have no sin, we deceive ourselves, and the truth is not in us.
⁹ If we confess our sins, He is faithful and just to forgive us our sins and to cleanse us from all unrighteousness.
¹⁰ If we say that we have not sinned, we make Him a liar, and His word is not in us.

What areas of my life can the Bible cleanse?
---

1. It can cleanse me from wrong thoughts. Sometimes we are tempted to think critically of others; God's Word can prevent this.

PSALM 1:1 KJV and v. 2 NKJV

¹ Blessed is the man that walketh not in the counsel of the ungodly, nor standeth in the way of sinners, nor sitteth in the seat of the scornful.
² But his delight is in the law of the Lord,
And in His law he meditates day and night.

On other occasion fearful thoughts
may race through our minds, the Scriptures
will prevent this also.

JOSHUA 1:7, 9 KJV and v. 8 NKJV

⁷ Only be thou strong and very courageous, that thou mayest observe to do according to all the law, which Moses my servant commanded thee: turn not from it to the right hand or to the left, that thou mayest prosper withersoever thou goest.
⁸ This Book of the Law shall not depart from your mouth, but you shall meditate in it day and night, that you may observe to do according to all that is written in it. For then you will make your way prosperous, and then you will have good success.
⁹ Have not I commanded thee? Be strong and of a good courage; be not afraid, neither be thou dismayed: for the Lord thy God is with thee whithersoever thou goest.

In fact, the Bible will establish our total
thought – life if we but allow it to do so.

Day 18: God's Word Cleanses

PHILIPPIANS 4:6-7 KJV and v. 8-9 NKJV

⁶ Be careful for nothing; but in every thing by prayer and supplication with thanksgiving let your requests be made known unto God.
⁷ And the peace of God, which passeth all understanding, shall keep your hearts and minds through Christ Jesus.
⁸ Finally, brethren, whatever things are true, whatever things are noble, whatever things are just, whatever things are pure, whatever things are lovely, whatever things are of good report, if there is any virtue and if there is anything praiseworthy—meditate on these things.
⁹ The things which you learned and received and heard and saw in me, these do, and the God of peace will be with you.

II PETER 1:3-4, 11 KJV and v. 5-10 NKJV

³ According as his divine power hath given unto us all things that pertain unto life and godliness, through the knowledge of him that hath called us to glory and virtue:
⁴ Whereby are given unto us exceeding great and precious promises: that by these ye might be partakers of the divine nature, having escaped the corruption that is in the world through lust.
⁵ But also for this very reason, giving all diligence, add to your faith virtue, to virtue knowledge,
⁶ to knowledge self-control, to self-control perseverance, to perseverance godliness,
⁷ to godliness brotherly kindness, and to brotherly kindness love.
⁸ For if these things are yours and abound, you will be neither barren nor unfruitful in the knowledge of our Lord Jesus Christ.
⁹ For he who lacks these things is shortsighted, even to blindness, and has forgotten that he was cleansed from his old sins.
¹⁰ Therefore, brethren, be even more diligent to make your call and election sure, for if you do these things you will never stumble;
¹¹ For so an entrance shall be ministered unto you abundantly into the everlasting kingdom of our Lord and Saviour Jesus Christ.

2. **It can cleanse me from wrong words.** Of all the Bible authors, James seems to be God's expert on the sins of the human tongue. In the first chapter of his book, he deals with this very thing and shows the absolute necessity of dependence upon the Scriptures to keep our words true.

JAMES 1:19-21, 27 KJV and v. 22-26 NKJV

[19] Wherefore, my beloved brethren, let every man be swift to hear, slow to speak, slow to wrath:
[20] For the wrath of man worketh not the righteousness of God.
[21] Wherefore lay apart all filthiness and superfluity of naughtiness, and receive with meekness the engrafted word, which is able to save your souls.
[22] But be doers of the word, and not hearers only, deceiving yourselves.
[23] For if anyone is a hearer of the word and not a doer, he is like a man observing his natural face in a mirror;
[24] for he observes himself, goes away, and immediately forgets what kind of man he was.
[25] But he who looks into the perfect law of liberty and continues in it, and is not a forgetful hearer but a doer of the work, this one will be blessed in what he does.
[26] If anyone among you thinks he is religious, and does not bridle his tongue but deceives his own heart, this one's religion is useless.
[27] Pure religion and undefiled before God and the Father is this, To visit the fatherless and widows in their affliction, and to keep himself unspotted from the world.

PSALM 119:172 NKJV

[172] My tongue shall speak of Your word,
For all Your commandments are righteousness.

3. It can cleanse me from wrong actions. Jesus promised us this would be the case.

JOHN 15:1-2, 4-5 KJV and v. 3 NKJV

¹ I am the true vine, and my Father is the husbandman.
² Every branch in me that beareth not fruit he taketh away: and every branch that beareth fruit, he purgeth it, that it may bring forth more fruit.
³ You are already clean because of the word which I have spoken to you.
⁴ Abide in me, and I in you. As the branch cannot bear fruit of itself, except it abide in the vine; no more can ye, except ye abide in me.
⁵ I am the vine, ye are the branches: He that abideth in me, and I in him, the same bringeth forth much fruit: for without me ye can do nothing.

Finally, God's Word will keep us from wrong thoughts, words, and actions or else wrong thoughts, words, and actions will keep us from God's Word.

DAY 19

———◆———

God's Word Confirms

JOHN 8:19-30, 32 KJV and v. 31 NKJV

[19] Then said they unto him, Where is thy Father? Jesus answered, Ye neither know me, nor my Father: if ye had known me, ye should have known my Father also.
[20] These words spake Jesus in the treasury, as he taught in the temple: and no man laid hands on him; for his hour was not yet come.
[21] Then said Jesus again unto them, I go my way, and ye shall seek me, and shall die in your sins: whither I go, ye cannot come.
[22] Then said the Jews, Will he kill himself? because he saith, Whither I go, ye cannot come.
[23] And he said unto them, Ye are from beneath; I am from above: ye are of this world; I am not of this world.
[24] I said therefore unto you, that ye shall die in your sins: for if ye believe not that I am he, ye shall die in your sins.
[25] Then said they unto him, Who art thou? And Jesus saith unto them, Even the same that I said unto you from the beginning.
[26] I have many things to say and to judge of you: but he that sent me is true; and I speak to the world those things which I have heard of him.
[27] They understood not that he spake to them of the Father.

Day 19: God's Word Confirms

²⁸ Then said Jesus unto them, When ye have lifted up the Son of man, then shall ye know that I am he, and that I do nothing of myself; but as my Father hath taught me, I speak these things.
²⁹ And he that sent me is with me: the Father hath not left me alone; for I do always those things that please him.
³⁰ As he spake these words, many believed on him.
³¹ Then Jesus said to those Jews who believed Him, "If you abide in My word, you are My disciples indeed.
³² And ye shall know the truth, and the truth shall make you free.

To confirm means to fully establish a truth or fact. The Bible should be used to confirm the truth in our own hearts.

---

1. **It confirms our salvation. Often Christians are troubled with doubts about their conversion experience. Did God really save them when they asked Him to do so? Are they still saved today? A number of verses may be used to confirm our salvation. One of the strongest is Jesus' own words in the Gospel of John.**

JOHN 5:24 NKJV

²⁴ "Most assuredly, I say to you, he who hears My word and believes in Him who sent Me has everlasting life, and shall not come into judgment, but has passed from death into life.

JOHN 6:32-34, 36, 38-39 KJV and v. 35, 37, and 40 NKJV

³² Then Jesus said unto them, Verily, verily, I say unto you, Moses gave you not that bread from heaven; but my Father giveth you the true bread from heaven.

33 For the bread of God is he which cometh down from heaven, and giveth life unto the world.
34 Then said they unto him, Lord, evermore give us this bread.
35 And Jesus said to them, "I am the bread of life. He who comes to Me shall never hunger, and he who believes in Me shall never thirst.
36 But I said unto you, That ye also have seen me, and believe not.
37 All that the Father gives Me will come to Me, and the one who comes to Me I will by no means cast out.
38 For I came down from heaven, not to do mine own will, but the will of him that sent me.
39 And this is the Father's will which hath sent me, that of all which he hath given me I should lose nothing, but should raise it up again at the last day.
40 And this is the will of Him who sent Me, that everyone who sees the Son and believes in Him may have everlasting life; and I will raise him up at the last day."

ACTS 10:24-44 KJV

24 And the morrow after they entered into Caesarea. And Cornelius waited for them, and he had called together his kinsmen and near friends.
25 And as Peter was coming in, Cornelius met him, and fell down at his feet, and worshipped him.
26 But Peter took him up, saying, Stand up; I myself also am a man.
27 And as he talked with him, he went in, and found many that were come together.
28 And he said unto them, Ye know how that it is an unlawful thing for a man that is a Jew to keep company, or come unto one of another nation; but God hath shewed me that I should not call any man common or unclean.
29 Therefore came I unto you without gainsaying, as soon as I was sent for: I ask therefore for what intent ye have sent for me?
30 And Cornelius said, Four days ago I was fasting until this hour; and at the ninth hour I prayed in my house, and, behold, a man stood before me in bright clothing,
31 And said, Cornelius, thy prayer is heard, and thine alms are had in remembrance in the sight of God.

³² Send therefore to Joppa, and call hither Simon, whose surname is Peter; he is lodged in the house of one Simon a tanner by the sea side: who, when he cometh, shall speak unto thee.

³³ Immediately therefore I sent to thee; and thou hast well done that thou art come. Now therefore are we all here present before God, to hear all things that are commanded thee of God.

³⁴ Then Peter opened his mouth, and said, Of a truth I perceive that God is no respecter of persons:

³⁵ But in every nation he that feareth him, and worketh righteousness, is accepted with him.

³⁶ The word which God sent unto the children of Israel, preaching peace by Jesus Christ: (he is Lord of all:)

³⁷ That word, I say, ye know, which was published throughout all Judaea, and began from Galilee, after the baptism which John preached;

³⁸ How God anointed Jesus of Nazareth with the Holy Ghost and with power: who went about doing good, and healing all that were oppressed of the devil; for God was with him.

³⁹ And we are witnesses of all things which he did both in the land of the Jews, and in Jerusalem; whom they slew and hanged on a tree:

⁴⁰ Him God raised up the third day, and shewed him openly;

⁴¹ Not to all the people, but unto witnesses chosen before God, even to us, who did eat and drink with him after he rose from the dead.

⁴² And he commanded us to preach unto the people, and to testify that it is he which was ordained of God to be the Judge of quick and dead.

⁴³ To him give all the prophets witness, that through his name whosoever believeth in him shall receive remission of sins.

⁴⁴ While Peter yet spake these words, the Holy Ghost fell on all them which heard the word.

ROMANS 8:1 NKJV and v. 2-11 KJV

¹ There is therefore now no condemnation to those who are in Christ Jesus, who do not walk according to the flesh, but according to the Spirit.

² For the law of the Spirit of life in Christ Jesus hath made me free from the law of sin and death.
³ For what the law could not do, in that it was weak through the flesh, God sending his own Son in the likeness of sinful flesh, and for sin, condemned sin in the flesh:
⁴ That the righteousness of the law might be fulfilled in us, who walk not after the flesh, but after the Spirit.
⁵ For they that are after the flesh do mind the things of the flesh; but they that are after the Spirit the things of the Spirit.
⁶ For to be carnally minded is death; but to be spiritually minded is life and peace.
⁷ Because the carnal mind is enmity against God: for it is not subject to the law of God, neither indeed can be.
⁸ So then they that are in the flesh cannot please God.
⁹ But ye are not in the flesh, but in the Spirit, if so be that the Spirit of God dwell in you. Now if any man have not the Spirit of Christ, he is none of his.
¹⁰ And if Christ be in you, the body is dead because of sin; but the Spirit is life because of righteousness.
¹¹ But if the Spirit of him that raised up Jesus from the dead dwell in you, he that raised up Christ from the dead shall also quicken your mortal bodies by his Spirit that dwelleth in you.

2. **It confirms the hand of God in all of life's bitter disappointments. Undoubtedly a most important verse of reassurance and comfort in the hour of great need is in Romans.**

ROMANS 8:22-27, 29-30 KJV and v. 28 NKJV

²² For we know that the whole creation groaneth and travaileth in pain together until now.
²³ And not only they, but ourselves also, which have the firstfruits of the Spirit, even we ourselves groan within ourselves, waiting for the adoption, to wit, the redemption of our body.

²⁴ For we are saved by hope: but hope that is seen is not hope: for what a man seeth, why doth he yet hope for?
²⁵ But if we hope for that we see not, then do we with patience wait for it.
²⁶ Likewise the Spirit also helpeth our infirmities: for we know not what we should pray for as we ought: but the Spirit itself maketh intercession for us with groanings which cannot be uttered.
²⁷ And he that searcheth the hearts knoweth what is the mind of the Spirit, because he maketh intercession for the saints according to the will of God.
²⁸ And we know that all things work together for good to those who love God, to those who are the called according to His purpose.
²⁹ For whom he did foreknow, he also did predestinate to be conformed to the image of his Son, that he might be the firstborn among many brethren.
³⁰ Moreover whom he did predestinate, them he also called: and whom he called, them he also justified: and whom he justified, them he also glorified.

> **3. It confirms our forgiveness when we sin, sometimes believers carry with them an unnecessary burden of guilt over past sins and failures, even though these have been confessed. They have difficulty believing God has truly forgiven and cleansed them. But time and again the Bible assures us that all confessed sin is instantly and eternally forgiven.**

PSALMS 32:1-4, 6-7 KJV and v. 5 NKJV

¹ Blessed is he whose transgression is forgiven, whose sin is covered.
² Blessed is the man unto whom the Lord imputeth not iniquity, and in whose spirit there is no guile.
³ When I kept silence, my bones waxed old through my roaring all the day long.

⁴ For day and night thy hand was heavy upon me: my moisture is turned into the drought of summer. Selah.
⁵ I acknowledged my sin to You,
And my iniquity I have not hidden.
I said, "I will confess my transgressions to the Lord,"
And You forgave the iniquity of my sin. Selah
⁶ For this shall every one that is godly pray unto thee in a time when thou mayest be found: surely in the floods of great waters they shall not come nigh unto him.
⁷ Thou art my hiding place; thou shalt preserve me from trouble; thou shalt compass me about with songs of deliverance. Selah.

PSALMS 103:1-11, 13-14 KJV and v. 12 NKJV

¹ Bless the Lord, O my soul: and all that is within me, bless his holy name.
² Bless the Lord, O my soul, and forget not all his benefits:
³ Who forgiveth all thine iniquities; who healeth all thy diseases;
⁴ Who redeemeth thy life from destruction; who crowneth thee with lovingkindness and tender mercies;
⁵ Who satisfieth thy mouth with good things; so that thy youth is renewed like the eagle's.
⁶ The Lord executeth righteousness and judgment for all that are oppressed.
⁷ He made known his ways unto Moses, his acts unto the children of Israel.
⁸ The Lord is merciful and gracious, slow to anger, and plenteous in mercy.
⁹ He will not always chide: neither will he keep his anger for ever.
¹⁰ He hath not dealt with us after our sins; nor rewarded us according to our iniquities.
¹¹ For as the heaven is high above the earth, so great is his mercy toward them that fear him.
¹² As far as the east is from the west,
So far has He removed our transgressions from us.
¹³ Like as a father pitieth his children, so the Lord pitieth them that fear him.
¹⁴ For he knoweth our frame; he remembereth that we are dust.

I JOHN 1:5-10 KJV

⁵ This then is the message which we have heard of him, and declare unto you, that God is light, and in him is no darkness at all.

⁶ If we say that we have fellowship with him, and walk in darkness, we lie, and do not the truth:

⁷ But if we walk in the light, as he is in the light, we have fellowship one with another, and the blood of Jesus Christ his Son cleanseth us from all sin.

⁸ If we say that we have no sin, we deceive ourselves, and the truth is not in us.

⁹ If we confess our sins, he is faithful and just to forgive us our sins, and to cleanse us from all unrighteousness.

¹⁰ If we say that we have not sinned, we make him a liar, and his word is not in us.

I JOHN 2:1-6 KJV

¹ My little children, these things write I unto you, that ye sin not. And if any man sin, we have an advocate with the Father, Jesus Christ the righteous:

² And he is the propitiation for our sins: and not for ours only, but also for the sins of the whole world.

³ And hereby we do know that we know him, if we keep his commandments.

₄ He that saith, I know him, and keepeth not his commandments, is a liar, and the truth is not in him.

⁵ But whoso keepeth his word, in him verily is the love of God perfected: hereby know we that we are in him.

⁶ He that saith he abideth in him ought himself also so to walk, even as he walked.

ISAIAH 38:17 NKJV

¹⁷ Indeed it was for my own peace that I had great bitterness; But You have lovingly delivered my soul from the pit of corruption, for You have cast all my sins behind Your back.

DAY 20

God's Word Equips

PROVERBS 22:17-20 KJV and v. 21 NKJV

[17] Bow down thine ear, and hear the words of the wise, and apply thine heart unto my knowledge.
[18] For it is a pleasant thing if thou keep them within thee; they shall withal be fitted in thy lips.
[19] That thy trust may be in the Lord, I have made known to thee this day, even to thee.
[20] Have not I written to thee excellent things in counsels and knowledge,
[21] That I may make you know the certainty of the words of truth,
That you may answer words of truth
To those who send to you?

In a general sense it can be said that the Bible was written to convict sinners of sin and to equip believers for service.

---

1. **It equips for evangelism. Philip the evangelist uses the fifty-third chapter of Isaiah to point the Ethiopian Eunuch to Christ.**

ACTS 8:26-35 NKJV

[26] Now an angel of the Lord spoke to Philip, saying, "Arise and go toward the south along the road which goes down from Jerusalem to Gaza." This is desert.

[27] So he arose and went. And behold, a man of Ethiopia, a eunuch of great authority under Candace the queen of the Ethiopians, who had charge of all her treasury, and had come to Jerusalem to worship,

[28] was returning. And sitting in his chariot, he was reading Isaiah the prophet.

[29] Then the Spirit said to Philip, "Go near and overtake this chariot."

[30] So Philip ran to him, and heard him reading the prophet Isaiah, and said, "Do you understand what you are reading?"

[31] And he said, "How can I, unless someone guides me?" And he asked Philip to come up and sit with him.

[32] The place in the Scripture which he read was this:

"He was led as a sheep to the slaughter;
And as a lamb before its shearer is silent,
So He opened not His mouth.

[33] In His humiliation His justice was taken away,
And who will declare His generation?
For His life is taken from the earth."

[34] So the eunuch answered Philip and said, "I ask you, of whom does the prophet say this, of himself or of some other man?"

[35] Then Philip opened his mouth, and beginning at this Scripture, preached Jesus to him.

2. **It equips for counseling others. In his two letters to Timothy, Paul constantly urge this young man to preach the Word of God.**

I TIMOTHY 1:3 NKJV, and v. 4-5 KJV

[3] As I urged you when I went into Macedonia—remain in Ephesus that you may charge some that they teach no other doctrine,
[4] Neither give heed to fables and endless genealogies, which minister questions, rather than godly edifying which is in faith: so do.
[5] Now the end of the commandment is charity out of a pure heart, and of a good conscience, and of faith unfeigned:

I TIMOTHY 4:1-5, 7-12, 16 KJV, and v. 6, 13-15 NKJV

[1] Now the Spirit speaketh expressly, that in the latter times some shall depart from the faith, giving heed to seducing spirits, and doctrines of devils;
[2] Speaking lies in hypocrisy; having their conscience seared with a hot iron;
[3] Forbidding to marry, and commanding to abstain from meats, which God hath created to be received with thanksgiving of them which believe and know the truth.
[4] For every creature of God is good, and nothing to be refused, if it be received with thanksgiving:
[5] For it is sanctified by the word of God and prayer.
[6] If you instruct the brethren in these things, you will be a good minister of Jesus Christ, nourished in the words of faith and of the good doctrine which you have carefully followed.
[7] But refuse profane and old wives' fables, and exercise thyself rather unto godliness.
[8] For bodily exercise profiteth little: but godliness is profitable unto all things, having promise of the life that now is, and of that which is to come.
[9] This is a faithful saying and worthy of all acceptation.

¹⁰ For therefore we both labour and suffer reproach, because we trust in the living God, who is the Saviour of all men, specially of those that believe.
¹¹ These things command and teach.
¹² Let no man despise thy youth; but be thou an example of the believers, in word, in conversation, in charity, in spirit, in faith, in purity.
¹³ Till I come, give attention to reading, to exhortation, to doctrine.
¹⁴ Do not neglect the gift that is in you, which was given to you by prophecy with the laying on of the hands of the eldership.
¹⁵ Meditate on these things; give yourself entirely to them, that your progress may be evident to all.
¹⁶ Take heed unto thyself, and unto the doctrine; continue in them: for in doing this thou shalt both save thyself, and them that hear thee.

II TIMOTHY 2:1-2, 15 NKJV

¹ You therefore, my son, be strong in the grace that is in Christ Jesus.
² And the things that you have heard from me among many witnesses, commit these to faithful men who will be able to teach others also.
¹⁵ Be diligent to present yourself approved to God, a worker who does not need to be ashamed, rightly dividing the word of truth.

3. **It equips for using one's spiritual gifts from God. A spiritual gift is an ability given by the Holy Spirit to the believer for the purpose of edifying the church and glorifying God. Paul says a knowledge of God's Word will provide us with the maturity we need to use our gifts in the most effective way.**

EPHESIANS 1:15-16, 20-23 KJV and v. 17-19 NKJV

15 Wherefore I also, after I heard of your faith in the Lord Jesus, and love unto all the saints,

16 Cease not to give thanks for you, making mention of you in my prayers;

17 That the God of our Lord Jesus Christ, the Father of glory, may give to you the spirit of wisdom and revelation in the knowledge of Him,

18 the eyes of your understanding being enlightened; that you may know what is the hope of His calling, what are the riches of the glory of His inheritance in the saints,

19 and what is the exceeding greatness of His power toward us who believe, according to the working of His mighty power

20 Which he wrought in Christ, when he raised him from the dead, and set him at his own right hand in the heavenly places,

21 Far above all principality, and power, and might, and dominion, and every name that is named, not only in this world, but also in that which is to come:

22 And hath put all things under his feet, and gave him to be the head over all things to the church,

23 Which is his body, the fulness of him that filleth all in all.

EPHESIANS 4:8-10, 15-16 KJV, and v. 7, 11-14 NKJV

7 But unto every one of us is given grace according to the measure of the gift of Christ.

8 Wherefore he saith, When he ascended up on high, he led captivity captive, and gave gifts unto men.

9 (Now that he ascended, what is it but that he also descended first into the lower parts of the earth?

10 He that descended is the same also that ascended up far above all heavens, that he might fill all things.)

11 And He Himself gave some to be apostles, some prophets, some evangelists, and some pastors and teachers,

12 for the equipping of the saints for the work of ministry, for the edifying of the body of Christ,

¹³ till we all come to the unity of the faith and of the knowledge of the Son of God, to a perfect man, to the measure of the stature of the fullness of Christ;
¹⁴ that we should no longer be children, tossed to and fro and carried about with every wind of doctrine, by the trickery of men, in the cunning craftiness of deceitful plotting,
¹⁵ But speaking the truth in love, may grow up into him in all things, which is the head, even Christ:
¹⁶ From whom the whole body fitly joined together and compacted by that which every joint supplieth, according to the effectual working in the measure of every part, maketh increase of the body unto the edifying of itself in love.

4. **It equips us for doing battle with Satan. Paul likens the believers' armor to that used by Roman foot soldiers. In this comparison the Word of God is likened to the soldier's sword.**

EPHESIANS 6:10-16, 18-20 KJV, and v. 17 NKJV

¹⁰ Finally, my brethren, be strong in the Lord, and in the power of his might.
¹¹ Put on the whole armour of God, that ye may be able to stand against the wiles of the devil.
¹² For we wrestle not against flesh and blood, but against principalities, against powers, against the rulers of the darkness of this world, against spiritual wickedness in high places.
¹³ Wherefore take unto you the whole armour of God, that ye may be able to withstand in the evil day, and having done all, to stand.
¹⁴ Stand therefore, having your loins girt about with truth, and having on the breastplate of righteousness;
¹⁵ And your feet shod with the preparation of the gospel of peace;

[16] Above all, taking the shield of faith, wherewith ye shall be able to quench all the fiery darts of the wicked.
[17] And take the helmet of salvation, and the sword of the Spirit, which is the word of God;
[18] Praying always with all prayer and supplication in the Spirit, and watching thereunto with all perseverance and supplication for all saints;
[19] And for me, that utterance may be given unto me, that I may open my mouth boldly, to make known the mystery of the gospel,
[20] For which I am an ambassador in bonds: that therein I may speak boldly, as I ought to speak.

DAY 21

Confession

II SAMUEL 11:1-27 NKJV

¹ It happened in the spring of the year, at the time when kings go out to battle, that David sent Joab and his servants with him, and all Israel; and they destroyed the people of Ammon and besieged Rabbah. But David remained at Jerusalem.

² Then it happened one evening that David arose from his bed and walked on the roof of the king's house. And from the roof he saw a woman bathing, and the woman was very beautiful to behold.

³ So David sent and inquired about the woman. And someone said, "Is this not Bathsheba, the daughter of Eliam, the wife of Uriah the Hittite?"

⁴ Then David sent messengers, and took her; and she came to him, and he lay with her, for she was cleansed from her impurity; and she returned to her house.

⁵ And the woman conceived; so she sent and told David, and said, "I am with child."

⁶ Then David sent to Joab, saying, "Send me Uriah the Hittite." And Joab sent Uriah to David.

⁷ When Uriah had come to him, David asked how Joab was doing, and how the people were doing, and how the war prospered.

⁸ And David said to Uriah, "Go down to your house and wash your feet." So Uriah departed from the king's house, and a gift of food from the king followed him.
⁹ But Uriah slept at the door of the king's house with all the servants of his lord, and did not go down to his house.
¹⁰ So when they told David, saying, "Uriah did not go down to his house," David said to Uriah, "Did you not come from a journey? Why did you not go down to your house?"
¹¹ And Uriah said to David, "The ark and Israel and Judah are dwelling in tents, and my lord Joab and the servants of my lord are encamped in the open fields. Shall I then go to my house to eat and drink, and to lie with my wife? As you live, and as your soul lives, I will not do this thing."
¹² Then David said to Uriah, "Wait here today also, and tomorrow I will let you depart." So Uriah remained in Jerusalem that day and the next.
¹³ Now when David called him, he ate and drank before him; and he made him drunk. And at evening he went out to lie on his bed with the servants of his lord, but he did not go down to his house.
¹⁴ In the morning it happened that David wrote a letter to Joab and sent it by the hand of Uriah.
¹⁵ And he wrote in the letter, saying, "Set Uriah in the forefront of the hottest battle, and retreat from him, that he may be struck down and die."
¹⁶ So it was, while Joab besieged the city, that he assigned Uriah to a place where he knew there were valiant men.
¹⁷ Then the men of the city came out and fought with Joab. And some of the people of the servants of David fell; and Uriah the Hittite died also.
¹⁸ Then Joab sent and told David all the things concerning the war,
¹⁹ and charged the messenger, saying, "When you have finished telling the matters of the war to the king,
²⁰ if it happens that the king's wrath rises, and he says to you: 'Why did you approach so near to the city when you fought? Did you not know that they would shoot from the wall?

²¹ Who struck Abimelech the son of Jerubbesheth? Was it not a woman who cast a piece of a millstone on him from the wall, so that he died in Thebez? Why did you go near the wall?'—then you shall say, 'Your servant Uriah the Hittite is dead also.' "
²² So the messenger went, and came and told David all that Joab had sent by him.
²³ And the messenger said to David, "Surely the men prevailed against us and came out to us in the field; then we drove them back as far as the entrance of the gate.
²⁴ The archers shot from the wall at your servants; and some of the king's servants are dead, and your servant Uriah the Hittite is dead also."
²⁵ Then David said to the messenger, "Thus you shall say to Joab: 'Do not let this thing displease you, for the sword devours one as well as another. Strengthen your attack against the city, and overthrow it.' So encourage him."
²⁶ When the wife of Uriah heard that Uriah her husband was dead, she mourned for her husband.
²⁷ And when her mourning was over, David sent and brought her to his house, and she became his wife and bore him a son. But the thing that David had done displeased the Lord.

II SAMUEL 12:1-14 KJV

¹ And the Lord sent Nathan unto David. And he came unto him, and said unto him, There were two men in one city; the one rich, and the other poor.
² The rich man had exceeding many flocks and herds:
³ But the poor man had nothing, save one little ewe lamb, which he had bought and nourished up: and it grew up together with him, and with his children; it did eat of his own meat, and drank of his own cup, and lay in his bosom, and was unto him as a daughter.
⁴ And there came a traveller unto the rich man, and he spared to take of his own flock and of his own herd, to dress for the wayfaring man that was come unto him; but took the poor man's lamb, and dressed it for the man that was come to him.

⁵ And David's anger was greatly kindled against the man; and he said to Nathan, As the Lord liveth, the man that hath done this thing shall surely die:

⁶ And he shall restore the lamb fourfold, because he did this thing, and because he had no pity.

⁷ And Nathan said to David, Thou art the man. Thus saith the Lord God of Israel, I anointed thee king over Israel, and I delivered thee out of the hand of Saul;

⁸ And I gave thee thy master's house, and thy master's wives into thy bosom, and gave thee the house of Israel and of Judah; and if that had been too little, I would moreover have given unto thee such and such things.

⁹ Wherefore hast thou despised the commandment of the Lord, to do evil in his sight? thou hast killed Uriah the Hittite with the sword, and hast taken his wife to be thy wife, and hast slain him with the sword of the children of Ammon.

¹⁰ Now therefore the sword shall never depart from thine house; because thou hast despised me, and hast taken the wife of Uriah the Hittite to be thy wife.

¹¹ Thus saith the Lord, Behold, I will raise up evil against thee out of thine own house, and I will take thy wives before thine eyes, and give them unto thy neighbour, and he shall lie with thy wives in the sight of this sun.

¹² For thou didst it secretly: but I will do this thing before all Israel, and before the sun.

¹³ And David said unto Nathan, I have sinned against the Lord. And Nathan said unto David, The Lord also hath put away thy sin; thou shalt not die.

¹⁴ Howbeit, because by this deed thou hast given great occasion to the enemies of the Lord to blaspheme, the child also that is born unto thee shall surely die.

One of the most remarkable chapters in the Old Testament is Psalm 51. This Psalm contains the actual words of confession uttered by King David after his great sins of adultery and murder.

Day 21: Confession

This prayer can serve as a pattern to the Christian when he is guilty of sin in his life today.

---

1. David begins his prayer by freely admitting his sin.

PSALM 51:3-4 NKJV

³ For I acknowledge my transgressions,
And my sin is always before me.
⁴ Against You, You only, have I sinned,
And done this evil in Your sight—
That You may be found just when You speak,
And blameless when You judge.

This honesty is vital in our confession. God will graciously forgive all our sins, but not on account of our excuses.

---

2. David then displays real sorrow over his sin.

ROMANS 3:23-26 KJV

²³ For all have sinned, and come short of the glory of God;
²⁴ Being justified freely by his grace through the redemption that is in Christ Jesus:
²⁵ Whom God hath set forth to be a propitiation through faith in his blood, to declare his righteousness for the remission of sins that are past, through the forbearance of God;
²⁶ To declare, I say, at this time his righteousness: that he might be just, and the justifier of him which believeth in Jesus.

PSALM 51:17 NKJV

¹⁷ The sacrifices of God are a broken spirit,
A broken and a contrite heart—
These, O God, You will not despise.

> Paul writes that the main characteristic of true confession is godly sorrow.

II CORINTHIANS 7:9, 11 KJV and v. 10 NKJV

⁹ Now I rejoice, not that ye were made sorry, but that ye sorrowed to repentance: for ye were made sorry after a godly manner, that ye might receive damage by us in nothing.
¹⁰ For godly sorrow produces repentance leading to salvation, not to be regretted; but the sorrow of the world produces death.
¹¹ For behold this selfsame thing, that ye sorrowed after a godly sort, what carefulness it wrought in you, yea, what clearing of yourselves, yea, what indignation, yea, what fear, yea, what vehement desire, yea, what zeal, yea, what revenge! In all things ye have approved yourselves to be clear in this matter.

3. David asks God's forgiveness.

PSALM 51:1, 7-9 NKJV

¹ Have mercy upon me, O God,
According to Your lovingkindness;
According to the multitude of Your tender mercies,
Blot out my transgressions.
⁷ Purge me with hyssop, and I shall be clean
Wash me, and I shall be whiter than snow.
⁸ Make me hear joy and gladness,
That the bones You have broken may rejoice.

⁹ Hide Your face from my sins,
And blot out all my iniquities.

4. David believes that God has heard him and will restore him.

PSALM 51:12-15 NKJV

¹² Restore to me the joy of Your salvation,
And uphold me by Your generous Spirit.
¹³ Then I will teach transgressors Your ways,
And sinners shall be converted to You.
¹⁴ Deliver me from the guilt of bloodshed, O God,
The God of my salvation,
And my tongue shall sing aloud of Your righteousness.
¹⁵ O Lord, open my lips,
And my mouth shall show forth Your praise.

In the New Testament the most important
single verse concerning confession is I John 1:9.

I JOHN 1:8, 10 KJV and v. 9 NKJV

⁸ If we say that we have no sin, we deceive ourselves, and the truth is not in us.
⁹ If we confess our sins, He is faithful and just to forgive us our sins and to cleanse us from all unrighteousness.
¹⁰ If we say that we have not sinned, we make him a liar, and his word is not in us.

> In essence John tells us the means of forgiveness and cleansing is the blood of Christ, while the method of this forgiveness and cleansing is the confession of the Christian.
> Like David, we must admit our sin, regret the actions of our sin, plead the blood of Christ, and believe that God has indeed done what He promised, namely, to cleanse us from sin and restore us to fellowship and service.

II SAMUEL 12:13-14 KJV

[13] And David said unto Nathan, I have sinned against the Lord. And Nathan said unto David, The Lord also hath put away thy sin; thou shalt not die.

[14] Howbeit, because by this deed thou hast given great occasion to the enemies of the Lord to blaspheme, the child also that is born unto thee shall surely die.

Day 22: Walking in the Spirit: Confession

²⁶ My flesh and my heart faileth: but God is the strength of my heart, and my portion for ever.
²⁷ For, lo, they that are far from thee shall perish: thou hast destroyed all them that go a whoring from thee.
²⁸ But it is good for me to draw near to God: I have put my trust in the Lord God, that I may declare all thy works.

PSALM 37:39-40 KJV

³⁹ But the salvation of the righteous is of the Lord: he is their strength in the time of trouble.
⁴⁰ And the Lord shall help them, and deliver them: he shall deliver them from the wicked, and save them, because they trust in him.

> An important prerequisite to walking in the Spirit is the confession of sin. Sin must be confessed in order to restore fellowship and to continue receiving God's power. Confession means that we agree with God about our sin. This involves much more than simply acknowledging the sin. Confession requires an attitude of sorrow for the sin and a willingness to turn from it. It does not mean that we will never commit the same again, but it does mean that the attitude of repentance is present.

I JOHN 1:1-4 KJV and vs 5-10 NKJV

¹ That which was from the beginning, which we have heard, which we have seen with our eyes, which we have looked upon, and our hands have handled, of the Word of life;
² (For the life was manifested, and we have seen it, and bear witness, and shew unto you that eternal life, which was with the Father, and was manifested unto us;)

³ That which we have seen and heard declare we unto you, that ye also may have fellowship with us: and truly our fellowship is with the Father, and with his Son Jesus Christ.
⁴ And these things write we unto you, that your joy may be full.
⁵ This is the message which we have heard from Him and declare to you, that God is light and in Him is no darkness at all.
⁶ If we say that we have fellowship with Him, and walk in darkness, we lie and do not practice the truth.
⁷ But if we walk in the light as He is in the light, we have fellowship with one another, and the blood of Jesus Christ His Son cleanses us from all sin.
⁸ If we say that we have no sin, we deceive ourselves, and the truth is not in us.
⁹ If we confess our sins, He is faithful and just to forgive us our sins and to cleanse us from all unrighteousness.
¹⁰ If we say that we have not sinned, we make Him a liar, and His word is not in us.

> Confession should be made at the moment the Christian becomes aware of sin. Apart from this rule, moreover, the Scriptures mention two specific times for confession:

---

1. Before the close of the day.

EPHESIANS 4:26 NKJV and v. 27-32 KJV

²⁶ "Be angry, and do not sin": do not let the sun go down on your wrath,
²⁷ Neither give place to the devil.
²⁸ Let him that stole steal no more: but rather let him labour, working with his hands the thing which is good, that he may have to give to him that needeth.

Day 22: Walking in the Spirit: Confession

²⁹ Let no corrupt communication proceed out of your mouth, but that which is good to the use of edifying, that it may minister grace unto the hearers.
³⁰ And grieve not the holy Spirit of God, whereby ye are sealed unto the day of redemption.
³¹ Let all bitterness, and wrath, and anger, and clamour, and evil speaking, be put away from you, with all malice:
³² And be ye kind one to another, tenderhearted, forgiving one another, even as God for Christ's sake hath forgiven you.

2. **Before the Lord's Supper is observed. Failure to do the latter is a special cause for discipline from the Lord.**

I CORINTHIANS 11:23-26 KJV and vs. 27-32 NKJV

²³ For I [Paul] have received of the Lord that which also I delivered unto you, that the Lord Jesus the same night in which he was betrayed took bread:
²⁴ And when he had given thanks, he brake it, and said, Take, eat: this is my body, which is broken for you: this do in remembrance of me.
²⁵ After the same manner also he took the cup, when he had supped, saying, this cup is the new testament in my blood: this do ye, as oft as ye drink it, in remembrance of me.
²⁶ For as often as ye eat this bread, and drink this cup, ye do shew the Lord's death till he come.
²⁷ Therefore whoever eats this bread or drinks this cup of the Lord in an unworthy manner will be guilty of the body and blood of the Lord.
²⁸ But let a man examine himself, and so let him eat of the bread and drink of the cup.
²⁹ For he who eats and drinks in an unworthy manner eats and drinks judgment to himself, not discerning the Lord's body.

³⁰ For this reason many are weak and sick among you, and many sleep.
³¹ For if we would judge ourselves, we would not be judged.
³² But when we are judged, we are chastened by the Lord, that we may not be condemned with the world.

Confession of sin should normally involve only those who have knowledge of the sin. This means that:

---

1. Private sins should be confessed privately

I JOHN 1:9 NKJV
⁹ If we confess our sins, He is faithful and just to forgive us our sins and to cleanse us from all unrighteousness.

2. Sins between individuals confessed between those involved

MATTHEW 5:20-22 KJV and vs. 23-24 NKJV
²⁰ For I say unto you, That except your righteousness shall exceed the righteousness of the scribes and Pharisees, ye shall in no case enter into the kingdom of heaven.
²¹ Ye have heard that it was said of them of old time, Thou shalt not kill; and whosoever shall kill shall be in danger of the judgment:

²² But I say unto you, That whosoever is angry with his brother without a cause shall be in danger of the judgment: and whosoever shall say to his brother, Raca, shall be in danger of the council: but whosoever shall say, Thou fool, shall be in danger of hell fire.
²³ Therefore if you bring your gift to the altar, and there remember that your brother has something against you,
²⁴ leave your gift there before the altar, and go your way. First be reconciled to your brother, and then come and offer your gift.

3. Public sins confessed publicly

MATTHEW 18:15-16, 18-20 KJV and v. 17 NKJV

¹⁵ Moreover if thy brother shall trespass against thee, go and tell him his fault between thee and him alone: if he shall hear thee, thou hast gained thy brother.
¹⁶ But if he will not hear thee, then take with thee one or two more, that in the mouth of two or three witnesses every word may be established.
¹⁷ And if he refuses to hear them, tell it to the church. But if he refuses even to hear the church, let him be to you like a heathen and a tax collector.
¹⁸ Verily I say unto you, Whatsoever ye shall bind on earth shall be bound in heaven: and whatsoever ye shall loose on earth shall be loosed in heaven.
¹⁹ Again I say unto you, That if two of you shall agree on earth as touching any thing that they shall ask, it shall be done for them of my Father which is in heaven.
²⁰ For where two or three are gathered together in my name, there am I in the midst of them.

Public confession normally is made for the edification of the church.

II CORINTHIANS 12:19-21 KJV

[19] Again, think ye that we excuse ourselves unto you? we speak before God in Christ: but we do all things, dearly beloved, for your edifying.

[20] For I [Paul] fear, lest, when I come, I shall not find you such as I would, and that I shall be found unto you such as ye would not: lest there be debates, envyings, wraths, strifes, backbitings, whisperings, swellings, tumults:

[21] And lest, when I come again, my God will humble me among you, and that I shall bewail many which have sinned already, and have not repented of the uncleanness and fornication and lasciviousness which they have committed.

II CORINTHIANS 13:1-14 KJV

[1] This is the third time I [Paul] am coming to you. In the mouth of two or three witnesses shall every word be established.

[2] I told you before, and foretell you, as if I were present, the second time; and being absent now I write to them which heretofore have sinned, and to all other, that, if I come again, I will not spare:

[3] Since ye seek a proof of Christ speaking in me, which to you-ward is not weak, but is mighty in you.

[4] For though he was crucified through weakness, yet he liveth by the power of God. For we also are weak in him, but we shall live with him by the power of God toward you.

[5] Examine yourselves, whether ye be in the faith; prove your own selves. Know ye not your own selves, how that Jesus Christ is in you, except ye be reprobates?

[6] But I trust that ye shall know that we are not reprobates.

[7] Now I pray to God that ye do no evil; not that we should appear approved, but that ye should do that which is honest, though we be as reprobates.

[8] For we can do nothing against the truth, but for the truth.

[9] For we are glad, when we are weak, and ye are strong: and this also we wish, even your perfection.

[10] Therefore I write these things being absent, lest being present I should use sharpness, according to the power which the Lord hath given me to edification, and not to destruction.

[11] Finally, brethren, farewell. Be perfect, be of good comfort, be of one mind, live in peace; and the God of love and peace shall be with you.
[12] Greet one another with an holy kiss.
[13] All the saints salute you.
[14] The grace of the Lord Jesus Christ, and the love of God, and the communion of the Holy Ghost, be with you all. Amen.

DAY 23

Walking in the Spirit: Yielding

ROMANS 12:1 NKJV and vs. 2 KJV

¹ I beseech you therefore, brethren, by the mercies of God, that you present your bodies a living sacrifice, holy, acceptable to God, which is your reasonable service.
² And be not conformed to this world: but be ye transformed by the renewing of your mind, that ye may prove what is that good, and acceptable, and perfect, will of God.

> Confession of sin in itself is not enough to enable the believer to automatically walk in the Spirit. He must then become a yielded instrument for God's service. What is to be yielded is simply himself.

ROMANS 6:4-12, 14 KJV and v. 13 NKJV

⁴ Therefore we are buried with him by baptism into death: that like as Christ was raised up from the dead by the glory of the Father, even so we also should walk in newness of life.

Day 23: Walking in the Spirit: Yielding

⁵ For if we have been planted together in the likeness of his death, we shall be also in the likeness of his resurrection:

⁶ Knowing this, that our old man is crucified with him, that the body of sin might be destroyed, that henceforth we should not serve sin.

⁷ For he that is dead is freed from sin.

⁸ Now if we be dead with Christ, we believe that we shall also live with him:

⁹ Knowing that Christ being raised from the dead dieth no more; death hath no more dominion over him.

¹⁰ For in that he died, he died unto sin once: but in that he liveth, he liveth unto God.

¹¹ Likewise reckon ye also yourselves to be dead indeed unto sin, but alive unto God through Jesus Christ our Lord.

¹² Let not sin therefore reign in your mortal body, that ye should obey it in the lusts thereof.

¹³ And do not present your members as instruments of unrighteousness to sin, but present yourselves to God as being alive from the dead, and your members as instruments of righteousness to God.

¹⁴ For sin shall not have dominion over you: for ye are not under the law, but under grace.

JAMES 4:7 NKJV and 8-10 KJV

⁷ Therefore submit to God. Resist the devil and he will flee from you.

⁸ Draw nigh to God, and he will draw nigh to you. Cleanse your hands, ye sinners; and purify your hearts, ye double minded.

⁹ Be afflicted, and mourn, and weep: let your laughter be turned to mourning, and your joy to heaviness.

¹⁰ Humble yourselves in the sight of the Lord, and he shall lift you up.

This involves both the body and the mind.

I CORINTHIANS 6:19 KJV and v. 20 NKJV

[19] What? know ye not that your body is the temple of the Holy Ghost which is in you, which ye have of God, and ye are not your own?

[20] For you were bought at a price; therefore glorify God in your body and in your spirit, which are God's.

Since it is with the body that actions conceived in the mind are carried out and with the mind that they are formulated. Stated another way, that which is conceived in the mind is carried out in the body; thus, one's whole being must be presented by a decisive act of the will to God for His service. Yielding must not be thought of simply as a willingness to do some specific thing. Rather, it consists of dedication by a person to do whatever God commands.

Yielding leads not only to dedication but also can result in separation:

ROMANS 12:2 NKJV

[2] And do not be conformed to this world, but be transformed by the renewing of your mind, that you may prove what is that good and acceptable and perfect will of God.

The same word translated "conformed" here is translated "fashioning" in 1 Peter 1:14 ref: *as obedient children not fashioning yourself according to the former lust in your ignorance.*

Day 23: Walking in the Spirit: Yielding

I JOHN 2:15-17 NKJV

¹⁵ Do not love the world or the things in the world. If anyone loves the world, the love of the Father is not in him.
¹⁶ For all that is in the world—the lust of the flesh, the lust of the eyes, and the pride of life—is not of the Father but is of the world.
¹⁷ And the world is passing away, and the lust of it; but he who does the will of God abides forever.

> Since the world is resolutely opposed to God, one cannot revel in its lusts and at the same time do the will of God.

I PETER 1:13-16 KJV

¹³ Wherefore gird up the loins of your mind, be sober, and hope to the end for the grace that is to be brought unto you at the revelation of Jesus Christ
¹⁴ As obedient children, not fashioning yourselves according to the former lusts in your ignorance:
¹⁵ But as he which hath called you is holy, so be ye holy in all manner of conversation;
¹⁶ Because it is written, Be ye holy; for I am holy.

> So the concept of separation involves being "unfashionable" in spirit, thought, values, and actions according to the world's standards. Finally, yielding includes transformation of the mind. This work is said to be accomplished through a lifetime of "renewing" the mind. Man's mind has been darkened by sin and must be brought to the place where it thinks as God thinks.

ROMANS 8:1-6, 8-11 KJV and v. 7 NKJV

[1] There is therefore now no condemnation to them which are in Christ Jesus, who walk not after the flesh, but after the Spirit.
[2] For the law of the Spirit of life in Christ Jesus hath made me free from the law of sin and death.
[3] For what the law could not do, in that it was weak through the flesh, God sending his own Son in the likeness of sinful flesh, and for sin, condemned sin in the flesh:
[4] That the righteousness of the law might be fulfilled in us, who walk not after the flesh, but after the Spirit.
[5] For they that are after the flesh do mind the things of the flesh; but they that are after the Spirit the things of the Spirit.
[6] For to be carnally minded is death; but to be spiritually minded is life and peace.
[7] Because the carnal mind is enmity against God; for it is not subject to the law of God, nor indeed can be.
[8] So then they that are in the flesh cannot please God.
[9] But ye are not in the flesh, but in the Spirit, if so be that the Spirit of God dwell in you. Now if any man have not the Spirit of Christ, he is none of his.
[10] And if Christ be in you, the body is dead because of sin; but the Spirit is life because of righteousness.
[11] But if the Spirit of him that raised up Jesus from the dead dwell in you, he that raised up Christ from the dead shall also quicken your mortal bodies by his Spirit that dwelleth in you.

COLOSSIANS 1:21 NKJV and 22-23 KJV

[21] And you, who once were alienated and enemies in your mind by wicked works, yet now He has reconciled
[22] In the body of his flesh through death, to present you holy and unblameable and unreproveable in his sight:

Day 23: Walking in the Spirit: Yielding

²³ If ye continue in the faith grounded and settled, and be not moved away from the hope of the gospel, which ye have heard, and which was preached to every creature which is under heaven; whereof I Paul am made a minister;

EPHESIANS 4:17-22, 24 KJV and v. 23 NKJV

¹⁷ This I say therefore, and testify in the Lord, that ye henceforth walk not as other Gentiles walk, in the vanity of their mind,

¹⁸ Having the understanding darkened, being alienated from the life of God through the ignorance that is in them, because of the blindness of their heart:

¹⁹ Who being past feeling have given themselves over unto lasciviousness, to work all uncleanness with greediness.

²⁰ But ye have not so learned Christ;

²¹ If so be that ye have heard him, and have been taught by him, as the truth is in Jesus:

²² That ye put off concerning the former conversation the old man, which is corrupt according to the deceitful lusts;

²³ and be renewed in the spirit of your mind,

²⁴ And that ye put on the new man, which after God is created in righteousness and true holiness.

This renewing is said to come especially through prayer to God in everything and through constant meditation on the Word of God.

PSALM 119:9-10 KJV

⁹ Wherewithal shall a young man cleanse his way? by taking heed thereto according to thy word.

¹⁰ With my whole heart have I sought thee: O let me not wander from thy commandments.

PHILIPPIANS 4:4-5 KJV and v. 6-7 NKJV

⁴ Rejoice in the Lord always: and again I say, Rejoice.
⁵ Let your moderation be known unto all men. The Lord is at hand.
⁶ Be anxious for nothing, but in everything by prayer and supplication, with thanksgiving, let your requests be made known to God;
⁷ and the peace of God, which surpasses all understanding, will guard your hearts and minds through Christ Jesus.

I JOHN 5:18-20 KJV

¹⁸ We know that whosoever is born of God sinneth not; but he that is begotten of God keepeth himself, and that wicked one toucheth him not.
¹⁹ And we know that we are of God, and the whole world lieth in wickedness.
²⁰ And we know that the Son of God is come, and hath given us an understanding, that we may know him that is true, and we are in him that is true, even in his Son Jesus Christ. This is the true God, and eternal life.

This transformation is a lifelong process that will not be completed until we are with Christ.

PHILIPPIANS 1:6 NKJV

⁶ being confident of this very thing, that He who has begun a good work in you will complete it until the day of Jesus Christ;

I JOHN 2:28-29 KJV

²⁸ And now, little children, abide in him; that, when he shall appear, we may have confidence, and not be ashamed before him at his coming.

Day 23: Walking in the Spirit: Yielding

²⁹ If ye know that he is righteous, ye know that every one that doeth righteousness is born of him.

I JOHN 3:1, 3 KJV and v. 2 NKJV

¹ Behold, what manner of love the Father hath bestowed upon us, that we should be called the sons of God: therefore the world knoweth us not, because it knew him not.
² Beloved, now we are children of God; and it has not yet been revealed what we shall be, but we know that when He is revealed, we shall be like Him, for we shall see Him as He is.
³ And every man that hath this hope in him purifieth himself, even as he is pure.

Along life's way, however, it brings a peace and delight that can only come from having embraced the mind of Christ.

DAY 24

———◆———

Walking in the Spirit: Filling

EPHESIANS 5:15-17, 19-21 KJV and vs. 18 NKJV

[15] See then that ye walk circumspectly, not as fools, but as wise,
[16] Redeeming the time, because the days are evil.
[17] Wherefore be ye not unwise, but understanding what the will of the Lord is.
[18] And do not be drunk with wine, in which is dissipation; but be filled with the Spirit,
[19] Speaking to yourselves in psalms and hymns and spiritual songs, singing and making melody in your heart to the Lord;
[20] Giving thanks always for all things unto God and the Father in the name of our Lord Jesus Christ;
[21] Submitting yourselves one to another in the fear of God.

To be filled with the Spirit is to be controlled by
the Spirit and is therefore crucial to successfully
living the Christian life.
Unlike the indwelling of the Spirit, filling is a
repeated experience. This is underscored

Day 24: Walking in the Spirit: Filling

by the use of the present tense ("be filled") as well as by biblical examples of Christians who were filled more than once:

ACTS 2:1-3 KJV and v. 4 NKJV

¹ And when the day of Pentecost was fully come, they were all with one accord in one place.
² And suddenly there came a sound from heaven as of a rushing mighty wind, and it filled all the house where they were sitting.
³ And there appeared unto them cloven tongues like as of fire, and it sat upon each of them.
⁴ And they were all filled with the Holy Spirit and began to speak with other tongues, as the Spirit gave them utterance.

ACTS 4:13-30 KJV and v. 31 NKJV

¹³ Now when they saw the boldness of Peter and John, and perceived that they were unlearned and ignorant men, they marvelled; and they took knowledge of them, that they had been with Jesus.
¹⁴ And beholding the man which was healed standing with them, they could say nothing against it.
¹⁵ But when they had commanded them to go aside out of the council, they conferred among themselves,
¹⁶ Saying, What shall we do to these men? for that indeed a notable miracle hath been done by them is manifest to all them that dwell in Jerusalem; and we cannot deny it.
¹⁷ But that it spread no further among the people, let us straitly threaten them, that they speak henceforth to no man in this name.
¹⁸ And they called them, and commanded them not to speak at all nor teach in the name of Jesus.
¹⁹ But Peter and John answered and said unto them, Whether it be right in the sight of God to hearken unto you more than unto God, judge ye.

²⁰ For we cannot but speak the things which we have seen and heard.
²¹ So when they had further threatened them, they let them go, finding nothing how they might punish them, because of the people: for all men glorified God for that which was done.
²² For the man was above forty years old, on whom this miracle of healing was shewed.
²³ And being let go, they went to their own company, and reported all that the chief priests and elders had said unto them.
²⁴ And when they heard that, they lifted up their voice to God with one accord, and said, Lord, thou art God, which hast made heaven, and earth, and the sea, and all that in them is:
²⁵ Who by the mouth of thy servant David hast said, Why did the heathen rage, and the people imagine vain things?
²⁶ The kings of the earth stood up, and the rulers were gathered together against the Lord, and against his Christ.
²⁷ For of a truth against thy holy child Jesus, whom thou hast anointed, both Herod, and Pontius Pilate, with the Gentiles, and the people of Israel, were gathered together,
²⁸ For to do whatsoever thy hand and thy counsel determined before to be done.
²⁹ And now, Lord, behold their threatenings: and grant unto thy servants, that with all boldness they may speak thy word,
³⁰ By stretching forth thine hand to heal; and that signs and wonders may be done by the name of thy holy child Jesus.
³¹ And when they had prayed, the place where they were assembled together was shaken; and they were all filled with the Holy Spirit, and they spoke the word of God with boldness.

> Just as important, we must observe that filling is a command to be obeyed, not an option. The next most important question is, how can someone be filled with the Spirit? The prerequisites are simply

confession of sin and yielding to God. The former means to agree with God about the person's sin; the latter means primarily dedication of himself to God. As the believer chooses to obey in these areas, he is filled with the Spirit and enabled to manifest Christlike character. This obedience may be accompanied by prayer but is not necessarily so. The certainty of being filled with the Spirit may be confirmed by the believer's faith and life.

The believer must, of course, believe God's Word that meeting the conditions will result in the filling. The spirit-filled person will exhibit the Christlike character described in Galatians 5 as the fruit of the Spirit. Included in that list are all the vibrant, attractive qualities desired by all Christians. How delightful it is that any Christian may possess them and be transformed by the filling of the Spirit.

GALATIANS 5:22-23 NKJV and v. 24-26 KJV

[22] But the fruit of the Spirit is love, joy, peace, longsuffering, kindness, goodness, faithfulness,
[23] gentleness, self-control. Against such there is no law.
[24] And they that are Christ's have crucified the flesh with the affections and lusts.
[25] If we live in the Spirit, let us also walk in the Spirit.
[26] Let us not be desirous of vain glory, provoking one another, envying one another.

GALATIANS 6:1-10 KJV

[1] Brethren, if a man be overtaken in a fault, ye which are spiritual, restore such an one in the spirit of meekness; considering thyself, lest thou also be tempted.

² Bear ye one another's burdens, and so fulfil the law of Christ.
³ For if a man think himself to be something, when he is nothing, he deceiveth himself.
⁴ But let every man prove his own work, and then shall he have rejoicing in himself alone, and not in another.
⁵ For every man shall bear his own burden.
⁶ Let him that is taught in the word communicate unto him that teacheth in all good things.
⁷ Be not deceived; God is not mocked: for whatsoever a man soweth, that shall he also reap.
⁸ For he that soweth to his flesh shall of the flesh reap corruption; but he that soweth to the Spirit shall of the Spirit reap life everlasting.
⁹ And let us not be weary in well doing: for in due season we shall reap, if we faint not.
¹⁰ As we have therefore opportunity, let us do good unto all men, especially unto them who are of the household of faith.

GALATIANS 5:19-21 KJV

¹⁹ Now the works of the flesh are manifest, which are these; Adultery, fornication, uncleanness, lasciviousness,
²⁰ Idolatry, witchcraft, hatred, variance, emulations, wrath, strife, seditions, heresies,
²¹ Envyings, murders, drunkenness, revellings, and such like: of the which I tell you before, as I have also told you in time past, that they which do such things shall not inherit the kingdom of God.

DAY 25

Everlasting Life

JOHN 5:24 NKJV

²⁴"Most assuredly, I say to you, he who hears My word and believes in Him who sent Me has everlasting life, and shall not come into judgment, but has passed from death into life.

> One benefit of finding new life in Christ is called in the Bible "everlasting [eternal] life." The character of this great reality may be summarized by carefully looking at each word. The word *life* stresses the quality of this new relationship to God.

JOHN 10:7-9, 11 KJV and v. 10 NKJV

⁷ Then said Jesus unto them again, Verily, verily, I say unto you, I am the door of the sheep.

⁸ All that ever came before me are thieves and robbers: but the sheep did not hear them.
⁹ I am the door: by me if any man enter in, he shall be saved, and shall go in and out, and find pasture.
¹⁰ The thief does not come except to steal, and to kill, and to destroy. I have come that they may have life, and that they may have it more abundantly.
¹¹ I am the good shepherd: the good shepherd giveth his life for the sheep.

> It does not mean, of course, that we are not physically alive before salvation; it simply stresses the fact that we enter a new, personal relationship with God that gives us a fullness of spiritual vitality that we lacked before.

JOHN 17:1-2, 4-5 KJV and v. 3 NKJV

¹ These words spake Jesus, and lifted up his eyes to heaven, and said, Father, the hour is come; glorify thy Son, that thy Son also may glorify thee:
² As thou hast given him power over all flesh, that he should give eternal life to as many as thou hast given him.
³ And this is eternal life, that they may know You, the only true God, and Jesus Christ whom You have sent.
⁴ I have glorified thee on the earth: I have finished the work which thou gavest me to do.
⁵ And now, O Father, glorify thou me with thine own self with the glory which I had with thee before the world was.

JOHN 17:13-26 KJV

¹³ And now come I to thee; and these things I speak in the world, that they might have my joy fulfilled in themselves.

Day 25: Everlasting Life

¹⁴ I have given them thy word; and the world hath hated them, because they are not of the world, even as I am not of the world.
¹⁵ I pray not that thou shouldest take them out of the world, but that thou shouldest keep them from the evil.
¹⁶ They are not of the world, even as I am not of the world.
¹⁷ Sanctify them through thy truth: thy word is truth.
¹⁸ As thou hast sent me into the world, even so have I also sent them into the world.
¹⁹ And for their sakes I sanctify myself, that they also might be sanctified through the truth.
²⁰ Neither pray I for these alone, but for them also which shall believe on me through their word;
²¹ That they all may be one; as thou, Father, art in me, and I in thee, that they also may be one in us: that the world may believe that thou hast sent me.
²² And the glory which thou gavest me I have given them; that they may be one, even as we are one:
²³ I in them, and thou in me, that they may be made perfect in one; and that the world may know that thou hast sent me, and hast loved them, as thou hast loved me.
²⁴ Father, I will that they also, whom thou hast given me, be with me where I am; that they may behold my glory, which thou hast given me: for thou lovedst me before the foundation of the world.
²⁵ O righteous Father, the world hath not known thee: but I have known thee, and these have known that thou hast sent me.
²⁶ And I have declared unto them thy name, and will declare it: that the love wherewith thou hast loved me may be in them, and I in them.

The word *everlasting* emphasizes life without end. Though it will not be completely fulfilled until our future redemption, it is still a present possession that can never perish.

JOHN 10:27, 29-30 KJV and v. 28 NKJV

²⁷ My sheep hear my voice, and I know them, and they follow me:
²⁸ And I give them eternal life, and they shall never perish; neither shall anyone snatch them out of My hand.
²⁹ My Father, which gave them me, is greater than all; and no man is able to pluck them out of my Father's hand.
³⁰ I and my Father are one.

> Everlasting life must not be conceived of as
> an exclusively future possession.
> Rather, its possession is clearly seen in our actions.
> Thus, "no murderer has eternal life abiding in
> Him." Indeed, love is the confirming evidence that
> we do, in fact, have eternal life.

I JOHN 3:13, 16-24 KJV and v. 14-15 NKJV

¹³ Marvel not, my brethren, if the world hate you.
¹⁴ We know that we have passed from death to life, because we love the brethren. He who does not love his brother abides in death.
¹⁵ Whoever hates his brother is a murderer, and you know that no murderer has eternal life abiding in him.
¹⁶ Hereby perceive we the love of God, because he laid down his life for us: and we ought to lay down our lives for the brethren.
¹⁷ But whoso hath this world's good, and seeth his brother have need, and shutteth up his bowels of compassion from him, how dwelleth the love of God in him?
¹⁸ My little children, let us not love in word, neither in tongue; but in deed and in truth.
¹⁹ And hereby we know that we are of the truth, and shall assure our hearts before him.
²⁰ For if our heart condemn us, God is greater than our heart, and knoweth all things.

Day 25: Everlasting Life

²¹ Beloved, if our heart condemn us not, then have we confidence toward God.
²² And whatsoever we ask, we receive of him, because we keep his commandments, and do those things that are pleasing in his sight.
²³ And this is his commandment, That we should believe on the name of his Son Jesus Christ, and love one another, as he gave us commandment.
²⁴ And he that keepeth his commandments dwelleth in him, and he in him. And hereby we know that he abideth in us, by the Spirit which he hath given us.

> The greatness of this spiritual reality constitutes a wonderful incentive to vigorously proclaim the Gospel to those who are still "dead in trespasses and sins."

EPHESIANS 2:1 NKJV and v. 2-10 KJV

¹ And you He made alive, who were dead in trespasses and sins,
² Wherein in time past ye walked according to the course of this world, according to the prince of the power of the air, the spirit that now worketh in the children of disobedience:
³ Among whom also we all had our conversation in times past in the lusts of our flesh, fulfilling the desires of the flesh and of the mind; and were by nature the children of wrath, even as others.
⁴ But God, who is rich in mercy, for his great love wherewith he loved us,
⁵ Even when we were dead in sins, hath quickened us together with Christ, (by grace ye are saved;)
⁶ And hath raised us up together, and made us sit together in heavenly places in Christ Jesus:

⁷ That in the ages to come he might shew the exceeding riches of his grace in his kindness toward us through Christ Jesus.
⁸ For by grace are ye saved through faith; and that not of yourselves: it is the gift of God:
⁹ Not of works, lest any man should boast.
¹⁰ For we are his workmanship, created in Christ Jesus unto good works, which God hath before ordained that we should walk in them.

DAY 26

God the Father of All

The Fatherhood of God applies in a general sense to everyone since all men and women are created by God in His image.

GENESIS 1:26-28 KJV

26 And God said, Let us make man in our image, after our likeness: and let them have dominion over the fish of the sea, and over the fowl of the air, and over the cattle, and over all the earth, and over every creeping thing that creepeth upon the earth.
27 So God created man in his own image, in the image of God created he him; male and female created he them.
28 And God blessed them, and God said unto them, Be fruitful, and multiply, and replenish the earth, and subdue it: and have dominion over the fish of the sea, and over the fowl of the air, and over every living thing that moveth upon the earth.

JOB 31:15 KJV

15 Did not he that made me in the womb make him? and did not one fashion us in the womb?

MALACHI 2:10 NKJV

[10] Have we not all one Father?
Has not one God created us?
Why do we deal treacherously with one another
By profaning the covenant of the fathers?

---

*Thus their creaturehood is derived
from his fatherhood.*

ECCLESIASTES 12:6, 8 KJV and v. 7 NKJV

[6] Or ever the silver cord be loosed, or the golden bowl be broken, or the pitcher be broken at the fountain, or the wheel broken at the cistern.
[7] Then the dust will return to the earth as it was,
And the spirit will return to God who gave it.
[8] Vanity of vanities, saith the preacher; all is vanity.

I CORINTHIANS 8:5-6 KJV

[5] For though there be that are called gods, whether in heaven or in earth, (as there be gods many, and lords many,)
[6] But to us there is but one God, the Father, of whom are all things, and we in him; and one Lord Jesus Christ, by whom are all things, and we by him.

HEBREWS 12:5-8, 10-11 KJV and v. 9 NKJV

[5] And ye have forgotten the exhortation which speaketh unto you as unto children, My son, despise not thou the chastening of the Lord, nor faint when thou art rebuked of him:
[6] For whom the Lord loveth he chasteneth, and scourgeth every son whom he receiveth.

⁷ If ye endure chastening, God dealeth with you as with sons; for what son is he whom the father chasteneth not?
⁸ But if ye be without chastisement, whereof all are partakers, then are ye bastards, and not sons.
⁹ Furthermore, we have had human fathers who corrected us, and we paid them respect. Shall we not much more readily be in subjection to the Father of spirits and live?
¹⁰ For they verily for a few days chastened us after their own pleasure; but he for our profit, that we might be partakers of his holiness.
¹¹ Now no chastening for the present seemeth to be joyous, but grievous: nevertheless afterward it yieldeth the peaceable fruit of righteousness unto them which are exercised thereby.

MALACHI 2:4-10 KJV

⁴ And ye shall know that I have sent this commandment unto you, that my covenant might be with Levi, saith the Lord of hosts.
⁵ My covenant was with him of life and peace; and I gave them to him for the fear wherewith he feared me, and was afraid before my name.
⁶ The law of truth was in his mouth, and iniquity was not found in his lips: he walked with me in peace and equity, and did turn many away from iniquity.
⁷ For the priest's lips should keep knowledge, and they should seek the law at his mouth: for he is the messenger of the Lord of hosts.
⁸ But ye are departed out of the way; ye have caused many to stumble at the law; ye have corrupted the covenant of Levi, saith the Lord of hosts.
⁹ Therefore have I also made you contemptible and base before all the people, according as ye have not kept my ways, but have been partial in the law.
¹⁰ Have we not all one father? hath not one God created us? why do we deal treacherously every man against his brother, by profaning the covenant of our fathers?

> Paul even agrees with a heathen poet that
> all men are God's offspring.

ACTS 17:28 NKJV and v. 29-31 KJV

[28] for in Him we live and move and have our being, as also some of your own poets have said, 'For we are also His offspring.'

[29] Forasmuch then as we are the offspring of God, we ought not to think that the Godhead is like unto gold, or silver, or stone, graven by art and man's device.

[30] And the times of this ignorance God winked at; but now commandeth all men every where to repent:

[31] Because he hath appointed a day, in the which he will judge the world in righteousness by that man whom he hath ordained; whereof he hath given assurance unto all men, in that he hath raised him from the dead.

> He [Paul] does not mean, of course,
> that everyone will have eternal life but that
> all men and women are the offspring of
> God in their created nature.

GENESIS 5:2 KJV

[2] Male and female created he them; and blessed them, and called their name Adam, in the day when they were created.

ROMANS 3:19-28 KJV

[19] Now we know that what things soever the law saith, it saith to them who are under the law: that every mouth may be stopped, and all the world may become guilty before God.

²⁰ Therefore by the deeds of the law there shall no flesh be justified in his sight: for by the law is the knowledge of sin.
²¹ But now the righteousness of God without the law is manifested, being witnessed by the law and the prophets;
²² Even the righteousness of God which is by faith of Jesus Christ unto all and upon all them that believe: for there is no difference:
²³ For all have sinned, and come short of the glory of God;
²⁴ Being justified freely by his grace through the redemption that is in Christ Jesus:
²⁵ Whom God hath set forth to be a propitiation through faith in his blood, to declare his righteousness for the remission of sins that are past, through the forbearance of God;
²⁶ To declare, I say, at this time his righteousness: that he might be just, and the justifier of him which believeth in Jesus.
²⁷ Where is boasting then? It is excluded. By what law? of works? Nay: but by the law of faith.
²⁸ Therefore we conclude that a man is justified by faith without the deeds of the law.

JAMES 3:2-8, 10-12 KJV and v. 9 NKJV

² For in many things we offend all. If any man offend not in word, the same is a perfect man, and able also to bridle the whole body.
³ Behold, we put bits in the horses' mouths, that they may obey us; and we turn about their whole body.
⁴ Behold also the ships, which though they be so great, and are driven of fierce winds, yet are they turned about with a very small helm, whithersoever the governor listeth.
⁵ Even so the tongue is a little member, and boasteth great things. Behold, how great a matter a little fire kindleth!
⁶ And the tongue is a fire, a world of iniquity: so is the tongue among our members, that it defileth the whole body, and setteth on fire the course of nature; and it is set on fire of hell.
⁷ For every kind of beasts, and of birds, and of serpents, and of things in the sea, is tamed, and hath been tamed of mankind:
⁸ But the tongue can no man tame; it is an unruly evil, full of deadly poison.

⁹ With it we bless our God and Father, and with it we curse men, who have been made in the similitude of God.
¹⁰ Out of the same mouth proceedeth blessing and cursing. My brethren, these things ought not so to be.
¹¹ Doth a fountain send forth at the same place sweet water and bitter?
¹² Can the fig tree, my brethren, bear olive berries? either a vine, figs? so can no fountain both yield salt water and fresh.

God is also the Father of all as Sustainer of Life. Every person is an object of His fatherly care and a candidate for His Kingdom.

MATTHEW 18:10 NKJV and v. 11 KJV

¹⁰ "Take heed that you do not despise one of these little ones, for I say to you that in heaven their angels always see the face of My Father who is in heaven.
¹¹ For the Son of man is come to save that which was lost.

LUKE 18:15, 17 KJV and v. 16 NKJV

¹⁵ And they brought unto him also infants, that he would touch them: but when his disciples saw it, they rebuked them.
¹⁶ But Jesus called them to Him and said, "Let the little children come to Me, and do not forbid them; for of such is the kingdom of God.
¹⁷ Verily I say unto you, Whosoever shall not receive the kingdom of God as a little child shall in no wise enter therein.

Furthermore, God is not willing that any should perish.

Day 26: God the Father of All

MATTHEW 18:14 NKJV

¹⁴ Even so it is not the will of your Father who is in heaven that one of these little ones should perish.

I TIMOTHY 2:1-3, 5-8 KJV, and v. 4 NKJV

¹ I exhort therefore, that, first of all, supplications, prayers, intercessions, and giving of thanks, be made for all men;
² For kings, and for all that are in authority; that we may lead a quiet and peaceable life in all godliness and honesty.
³ For this is good and acceptable in the sight of God our Saviour;
⁴ who desires all men to be saved and to come to the knowledge of the truth.
⁵ For there is one God, and one mediator between God and men, the man Christ Jesus;
⁶ Who gave himself a ransom for all, to be testified in due time.
⁷ Whereunto I [Paul] am ordained a preacher, and an apostle, (I speak the truth in Christ, and lie not;) a teacher of the Gentiles in faith and verity.
⁸ I will therefore that men pray every where, lifting up holy hands, without wrath and doubting.

II PETER 3:9-18 KJV

⁹ The Lord is not slack concerning his promise, as some men count slackness; but is longsuffering to us-ward, not willing that any should perish, but that all should come to repentance.
¹⁰ But the day of the Lord will come as a thief in the night; in the which the heavens shall pass away with a great noise, and the elements shall melt with fervent heat, the earth also and the works that are therein shall be burned up.
¹¹ Seeing then that all these things shall be dissolved, what manner of persons ought ye to be in all holy conversation and godliness,
¹² Looking for and hasting unto the coming of the day of God, wherein the heavens being on fire shall be dissolved, and the elements shall melt with fervent heat?

¹³ Nevertheless we, according to his promise, look for new heavens and a new earth, wherein dwelleth righteousness.
¹⁴ Wherefore, beloved, seeing that ye look for such things, be diligent that ye may be found of him in peace, without spot, and blameless.
¹⁵ And account that the longsuffering of our Lord is salvation; even as our beloved brother Paul also according to the wisdom given unto him hath written unto you;
¹⁶ As also in all his epistles, speaking in them of these things; in which are some things hard to be understood, which they that are unlearned and unstable wrest, as they do also the other scriptures, unto their own destruction.
¹⁷ Ye therefore, beloved, seeing ye know these things before, beware lest ye also, being led away with the error of the wicked, fall from your own steadfastness.
¹⁸ But grow in grace, and in the knowledge of our Lord and Saviour Jesus Christ. To him be glory both now and for ever. Amen.

Even when men and women reject God He still provides for them as He does believers with rain, fruitful seasons, food, and gladness.

ACTS 14:13-16 KJV, and v. 17 NKJV

¹³ Then the priest of Jupiter, which was before their city, brought oxen and garlands unto the gates, and would have done sacrifice with the people.
¹⁴ Which when the apostles, Barnabas and Paul, heard of, they rent their clothes, and ran in among the people, crying out,
¹⁵ And saying, Sirs, why do ye these things? We also are men of like passions with you, and preach unto you that ye should turn from these vanities unto the living God, which made heaven, and earth, and the sea, and all things that are therein:

¹⁶ Who in times past suffered all nations to walk in their own ways. ¹⁷ Nevertheless He did not leave Himself without witness, in that He did good, gave us rain from heaven and fruitful seasons, filling our hearts with food and gladness."

MATTHEW 5:43-44, 46-48 KJV and v. 45 NKJV

⁴³ Ye have heard that it hath been said, Thou shalt love thy neighbour, and hate thine enemy.
⁴⁴ But I say unto you, Love your enemies, bless them that curse you, do good to them that hate you, and pray for them which despitefully use you, and persecute you;
⁴⁵ that you may be sons of your Father in heaven; for He makes His sun rise on the evil and on the good, and sends rain on the just and on the unjust.
⁴⁶ For if ye love them which love you, what reward have ye? do not even the publicans the same?
⁴⁷ And if ye salute your brethren only, what do ye more than others? do not even the publicans so?
⁴⁸ Be ye therefore perfect, even as your Father which is in heaven is perfect.

ROMANS 1:20 KJV

²⁰ For the invisible things of him from the creation of the world are clearly seen, being understood by the things that are made, even his eternal power and Godhead; so that they are without excuse:

TITUS 2:11-15 KJV

¹¹ For the grace of God that bringeth salvation hath appeared to all men,
¹² Teaching us that, denying ungodliness and worldly lusts, we should live soberly, righteously, and godly, in this present world;
¹³ Looking for that blessed hope, and the glorious appearing of the great God and our Saviour Jesus Christ;
¹⁴ Who gave himself for us, that he might redeem us from all iniquity, and purify unto himself a peculiar people, zealous of good works.

¹⁵ These things speak, and exhort, and rebuke with all authority. Let no man despise thee.

EPHESIANS 4:1-6 KJV

¹ I [Paul] therefore, the prisoner of the Lord, beseech you that ye walk worthy of the vocation wherewith ye are called,
² With all lowliness and meekness, with longsuffering, forbearing one another in love;
³ Endeavouring to keep the unity of the Spirit in the bond of peace.
⁴ There is one body, and one Spirit, even as ye are called in one hope of your calling;
⁵ One Lord, one faith, one baptism,
⁶ One God and Father of all, who is above all, and through all, and in you all.

ACTS 17:29-31 KJV

²⁹ Forasmuch then as we are the offspring of God, we ought not to think that the Godhead is like unto gold, or silver, or stone, graven by art and man's device.
³⁰ And the times of this ignorance God winked at; but now commandeth all men every where to repent:
³¹ Because he hath appointed a day, in the which he will judge the world in righteousness by that man whom he hath ordained; whereof he hath given assurance unto all men, in that he hath raised him from the dead.

DAY 27

---·◆·---

Temptation by the World

I JOHN 2:15 NKJV and v. 16-17 KJV

¹⁵ Do not love the world or the things in the world. If anyone loves the world, the love of the Father is not in him.
¹⁶ For all that is in the world, the lust of the flesh, and the lust of the eyes, and the pride of life, is not of the Father, but is of the world.
¹⁷ And the world passeth away, and the lust thereof: but he that doeth the will of God abideth for ever.

ROMANS 12:2 KJV

² And be not conformed to this world: but be ye transformed by the renewing of your mind, that ye may prove what is that good, and acceptable, and perfect, will of God.

> The term *world* does not always refer to the universe as created by God. It often is used to describe the community of sinful humanity that possesses a spirit of rebellion against God.

I JOHN 5:18, 20 KJV and v. 19 NKJV

[18] We know that whosoever is born of God sinneth not; but he that is begotten of God keepeth himself, and that wicked one toucheth him not.

[19] We know that we are of God, and the whole world lies under the sway of the wicked one.

[20] And we know that the Son of God is come, and hath given us an understanding, that we may know him that is true, and we are in him that is true, even in his Son Jesus Christ. This is the true God, and eternal life.

Because of its opposition to God, the world values those things which are contrary to God's will: the lust of the flesh, and the lust of the eyes, and the pride of life.

I JOHN 2:16 NKJV

[26] For all that is in the world—the lust of the flesh, the lust of the eyes, and the pride of life—is not of the Father but is of the world.

Its temptation to the believer are thus two-fold: lust for the sensual and pride in mastery of his own life. Attraction of the world is amplified by Satan who is head of its system. He is called the Prince of this World, and the whole world is said to be under his power where wickedness can also be translated *wicked one*.

Day 27: Temptation by the World

EPHESIANS 2:1-10 KJV

[1] And you hath he [God] quickened, who were dead in trespasses and sins;

[2] Wherein in time past ye walked according to the course of this world, according to the prince of the power of the air, the spirit that now worketh in the children of disobedience:

[3] Among whom also we all had our conversation in times past in the lusts of our flesh, fulfilling the desires of the flesh and of the mind; and were by nature the children of wrath, even as others.

[4] But God, who is rich in mercy, for his great love wherewith he loved us,

[5] Even when we were dead in sins, hath quickened us together with Christ, (by grace ye are saved;)

[6] And hath raised us up together, and made us sit together in heavenly places in Christ Jesus:

[7] That in the ages to come he might shew the exceeding riches of his grace in his kindness toward us through Christ Jesus.

[8] For by grace are ye saved through faith; and that not of yourselves: it is the gift of God:

[9] Not of works, lest any man should boast.

[10] For we are his workmanship, created in Christ Jesus unto good works, which God hath before ordained that we should walk in them.

GALATIANS 1:3-4 KJV

[3] Grace be to you and peace from God the Father, and from our Lord Jesus Christ,

[4] Who gave himself for our sins, that he might deliver us from this present evil world, according to the will of God and our Father:

JOHN 12:31 NKJV and v. 32-33 KJV

[31] Now is the judgment of this world; now the ruler of this world will be cast out.

[32] And I, if I [Jesus] be lifted up from the earth, will draw all men unto me.

⁳³ This he said, signifying what death he should die.

Some of the tragic effects that love of the world
will produce in the believer's life are.

---

1. A turning away from the Lord's work and other believers.

II TIMOTHY 4:10 NKJV
¹⁰ for Demas has forsaken me, having loved this present world, and has departed for Thessalonica—Crescens for Galatia, Titus for Dalmatia.

II TIMOTHY 3:1-9 KJV
¹ This know also, that in the last days perilous times shall come.
² For men shall be lovers of their own selves, covetous, boasters, proud, blasphemers, disobedient to parents, unthankful, unholy,
³ Without natural affection, trucebreakers, false accusers, incontinent, fierce, despisers of those that are good,
⁴ Traitors, heady, highminded, lovers of pleasures more than lovers of God;
⁵ Having a form of godliness, but denying the power thereof: from such turn away.
⁶ For of this sort are they which creep into houses, and lead captive silly women laden with sins, led away with divers lusts,
⁷ Ever learning, and never able to come to the knowledge of the truth.
⁸ Now as Jannes and Jambres withstood Moses, so do these also resist the truth: men of corrupt minds, reprobate concerning the faith.

Day 27: Temptation by the World

⁹ But they shall proceed no further: for their folly shall be manifest unto all men, as their's also was.

2. Alienation from God

JAMES 4:4 NKJV

⁴ Adulterers and adulteresses! Do you not know that friendship with the world is enmity with God? Whoever therefore wants to be a friend of the world makes himself an enemy of God.

3. Corrupting sins

II PETER 1:1-3 KJV and v. 4 NKJV

¹ Simon Peter, a servant and an apostle of Jesus Christ, to them that have obtained like precious faith with us through the righteousness of God and our Saviour Jesus Christ:
² Grace and peace be multiplied unto you through the knowledge of God, and of Jesus our Lord,
³ According as his divine power hath given unto us all things that pertain unto life and godliness, through the knowledge of him that hath called us to glory and virtue:
⁴ by which have been given to us exceedingly great and precious promises, that through these you may be partakers of the divine nature, having escaped the corruption that is in the world through lust.

4. Deception by false teachers

I JOHN 4:1 NKJV and v. 2-6 KJV

¹ Beloved, believe not every spirit, but try the spirits whether they are of God: because many false prophets are gone out into the world.
² Hereby know ye the Spirit of God: Every spirit that confesseth that Jesus Christ is come in the flesh is of God:
³ And every spirit that confesseth not that Jesus Christ is come in the flesh is not of God: and this is that spirit of antichrist, whereof ye have heard that it should come; and even now already is it in the world.
⁴ Ye are of God, little children, and have overcome them: because greater is he that is in you, than he that is in the world.
⁵ They are of the world: therefore speak they of the world, and the world heareth them.
⁶ We are of God: he that knoweth God heareth us; he that is not of God heareth not us. Hereby know we the spirit of truth, and the spirit of error.

II JOHN 6, 8-9 KJV and v. 7 NKJV

⁶ And this is love, that we walk after his commandments. This is the commandment, That, as ye have heard from the beginning, ye should walk in it.
⁷ For many deceivers have gone out into the world who do not confess Jesus Christ as coming in the flesh. This is a deceiver and an antichrist.
⁸ Look to yourselves, that we lose not those things which we have wrought, but that we receive a full reward.
⁹ Whosoever transgresseth, and abideth not in the doctrine of Christ, hath not God. He that abideth in the doctrine of Christ, he hath both the Father and the Son.

Day 27: Temptation by the World

> The solution to the love of the world is
> to have a greater love for the father.
> The Christian who seeks daily to please God in
> everything and who strives for spiritual growth
> through prayer, study of God's Word,
> and witnessing need not fall prey to the
> temptations of the world.

I JOHN 2:15 NKJV

[15] Do not love the world or the things in the world. If anyone loves the world, the love of the Father is not in him.

DAY 28

Temptation by the Flesh

MARK 14:38 NKJV

38 Watch and pray, lest you enter into temptation. The spirit indeed is willing, but the flesh is weak."

LUKE 21:34-36 KJV

34 And take heed to yourselves, lest at any time your hearts be overcharged with surfeiting, and drunkenness, and cares of this life, and so that day come upon you unawares.
35 For as a snare shall it come on all them that dwell on the face of the whole earth.
36 Watch ye therefore, and pray always, that ye may be accounted worthy to escape all these things that shall come to pass, and to stand before the Son of man.

> Flesh in the Bible often means something other than the substance of the human body. It is used constantly to refer to the carnal, sinful principles within man that is opposed to God.

Day 28: Temptation by the Flesh

ROMANS 8:1-6, 8 KJV and v. 7 NKJV

¹ There is therefore now no condemnation to them which are in Christ Jesus, who walk not after the flesh, but after the Spirit.
² For the law of the Spirit of life in Christ Jesus hath made me free from the law of sin and death.
³ For what the law could not do, in that it was weak through the flesh, God sending his own Son in the likeness of sinful flesh, and for sin, condemned sin in the flesh:
⁴ That the righteousness of the law might be fulfilled in us, who walk not after the flesh, but after the Spirit.
⁵ For they that are after the flesh do mind the things of the flesh; but they that are after the Spirit the things of the Spirit.
⁶ For to be carnally minded is death; but to be spiritually minded is life and peace.
⁷ Because the carnal mind is enmity against God; for it is not subject to the law of God, nor indeed can be.
⁸ So then they that are in the flesh cannot please God.

ROMANS 7:14 KJV and 15-25 NKJV

¹⁴ For we know that the law is spiritual: but I am carnal, sold under sin.
¹⁵ For what I am doing, I do not understand. For what I will to do, that I do not practice; but what I hate, that I do.
¹⁶ If, then, I do what I will not to do, I agree with the law that it is good.
¹⁷ But now, it is no longer I who do it, but sin that dwells in me. ¹⁸ For I know that in me (that is, in my flesh) nothing good dwells; for to will is present with me, but how to perform what is good I do not find.
¹⁹ For the good that I will to do, I do not do; but the evil I will not to do, that I practice.
²⁰ Now if I do what I will not to do, it is no longer I who do it, but sin that dwells in me.
²¹ I find then a law, that evil is present with me, the one who wills to do good.

²² For I delight in the law of God according to the inward man.
²³ But I see another law in my members, warring against the law of my mind, and bringing me into captivity to the law of sin which is in my members.
²⁴ O wretched man that I am! Who will deliver me from this body of death?
²⁵ I thank God—through Jesus Christ our Lord! So then, with the mind I myself serve the law of God, but with the flesh the law of sin.

ROMANS 8:9-11 KJV

⁹ But ye are not in the flesh, but in the Spirit, if so be that the Spirit of God dwell in you. Now if any man have not the Spirit of Christ, he is none of his.
¹⁰ And if Christ be in you, the body is dead because of sin; but the Spirit is life because of righteousness.
¹¹ But if the Spirit of him that raised up Jesus from the dead dwell in you, he that raised up Christ from the dead shall also quicken your mortal bodies by his Spirit that dwelleth in you.

The actions produced by the flesh are given in detail in Galatians.

GALATIANS 5:19-21 NKJV

¹⁹ Now the works of the flesh are evident, which are: adultery, fornication, uncleanness, lewdness,
²⁰ idolatry, sorcery, hatred, contentions, jealousies, outbursts of wrath, selfish ambitions, dissensions, heresies,
²¹ envy, murders, drunkenness, revelries, and the like; of which I tell you beforehand, just as I also told you in time past, that those who practice such things will not inherit the kingdom of God.

> Among these are all types of sexual immorality, impurity, hatred, anger, false religions, envy, and drunkenness. A person whose life is characterized by these sins cannot be a true Christian and is under the wrath of God.

EPHESIANS 2:1-2 KJV and v. 3 NKJV

¹ And you hath he quickened, who were dead in trespasses and sins;
² Wherein in time past ye walked according to the course of this world, according to the prince of the power of the air, the spirit that now worketh in the children of disobedience:
³ Among whom also we all once conducted ourselves in the lusts of our flesh, fulfilling the desires of the flesh and of the mind, and were by nature children of wrath, just as the others.

I CORINTHIANS 6:9-11 KJV

⁹ Know ye not that the unrighteous shall not inherit the kingdom of God? Be not deceived: neither fornicators, nor idolaters, nor adulterers, nor effeminate, nor abusers of themselves with mankind,
¹⁰ Nor thieves, nor covetous, nor drunkards, nor revilers, nor extortioners, shall inherit the kingdom of God.
¹¹ And such were some of you: but ye are washed, but ye are sanctified, but ye are justified in the name of the Lord Jesus, and by the Spirit of our God.

> Though the flesh is not eradicated for the Christian, he does not have to obey it. He possesses a new nature empowered by the Holy Spirit, since the flesh and the Spirit are totally

opposed to each other, the one whom the believer allows to dominate him will take charge in his life and produce its own fruit.

The solution to the urges of the flesh lies in acknowledging that the power of sin was nullified by Jesus' death and in living under the control of the Spirit's power.

GALATIANS 5:16 NKJV and v. 17-18 KJV

[16] I say then: Walk in the Spirit, and you shall not fulfill the lust of the flesh.

[17] For the flesh lusteth against the Spirit, and the Spirit against the flesh: and these are contrary the one to the other: so that ye cannot do the things that ye would.

[18] But if ye be led of the Spirit, ye are not under the law.

ROMANS 8:1-2 KJV

[1] There is therefore now no condemnation to them which are in Christ Jesus, who walk not after the flesh, but after the Spirit.

[2] For the law of the Spirit of life in Christ Jesus hath made me free from the law of sin and death.

ROMANS 5:20-21 KJV

[20] Moreover the law entered, that the offence might abound. But where sin abounded, grace did much more abound:

[21] That as sin hath reigned unto death, even so might grace reign through righteousness unto eternal life by Jesus Christ our Lord.

ROMANS 6:1-10, 12-14 KJV, and v. 11 NKJV

[1] What shall we say then? Shall we continue in sin, that grace may abound?

[2] God forbid. How shall we, that are dead to sin, live any longer therein?

Day 28: Temptation by the Flesh

³ Know ye not, that so many of us as were baptized into Jesus Christ were baptized into his death?

⁴ Therefore we are buried with him by baptism into death: that like as Christ was raised up from the dead by the glory of the Father, even so we also should walk in newness of life.

⁵ For if we have been planted together in the likeness of his death, we shall be also in the likeness of his resurrection:

⁶ Knowing this, that our old man is crucified with him, that the body of sin might be destroyed, that henceforth we should not serve sin.

⁷ For he that is dead is freed from sin.

⁸ Now if we be dead with Christ, we believe that we shall also live with him:

⁹ Knowing that Christ being raised from the dead dieth no more; death hath no more dominion over him.

¹⁰ For in that he died, he died unto sin once: but in that he liveth, he liveth unto God.

¹¹ Likewise you also, reckon yourselves to be dead indeed to sin, but alive to God in Christ Jesus our Lord.

¹² Let not sin therefore reign in your mortal body, that ye should obey it in the lusts thereof.

¹³ Neither yield ye your members as instruments of unrighteousness unto sin: but yield yourselves unto God, as those that are alive from the dead, and your members as instruments of righteousness unto God.

¹⁴ For sin shall not have dominion over you: for ye are not under the law, but under grace.

> The latter is a moment-by-moment dependence in faith on the Spirit's power. The believer must choose by an act of his will to benefit from the Spirit's enablement.

I JOHN 4:4 KJV

⁴ Ye are of God, little children, and have overcome them: because greater is he that is in you, than he that is in the world.

1 JOHN 2:17 KJV

¹⁷ And the world passeth away, and the lust thereof: but he that doeth the will of God abideth for ever.

DAY 29

———◆———

Temptation by Satan

I CHRONICLES 21:1 NKJV and v. 2-8 KJV

¹ Now Satan stood up against Israel, and moved David to number Israel.
² And David said to Joab and to the rulers of the people, Go, number Israel from Beersheba even to Dan; and bring the number of them to me, that I may know it.
³ And Joab answered, The Lord make his people an hundred times so many more as they be: but, my lord the king, are they not all my lord's servants? why then doth my lord require this thing? why will he be a cause of trespass to Israel?
⁴ Nevertheless the king's word prevailed against Joab. Wherefore Joab departed, and went throughout all Israel, and came to Jerusalem.
⁵ And Joab gave the sum of the number of the people unto David. And all they of Israel were a thousand thousand and an hundred thousand men that drew sword: and Judah was four hundred threescore and ten thousand men that drew sword.
⁶ But Levi and Benjamin counted he not among them: for the king's word was abominable to Joab.
⁷ And God was displeased with this thing; therefore he smote Israel.

⁸ And David said unto God, I have sinned greatly, because I have done this thing: but now, I beseech thee, do away the iniquity of thy servant; for I have done very foolishly.

The role of Satan against the Christian is well summed up by the meaning of the name Satan: "adversary." He is also called "the devil" meaning "accuser." He can appear as a hideous dragon or as a beautifully deceptive "Angel of Light."

---

2 CORINTHIANS 11:12-13, 15 KJV and v. 14 NKJV

¹² But what I do, that I [Paul] will do, that I may cut off occasion from them which desire occasion; that wherein they glory, they may be found even as we.
¹³ For such are false apostles, deceitful workers, transforming themselves into the apostles of Christ.
¹⁴ And no wonder! For Satan himself transforms himself into an angel of light.
¹⁵ Therefore it is no great thing if his ministers also be transformed as the ministers of righteousness; whose end shall be according to their works.

He stands hatefully opposed to all the work of God and resourcefully promotes defiance among men.

Day 29: Temptation by Satan

JOB 2:1-3, 6-7 KJV and v. 4-5 NKJV

¹ Again there was a day when the sons of God came to present themselves before the Lord, and Satan came also among them to present himself before the Lord.
² And the Lord said unto Satan, From whence comest thou? And Satan answered the Lord, and said, From going to and fro in the earth, and from walking up and down in it.
³ And the Lord said unto Satan, Hast thou considered my servant Job, that there is none like him in the earth, a perfect and an upright man, one that feareth God, and escheweth evil? and still he holdeth fast his integrity, although thou movedst me against him, to destroy him without cause.
⁴ So Satan answered the Lord and said, "Skin for skin! Yes, all that a man has he will give for his life.
⁵ But stretch out Your hand now, and touch his bone and his flesh, and he will surely curse You to Your face!"
⁶ And the Lord said unto Satan, Behold, he is in thine hand; but save his life.
⁷ So went Satan forth from the presence of the Lord, and smote Job with sore boils from the sole of his foot unto his crown.

MARK 4:2-14 KJV and v. 15 NKJV

² And he [Jesus] taught them many things by parables, and said unto them in his doctrine,
³ Hearken; Behold, there went out a sower to sow:
⁴ And it came to pass, as he sowed, some fell by the way side, and the fowls of the air came and devoured it up.
⁵ And some fell on stony ground, where it had not much earth; and immediately it sprang up, because it had no depth of earth:
⁶ But when the sun was up, it was scorched; and because it had no root, it withered away.
⁷ And some fell among thorns, and the thorns grew up, and choked it, and it yielded no fruit.
⁸ And other fell on good ground, and did yield fruit that sprang up and increased; and brought forth, some thirty, and some sixty, and some an hundred.

⁹ And he said unto them, He that hath ears to hear, let him hear.
¹⁰ And when he was alone, they that were about him with the twelve asked of him the parable.
¹¹ And he said unto them, Unto you it is given to know the mystery of the kingdom of God: but unto them that are without, all these things are done in parables:
¹² That seeing they may see, and not perceive; and hearing they may hear, and not understand; lest at any time they should be converted, and their sins should be forgiven them.
¹³ And he said unto them, Know ye not this parable? and how then will ye know all parables?
¹⁴ The sower soweth the word.
¹⁵ And these are the ones by the wayside where the word is sown. When they hear, Satan comes immediately and takes away the word that was sown in their hearts.

When Satan sinned he was expelled from heaven, although apparently he still had some access to God.

LUKE 10:18 NKJV and v. 19-20 KJV

¹⁸ And He [Jesus] said to them, "I saw Satan fall like lightning from heaven.
¹⁹ Behold, I give unto you power to tread on serpents and scorpions, and over all the power of the enemy: and nothing shall by any means hurt you.
²⁰ Notwithstanding in this rejoice not, that the spirits are subject unto you; but rather rejoice, because your names are written in heaven.

Day 29: Temptation by Satan

> A multitude of angels cast in their lot with him [Satan] in his fall and subsequently became the demons mentioned often in the Bible.

REVELATION 12:7 NKJV and v. 8-9 KJV

[7] And war broke out in heaven: Michael and his angels fought with the dragon; and the dragon and his angels fought,
[8] And prevailed not; neither was their place found any more in heaven.
[9] And the great dragon was cast out, that old serpent, called the Devil, and Satan, which deceiveth the whole world: he was cast out into the earth, and his angels were cast out with him.

MATTHEW 12:22-23 and 25-26 KJV and v. 24 NKJV

[22] Then was brought unto him [Jesus] one possessed with a devil, blind, and dumb: and he healed him, insomuch that the blind and dumb both spake and saw.
[23] And all the people were amazed, and said, Is not this the son of David?
[24] Now when the Pharisees heard it they said, "This fellow does not cast out demons except by Beelzebub, the ruler of the demons."
[25] And Jesus knew their thoughts, and said unto them, Every kingdom divided against itself is brought to desolation; and every city or house divided against itself shall not stand:
[26] And if Satan cast out Satan, he is divided against himself; how shall then his kingdom stand?

> Although Satan's doom was secured by Jesus' death on the cross, he will continue to hinder God's program until he and his angels are cast into the lake of fire.

REVELATION 20:10 NKJV

[10] The devil, who deceived them, was cast into the lake of fire and brimstone where the beast and the false prophet are. And they will be tormented day and night forever and ever.

COLOSSIANS 2:8-15 KJV

[8] Beware lest any man spoil you through philosophy and vain deceit, after the tradition of men, after the rudiments of the world, and not after Christ.
[9] For in him dwelleth all the fulness of the Godhead bodily.
[10] And ye are complete in him, which is the head of all principality and power:
[11] In whom also ye are circumcised with the circumcision made without hands, in putting off the body of the sins of the flesh by the circumcision of Christ:
[12] Buried with him in baptism, wherein also ye are risen with him through the faith of the operation of God, who hath raised him from the dead.
[13] And you, being dead in your sins and the uncircumcision of your flesh, hath he quickened together with him, having forgiven you all trespasses;
[14] Blotting out the handwriting of ordinances that was against us, which was contrary to us, and took it out of the way, nailing it to his cross;
[15] And having spoiled principalities and powers, he made a shew of them openly, triumphing over them in it.

The terrifying work of Satan in the believer is described in Scipture as follows.

---

1. He blinds their minds.

Day 29: Temptation by Satan

II CORINTHIANS 4:4 NKJV and v. 3, 5-7 KJV

³ But if our gospel be hid, it is hid to them that are lost:
⁴ Whose minds the god of this age has blinded, who do not believe, lest the light of the gospel of the glory of Christ, who is the image of God, should shine on them.
⁵ For we preach not ourselves, but Christ Jesus the Lord; and ourselves your servants for Jesus' sake.
⁶ For God, who commanded the light to shine out of darkness, hath shined in our hearts, to give the light of the knowledge of the glory of God in the face of Jesus Christ.
⁷ But we have this treasure in earthen vessels, that the excellency of the power may be of God, and not of us.

2. He takes the Word of God from their hearts.

LUKE 8:11 KJV and v. 12 NKJV

¹¹ Now the parable is this: The seed is the word of God.
¹² Those by the wayside are the ones who hear; then the devil comes and takes away the word out of their hearts, lest they should believe and be saved.

3. He controls them.

ACTS 13:6-7, 9-10 KJV and v. 8 NKJV

⁶ And when they had gone through the isle unto Paphos, they found a certain sorcerer, a false prophet, a Jew, whose name was Barjesus:
⁷ Which was with the deputy of the country, Sergius Paulus, a prudent man; who called for Barnabas and Saul, and desired to hear the word of God.
⁸ But Elymas the sorcerer (for so his name is translated) withstood them, seeking to turn the proconsul away from the faith.

⁹ Then Saul, (who also is called Paul,) filled with the Holy Ghost, set his eyes on him.
¹⁰ And said, O full of all subtilty and all mischief, thou child of the devil, thou enemy of all righteousness, wilt thou not cease to pervert the right ways of the Lord?

4. In regard to Christians, Satan may accuse them.

REVELATION 12:10 NKJV

¹⁰ Then I [John] heard a loud voice saying in heaven, "Now salvation, and strength, and the kingdom of our God, and the power of His Christ have come, for the accuser of our brethren, who accused them before our God day and night, has been cast down.

5. Devour their testimony for Christ.

I PETER 5:6-7, 9-11 KJV and v. 8 NKJV

⁶ Humble yourselves therefore under the mighty hand of God, that he may exalt you in due time:
⁷ Casting all your care upon him; for he careth for you.
⁸ Be sober, be vigilant; because your adversary the devil walks about like a roaring lion, seeking whom he may devour.
⁹ Whom resist steadfast in the faith, knowing that the same afflictions are accomplished in your brethren that are in the world.
¹⁰ But the God of all grace, who hath called us unto his eternal glory by Christ Jesus, after that ye have suffered a while, make you perfect, stablish, strengthen, settle you.
¹¹ To him be glory and dominion for ever and ever. Amen.

6. Deceive them.

Day 29: Temptation by Satan

II CORINTHIANS 11:3-4 KJV

³ But I [Paul] fear, lest by any means, as the serpent beguiled Eve through his subtilty, so your minds should be corrupted from the simplicity that is in Christ.
⁴ For if he that cometh preacheth another Jesus, whom we have not preached, or if ye receive another spirit, which ye have not received, or another gospel, which ye have not accepted, ye might well bear with him.

7. Hinder their work.

I THESSALONIANS 2:17 KJV and v.18 NKJV

¹⁷ But we, brethren, being taken from you for a short time in presence, not in heart, endeavoured the more abundantly to see your face with great desire.
¹⁸ Therefore we wanted to come to you—even I, Paul, time and again—but Satan hindered us.

8. Tempt them to immorality.

I CORINTHIANS 7:2-4 KJV and v. 5 NKJV

² Nevertheless, to avoid fornication, let every man have his own wife, and let every woman have her own husband.
³ Let the husband render unto the wife due benevolence: and likewise also the wife unto the husband.
⁴ The wife hath not power of her own body, but the husband: and likewise also the husband hath not power of his own body, but the wife.
⁵ Do not deprive one another except with consent for a time, that you may give yourselves to fasting and prayer; and come together again so that Satan does not tempt you because of your lack of self-control.

9. And even be used by God to discipline Christians.

I CORINTHIANS 5:1-4, 6-7 KJV and v. 5 NKJV

¹ It is reported commonly that there is fornication among you, and such fornication as is not so much as named among the Gentiles, that one should have his father's wife.
² And ye are puffed up, and have not rather mourned, that he that hath done this deed might be taken away from among you.
³ For I [Paul] verily, as absent in body, but present in spirit, have judged already, as though I were present, concerning him that hath so done this deed,
⁴ In the name of our Lord Jesus Christ, when ye are gathered together, and my spirit, with the power of our Lord Jesus Christ,
⁵ deliver such a one to Satan for the destruction of the flesh, that his spirit may be saved in the day of the Lord Jesus.
⁶ Your glorying is not good. Know ye not that a little leaven leaveneth the whole lump?
⁷ Purge out therefore the old leaven, that ye may be a new lump, as ye are unleavened. For even Christ our passover is sacrificed for us:

II CORINTHIANS 12:7 NKJV and v. 8-10 KJV

⁷ And lest I [Paul] should be exalted above measure by the abundance of the revelations, a thorn in the flesh was given to me, a messenger of Satan to buffet me, lest I be exalted above measure.
⁸ For this thing I besought the Lord thrice, that it might depart from me.
⁹ And he said unto me, My grace is sufficient for thee: for my strength is made perfect in weakness. Most gladly therefore will I rather glory in my infirmities, that the power of Christ may rest upon me.
¹⁰ Therefore I take pleasure in infirmities, in reproaches, in necessities, in persecutions, in distresses for Christ's sake: for when I am weak, then am I strong.

Day 29: Temptation by Satan

I TIMOTHY 1:18-20 KJV

[18] This charge I [Paul] commit unto thee, son Timothy, according to the prophecies which went before on thee, that thou by them mightest war a good warfare;
[19] Holding faith, and a good conscience; which some having put away concerning faith have made shipwreck:
[20] Of whom is Hymenaeus and Alexander; whom I have delivered unto Satan, that they may learn not to blaspheme.

The Christian's response to Satan is:

---

1. To recognize his power and deception.

EPHESIANS 6:10, 12-20 KJV and v. 11 NKJV

[10] Finally, my brethren, be strong in the Lord, and in the power of his might.
[11] Put on the whole armor of God, that you may be able to stand against the wiles of the devil.
[12] For we wrestle not against flesh and blood, but against principalities, against powers, against the rulers of the darkness of this world, against spiritual wickedness in high places.
[13] Wherefore take unto you the whole armour of God, that ye may be able to withstand in the evil day, and having done all, to stand.
[14] Stand therefore, having your loins girt about with truth, and having on the breastplate of righteousness;
[15] And your feet shod with the preparation of the gospel of peace;
[16] Above all, taking the shield of faith, wherewith ye shall be able to quench all the fiery darts of the wicked.
[17] And take the helmet of salvation, and the sword of the Spirit, which is the word of God:

¹⁸ Praying always with all prayer and supplication in the Spirit, and watching thereunto with all perseverance and supplication for all saints;
¹⁹ And for me, that utterance may be given unto me, that I [Paul] may open my mouth boldly, to make known the mystery of the gospel,
²⁰ For which I am an ambassador in bonds: that therein I may speak boldly, as I ought to speak.

II CORINTHIANS 2:4-10 KJV and v. 11 NKJV

⁴ For out of much affliction and anguish of heart I [Paul] wrote unto you with many tears; not that ye should be grieved, but that ye might know the love which I have more abundantly unto you.
⁵ But if any have caused grief, he hath not grieved me, but in part: that I may not overcharge you all.
⁶ Sufficient to such a man is this punishment, which was inflicted of many.
⁷ So that contrariwise ye ought rather to forgive him, and comfort him, lest perhaps such a one should be swallowed up with overmuch sorrow.
⁸ Wherefore I beseech you that ye would confirm your love toward him.
⁹ For to this end also did I write, that I might know the proof of you, whether ye be obedient in all things.
¹⁰ To whom ye forgive any thing, I forgive also: for if I forgave any thing, to whom I forgave it, for your sakes forgave I it in the person of Christ;
¹¹ lest Satan should take advantage of us; for we are not ignorant of his devices.

2. To adhere steadfastly to the faith.

Day 29: Temptation by Satan

I PETER 5:8, 10 KJV and v. 9 NKJV

[8] Be sober, be vigilant; because your adversary the devil, as a roaring lion, walketh about, seeking whom he may devour:
[9] Resist him, steadfast in the faith, knowing that the same sufferings are experienced by your brotherhood in the world.
[10] But the God of all grace, who hath called us unto his eternal glory by Christ Jesus, after that ye have suffered a while, make you perfect, stablish, strengthen, settle you.

3. To resist him openly.

JAMES 4:7 NKJV and v. 8 KJV

[7] Therefore submit to God. Resist the devil and he will flee from you.
[8] Draw nigh to God, and he will draw nigh to you. Cleanse your hands, ye sinners; and purify your hearts, ye double minded.

4. And not to give him opportunities.

EPHESIANS 4:20-26, 28-30 KJV and v. 27 NKJV

[20] But ye have not so learned Christ;
[21] If so be that ye have heard him, and have been taught by him, as the truth is in Jesus:
[22] That ye put off concerning the former conversation the old man, which is corrupt according to the deceitful lusts;
[23] And be renewed in the spirit of your mind;
[24] And that ye put on the new man, which after God is created in righteousness and true holiness.
[25] Wherefore putting away lying, speak every man truth with his neighbour: for we are members one of another.

²⁶ Be ye angry, and sin not: let not the sun go down upon your wrath:
²⁷ nor give place to the devil.
²⁸ Let him that stole steal no more: but rather let him labour, working with his hands the thing which is good, that he may have to give to him that needeth.
²⁹ Let no corrupt communication proceed out of your mouth, but that which is good to the use of edifying, that it may minister grace unto the hearers.
³⁰ And grieve not the holy Spirit of God, whereby ye are sealed unto the day of redemption.

> In practice, the best way to oppose him [Satan] is to be a growing Christian. Also, in the light of his tremendous power to blind men to the Gospel. Christians must always be aggressively and compassionately witnessing to the lost in order to snatch them from Satan's control.

ACTS 26:15-17 KJV and v. 18 NKJV

¹⁵ And I [Saul, later named Paul] said, Who art thou, Lord? And he said, I am Jesus whom thou persecutest.
¹⁶ But rise, and stand upon thy feet: for I have appeared unto thee for this purpose, to make thee a minister and a witness both of these things which thou hast seen, and of those things in the which I will appear unto thee;
¹⁷ Delivering thee from the people, and from the Gentiles, unto whom now I send thee,
¹⁸ to open their eyes, in order to turn them from darkness to light, and from the power of Satan to God, that they may receive forgiveness of sins and an inheritance among those who are sanctified by faith in Me.'

Day 29: Temptation by Satan

Believers can respond to temptation by
Satan with confidence. We know that nothing can
separate us from the love of God.

ROMANS 8:26-27 KJV and v. 28-39 NKJV

[26] Likewise the Spirit also helpeth our infirmities: for we know not what we should pray for as we ought: but the Spirit itself maketh intercession for us with groanings which cannot be uttered.

[27] And he that searcheth the hearts knoweth what is the mind of the Spirit, because he maketh intercession for the saints according to the will of God.

[28] And we know that all things work together for good to those who love God, to those who are the called according to His purpose.

[29] For whom He foreknew, He also predestined to be conformed to the image of His Son, that He might be the firstborn among many brethren.

[30] Moreover whom He predestined, these He also called; whom He called, these He also justified; and whom He justified, these He also glorified.

[31] God is for us, who can be against us?

[32] He who did not spare His own Son, but delivered Him up for us all, how shall He not with Him also freely give us all things?

[33] Who shall bring a charge against God's elect? It is God who justifies.

[34] Who is he who condemns? It is Christ who died, and furthermore is also risen, who is even at the right hand of God, who also makes intercession for us.

[35] Who shall separate us from the love of Christ? Shall tribulation, or distress, or persecution, or famine, or nakedness, or peril, or sword?

[36] As it is written: "For Your sake we are killed all day long; We are accounted as sheep for the slaughter."

[37] Yet in all these things we are more than conquerors through Him who loved us.

[38] For I am persuaded that neither death nor life, nor angels nor principalities nor powers, nor things present nor things to come, [39] nor height nor depth, nor any other created thing, shall be able to separate us from the love of God which is in Christ Jesus our Lord.

DAY 30

———•———

Meditating Upon God's Word

JOSHUA 1:8 NKJV

⁸ This Book of the Law shall not depart from your mouth, but you shall meditate in it day and night, that you may observe to do according to all that is written in it. For then you will make your way prosperous, and then you will have good success.

Joshua had just succeeded Moses in the leadership of the nation Israel. Moses had led the nation for forty years and had the benefit that all the wisdom and culture of Egypt and the King's household could provide. Moses was a seasoned, multi-talented man who had walked closely with God. Joshua, by contrast, was relatively untried.
He was assuming an awesome responsibility in taking command of two-and-a-half million people. If anyone needed a formula for success, Joshua did.

> Likely there were many well-meaning people with all kinds of advice and formulas to help Joshua in the seemingly impossible task that lay ahead. What comfort and assurance it must have been as the Lord (Yahweh) spoke directly to Joshua, assuring him of His presence with him as He had been with Moses, and giving him the key to success – meditating upon God's Word.

JOSHUA 1:1-4, 6-9 KJV and v. 5 NKJV

[1] Now after the death of Moses the servant of the Lord it came to pass, that the Lord spake unto Joshua the son of Nun, Moses' minister, saying,

[2] Moses my servant is dead; now therefore arise, go over this Jordan, thou, and all this people, unto the land which I do give to them, even to the children of Israel.

[3] Every place that the sole of your foot shall tread upon, that have I given unto you, as I said unto Moses.

[4] From the wilderness and this Lebanon even unto the great river, the river Euphrates, all the land of the Hittites, and unto the great sea toward the going down of the sun, shall be your coast.

[5] No man shall be able to stand before you all the days of your life; as I was with Moses, so I will be with you. I will not leave you nor forsake you.

[6] Be strong and of a good courage: for unto this people shalt thou divide for an inheritance the land, which I sware unto their fathers to give them.

[7] Only be thou strong and very courageous, that thou mayest observe to do according to all the law, which Moses my servant commanded thee: turn not from it to the right hand or to the left, that thou mayest prosper withersoever thou goest.

[8] This book of the law shall not depart out of thy mouth; but thou shalt meditate therein day and night, that thou mayest observe to do according to all that is written therein: for then thou shalt make thy way prosperous, and then thou shalt have good success.

Day 30: Meditating Upon God's Word

⁹ Have not I commanded thee? Be strong and of a good courage; be not afraid, neither be thou dismayed: for the Lord thy God is with thee whithersoever thou goest.

Joshua is to meditate upon the Word of God day and night (i.e., at all times), and is promised (1) prosperity and (2) good success in the God-given task that lies ahead. Reading and memorizing God's Word provides the basis for meditating upon God's Word. You meditate upon the Word of God by rehearsing its thoughts over and over in order to understand its implications for the situations of life. Meditating upon the Word of God will guarantee prosperity and success in the new life.

DAY 31

Obedience to God's Word

DEUTERONOMY 31:12 NKJV and v.13 KJV

¹² Gather the people together, men and women and little ones, and the stranger who is within your gates, that they may hear and that they may learn to fear the Lord your God and carefully observe all the words of this law,

¹³ And that their children, which have not known any thing, may hear, and learn to fear the Lord your God, as long as ye live in the land whither ye go over Jordan to possess it.

Reading, memorizing and meditating upon the Word of God are of no value without obedience to the Word of God. To obey the Word of God, you do what the Word of God indicates should be done in any situation. Obedience to the Word of God is the only way that the child of God can be pleasing to God in the new life.

Day 31: Obedience to God's Word

Obedience to God's Word results in:

---

1. Being treasured by God

EXODUS 19:3-4, 6-8 KJV and v. 5 NKJV

³ And Moses went up unto God, and the Lord called unto him out of the mountain, saying, Thus shalt thou say to the house of Jacob, and tell the children of Israel;
⁴ Ye have seen what I did unto the Egyptians, and how I bare you on eagles' wings, and brought you unto myself.
⁵ Now therefore, if you will indeed obey My voice and keep My covenant, then you shall be a special treasure to Me above all people; for all the earth is Mine.
⁶ And ye shall be unto me a kingdom of priests, and an holy nation. These are the words which thou shalt speak unto the children of Israel.
⁷ And Moses came and called for the elders of the people, and laid before their faces all these words which the Lord commanded him.
⁸ And all the people answered together, and said, All that the Lord hath spoken we will do. And Moses returned the words of the people unto the Lord.

2. Blessedness (happiness) in life

PSALM 119:2 NKJV

² Blessed are those who keep His testimonies,
Who seek Him with the whole heart!

3. Not being ashamed

PSALM 119:4-6 NKJV

⁴ You have commanded us to keep Your precepts diligently.
⁵ Oh, that my ways were directed to keep Your statutes!
⁶ Then I would not be ashamed, when I look into all Your commandments.

4. Understanding

PSALM 119:99 KJV and v. 100 NKJV

⁹⁹ I have more understanding than all my teachers: for thy testimonies are my meditation.
¹⁰⁰ I understand more than the ancients, because I keep Your precepts.

5. Avoidance of evil

PSALM 119:101 NKJV

¹⁰¹ I have restrained my feet from every evil way,
That I may keep Your word.

6. Guidance for life

PSALM 119:105 NKJV

¹⁰⁵ Your word is a lamp to my feet and a light to my path.

7. Safety and freedom from anxiety

Day 31: Obedience to God's Word

PROVERBS 1:33 NKJV

33 But whoever listens to me will dwell safely, and will be secure, without fear of evil."

8. **Life**

PROVERBS 19:15, 17 KJV and v. 16 NKJV

15 Slothfulness casteth into a deep sleep; and an idle soul shall suffer hunger.
16 He who keeps the commandment keeps his soul, but he who is careless of his ways will die.
17 He that hath pity upon the poor lendeth unto the Lord; and that which he hath given will he pay him again.

EXEKIEL 18:19 NKJV and 20-21 KJV

19 "Yet you say, 'Why should the son not bear the guilt of the father?' Because the son has done what is lawful and right, and has kept all My statutes and done them, he shall surely live.
20 The soul that sinneth, it shall die. The son shall not bear the iniquity of the father, neither shall the father bear the iniquity of the son: the righteousness of the righteous shall be upon him, and the wickedness of the wicked shall be upon him.
21 But if the wicked will turn from all his sins that he hath committed, and keep all my statutes, and do that which is lawful and right, he shall surely live, he shall not die.

JOHN 8:51 NKJV

51 Most assuredly, I [Jesus] say to you, if anyone keeps My word he shall never see death."

9. God's blessing

ISAIAH 1:18 KJV and v. 19-20 NKJV

[18] Come now, and let us reason together, saith the Lord: though your sins be as scarlet, they shall be as white as snow; though they be red like crimson, they shall be as wool.

[19] If you are willing and obedient,	SPIRIT
You shall eat the good of the land;	vs
[20] But if you refuse and rebel,	FLESH
You shall be devoured by the sword";	
For the mouth of the Lord has spoken.	(deciding factor) ↓

PSALM 103:1-5 KJV

[1] Bless the Lord, O my soul:	SOUL
and all that is within me,	
bless his holy name.	
[2] Bless the Lord, O my soul,	(blessings)
and forget not all his benefits:	BENEFITS

[3] Who forgiveth all thine iniquities;
who healeth all thy diseases;
[4] Who redeemeth thy life from destruction;
who crowneth thee with lovingkindness and tender mercies;
[5] Who satisfieth thy mouth with good things;
so that thy youth is renewed like the eagle's.

10. Greatness in the kingdom of heaven

MATTHEW 5:19 NKJV

[19] Whoever therefore breaks one of the least of these commandments, and teaches men so, shall be called least in the kingdom of heaven; but whoever does and teaches them, he shall be called great in the kingdom of heaven.

11. Bearing fruit for God

MATTHEW 13:23 NKJV

²³ But he who received seed on the good ground is he who hears the word and understands it, who indeed bears fruit and produces: some a hundredfold, some sixty, some thirty."

12. Manifesting love for God

JOHN 14:23 NKJV

²³ Jesus answered and said to him, "If anyone loves Me, he will keep My word; and My Father will love him, and We will come to him and make Our home with him.

I JOHN 2:5 NKJV and v. 6 KJV

⁵ But whoever keeps His word, truly the love of God is perfected in him. By this we know that we are in Him.
⁶ He that saith he abideth in him ought himself also so to walk, even as he walked.

13. Promise of God's presence

II JOHN v. 8 KJV and 9 NKJV

⁸ Look to yourselves, that we lose not those things which we have wrought, but that we receive a full reward.
⁹ Whoever transgresses and does not abide in the doctrine of Christ does not have God. He who abides in the doctrine of Christ has both the Father and the Son.

14. Abiding in the love of God

JOHN 15:7-9, 11 KJV and v. 10 NKJV

[7] If ye abide in me, and my words abide in you, ye shall ask what ye will, and it shall be done unto you.
[8] Herein is my Father glorified, that ye bear much fruit; so shall ye be my disciples.
[9] As the Father hath loved me, so have I loved you: continue ye in my love.
[10] If you keep My commandments, you will abide in My love, just as I have kept My Father's commandments and abide in His love.
[11] These things have I spoken unto you, that my joy might remain in you, and that your joy might be full.

15. Evidence of the doctrine that has been taught

ROMANS 6:16, 18 KJV and v. 17 NKJV

[16] Know ye not, that to whom ye yield yourselves servants to obey, his servants ye are to whom ye obey; whether of sin unto death, or of obedience unto righteousness?
[17] But God be thanked that though you were slaves of sin, yet you obeyed from the heart that form of doctrine to which you were delivered.
[18] Being then made free from sin, ye became the servants of righteousness.

16. Assurance of salvation

Day 31: Obedience to God's Word

I JOHN 2:1-2, 4-6 KJV and v. 3 NKJV

[1] My little children, these things write I [John] unto you, that ye sin not. And if any man sin, we have an advocate with the Father, Jesus Christ the righteous:
[2] And he is the propitiation for our sins: and not for ours only, but also for the sins of the whole world.
[3] Now by this we know that we know Him, if we keep His commandments.
[4] He that saith, I know him, and keepeth not his commandments, is a liar, and the truth is not in him.
[5] But whoso keepeth his word, in him verily is the love of God perfected: hereby know we that we are in him.
[6] He that saith he abideth in him ought himself also so to walk, even as he walked.

17. Eternal life

I JOHN 2:17 NKJV

[17] And the world is passing away, and the lust of it; but he who does the will of God abides forever.

18. Dwelling in God

I JOHN 3:18-23 KJV and v. 24 NKJV

[18] My little children, let us not love in word, neither in tongue; but in deed and in truth.
[19] And hereby we know that we are of the truth, and shall assure our hearts before him.
[20] For if our heart condemn us, God is greater than our heart, and knoweth all things.
[21] Beloved, if our heart condemn us not, then have we confidence toward God.

[22] And whatsoever we ask, we receive of him, because we keep his commandments, and do those things that are pleasing in his sight.
[23] And this is his commandment, That we should believe on the name of his Son Jesus Christ, and love one another, as he gave us commandment.
[24] Now he who keeps His commandments abides in Him, and He in him. And by this we know that He abides in us, by the Spirit whom He has given us.

19. Love of God's children

I JOHN 5:1, 3-5 KJV and v. 2 NKJV

[1] Whosoever believeth that Jesus is the Christ is born of God: and every one that loveth him that begat loveth him also that is begotten of him.
[2] By this we know that we love the children of God, when we love God and keep His commandments.
[3] For this is the love of God, that we keep his commandments: and his commandments are not grievous.
[4] For whatsoever is born of God overcometh the world: and this is the victory that overcometh the world, even our faith.
[5] Who is he that overcometh the world, but he that believeth that Jesus is the Son of God?

20. Entrance into heaven

I PETER 1:3-5 KJV

[3] Blessed be the God and Father of our Lord Jesus Christ, which according to his abundant mercy hath begotten us again unto a lively hope by the resurrection of Jesus Christ from the dead,
[4] To an inheritance incorruptible, and undefiled, and that fadeth not away, reserved in heaven for you,

⁵ Who are kept by the power of God through faith unto salvation ready to be revealed in the last time.

II PETER 1:1-11 KJV

¹ Simon Peter, a servant and an apostle of Jesus Christ, to them that have obtained like precious faith with us through the righteousness of God and our Saviour Jesus Christ:
² Grace and peace be multiplied unto you through the knowledge of God, and of Jesus our Lord,
³ According as his divine power hath given unto us all things that pertain unto life and godliness, through the knowledge of him that hath called us to glory and virtue:
⁴ Whereby are given unto us exceeding great and precious promises: that by these ye might be partakers of the divine nature, having escaped the corruption that is in the world through lust.
⁵ And beside this, giving all diligence, add to your faith virtue; and to virtue knowledge;
⁶ And to knowledge temperance; and to temperance patience; and to patience godliness;
⁷ And to godliness brotherly kindness; and to brotherly kindness charity.
⁸ For if these things be in you, and abound, they make you that ye shall neither be barren nor unfruitful in the knowledge of our Lord Jesus Christ.
⁹ But he that lacketh these things is blind, and cannot see afar off, and hath forgotten that he was purged from his old sins.
¹⁰ Wherefore the rather, brethren, give diligence to make your calling and election sure: for if ye do these things, ye shall never fall:
¹¹ For so an entrance shall be ministered unto you abundantly into the everlasting kingdom of our Lord and Saviour Jesus Christ.

ROMANS 14:17-19 KJV

¹⁷ For the kingdom of God is not meat and drink; but righteousness, and peace, and joy in the Holy Ghost.

¹⁸ For he that in these things serveth Christ is acceptable to God, and approved of men.
¹⁹ Let us therefore follow after the things which make for peace, and things wherewith one may edify another.

I JOHN 2:24-25 KJV

²⁴ Let that therefore abide in you, which ye have heard from the beginning. If that which ye have heard from the beginning shall remain in you, ye also shall continue in the Son, and in the Father.
²⁵ And this is the promise that he hath promised us, even eternal life.

JOHN 3:16 KJV

¹⁶ For God so loved the world, that he gave his only begotten Son, that whosoever believeth in him should not perish, but have everlasting life.

I JOHN 2:26-29 KJV

²⁶ These things have I [John] written unto you concerning them that seduce you.
²⁷ But the anointing which ye have received of him abideth in you, and ye need not that any man teach you: but as the same anointing teacheth you of all things, and is truth, and is no lie, and even as it hath taught you, ye shall abide in him.
²⁸ And now, little children, abide in him; that, when he shall appear, we may have confidence, and not be ashamed before him at his coming.
²⁹ If ye know that he is righteous, ye know that every one that doeth righteousness is born of him.

I JOHN 3:1-3 KJV

¹ Behold, what manner of love the Father hath bestowed upon us, that we should be called the sons of God: therefore the world knoweth us not, because it knew him not.

² Beloved, now are we the sons of God, and it doth not yet appear what we shall be: but we know that, when he shall appear, we shall be like him; for we shall see him as he is.

³ And every man that hath this hope in him purifieth himself, even as he is pure.

REVELATION 22:7 NKJV

⁷ "Behold, I [Jesus] am coming quickly! Blessed is he who keeps the words of the prophecy of this book."

INDEX

Search by Topic
(Alphabetical Order)

~ A ~

Abide	165	I John 2:24
	173	John 15:4
	181	I John 2:6
	273	I John 2:6
	273	II John 9
	274	John 15:7
Abolished	33	Ephesians 2:15
Abominable	249	I Chronicle 21:6
Abundantly	9	John 10:10
	50	Ephesians 3:20
Accepted	141	Ephesians 1:6
Access	46	Romans 5:2
	85	Romans 5:2

Index

Accuser	256	Revelation 12:10
Adoption	19	Romans 8:15
	24	Galatians 4:5
Adulterers	239	James 4:4
Adversary	256	I Peter 5:8
Advocate	181	I John 2:1
	275	I John 2:1
Affection	163	Galatians 5:24
Affirm	114	Titus 3:8
Afflicted	105	Isaiah 53:4
Affliction	172	James 1:27
Afraid	149	Acts 18:9
	267	Joshua 1:9
Alienated	210	Colossians 1:21
	211	Ephesians 4:18
Ambassador	43	II Corinthians 5:20
	188	Ephesians 6:20
Angry	200	Ephesians 4:26
	203	Matthew 5:22
Anointed	177	Acts 10:38
Anointing	79	I John 2:27
Antichrist	240	I John 4:3
		II John 7

Anxious	212	Philippians 4:6
Armour	187	Ephesians 6:11
	259	Ephesians 6:13
Ashamed	56	II Timothy 1:8
Ask	114	John 14:14
Assurance	74	Hebrews 10:22
	228	Acts 17:31
Assure	275	I John 3:19
Assuredly	175	John 5:24
Authority	136	John 16:13
Awake	37	Ephesians 5:14
	59	Romans 13:11

⇛ B ⇚

Baptized	157	Acts 1:5
Beginning	24	John 1:1
Believe	19	John 3:18
	55	Romans 4:3
	85	John 5:24
	89	Acts 16:31
	90	John 3:36
	119	John 20:25
	276	I John 5:1
Benefits	180	Psalm 103:2

Bewitched	73	Galatians 3:1
Blameless	12	I Thessalonians 5:23
	80	I Thessalonians 5:23
Blaspheme	192	II Samuel 12:14
	121	Acts 26:11
Blessed	27	Ephesians 1:3
	119	John 20:29
	179	Psalm 32:1
	279	Revelation 22:7
Blinded	109	II Peter 1:9
	255	II Corinthians 4:4
Blindness	34	Ephesians 4:18
Blood	141	Ephesians 1:7
	144	Hebrews 9:18
	144	Hebrews 9:22
Boldly	63	Hebrews 4:16
Boldness	74	Hebrews 10:19
	215	Acts 4:13
Bondage	19	Romans 8:15
Born Again	6	Romans 3:5-7
	16	John 3:3
Bread	176	John 6:35
Buried	206	Romans 6:4

C

Term	Page	Reference
Call	57	Romans 10:12
Called	234	Ephesians 4:4
Calling	49	Ephesians 1:18
	93	I Corinthians 1:26
	95	II Peter 1:10
Captivity	244	Romans 7:23
Care	242	Luke 21:34
	256	I Peter 5:7
Carnal	72	Romans 8:7
	73	I Corinthians 3:1
Carnally	139	Romans 8:6
Chastened	202	I Corinthians 11:32
Chastening	58	Hebrews 12:5
Children	19	Romans 8:16
	230	Luke 18:16
Chosen	91	I Peter 2:9
	94	I Corinthians 1:27
	141	Ephesians 1:4
Christlike	217	Galatians 5:24
Citizen	34	Ephesians 2:19
Clean	167	Psalm 51:7
Cleanse	167	Psalm 119:9
	169	I John 1:7

Index

Clothed	38	Isaiah 61:10
Comfort	54	II Corinthians 1:3
	55	II Corinthians 1:4
	260	II Corinthians 2:7
Commit	185	II Timothy 2:2
Communion	205	II Corinthians 13:14
Compassion	222	I John 3:17
Condemned	19	John 3:18
Conduct	34	Ephesians 4:22
Confess	29	Philippians 2:11
	106	Romans 10:9
	195	I John 1:9
Confidence	17	I John 2:28
	75	Hebrews 10:35
	223	I John 3:21
Confident	57	II Corinthians 5:6
	92	Philippians 1:6
Confirm	54	I Corinthians 1:8
Conformed	67	Romans 12:2
	263	Romans 8:29
Conquerors	88	Romans 8:37
Conscience	184	I Timothy 1:5
Consecrated	74	Hebrews 10:20
Contemptible	227	Malachi 2:9

Contention	244	Galatians 5:20
Contrary	68	Galatians 5:17
	120	Acts 26:9
Convict	116	John 16:8
Corruption	11	II Peter 1:3-4
	218	Galatians 6:8
Counsel	40	Psalm 16:7
	182	Proverbs 22:20
Counselor	23	Isaiah 9:6
Courage	266	Joshua 1:6
Courageous	266	Joshua 1:7
Covenant	33	Ephesians 2:12
	115	Isaiah 59:21
	148	Hebrews 10:16
	227	Malachi 2:5
Created	225	Genesis 1:27
	226	Malachi 2:10
Creation	5	2 Corinthians 5:17
Cross	81	Colossians 1:20
	102	I Corinthians 1:18

Darkness	36	Ephesians 5:8
Deceived	74	Galatians 6:7
	150	I Corinthians 6:9

Index

Deceiver	240	II John 7
Deceiveth	253	Revelation 12:9
Deeds	15	Romans 3:28
Delight	107	Psalm 1:2
	244	Romans 7:22
Deliver	89	Colossians 1:13
	95	II Corinthians 1:10
	237	Galatians 1:4
	244	Romans 7:24
	258	I Corinthians 5:5
Denying	238	II Timothy 3:5
Diligence	78	Hebrews 6:11
	277	II Peter 1:10
Diligent	171	II Peter 1:10
Discipline	9	I Corinthians 9:27
Dishonor	101	Romans 1:24
Displeased	191	II Samuel 11:27
Divided	253	Matthew 12:25
Divine	171	II Peter 1:3
Doctrine	66	Romans 6:17
Dominion	32	Romans 6:14
	225	Genesis 1:26
Door	143	John 10:9
	157	John 20:19

Dust	180	Psalm 103:14
Dwell	161	Ephesians 3:17

E

Eagle	272	Psalm 103:5
Edification	204	II Corinthaisn 13:10
Edifying	186	Ephesians 4:12
	204	II Corinthians 12:19
Elect	36	Colossians 3:12
Endure	58	Hebrews 12:7
	78	Hebrews 6:15
Enemies	47	Romans 5:10
Enemy	115	Isaiah 59:19
Envious	197	Psalm 73:3
Equipping	186	Ephesians 4:12
Error	101	Romans 1:27
Eternal Life	65	I John 5:11
	76	John 17:2
	220	John 17:3
Evangelist	186	Ephesians 4:11
Everlasting Life	219	John 5:24
	278	John 3:16

Evidence	103	Hebrews 11:1
Evil	193	Psalm 51:4
Exalted	29	Philippians 2:9
Examine	201	I Corinthians 11:28
	204	II Corinthians 13:5
Exhorting	148	Hebrews 10:25
Expectation	87	Romans 8:19

⇛ F ⇚

Faith	45	Romans 4:16
	55	Romans 4:5
	56	Romans 10:6
	57	Romans 10:17
	103	II Corinthians 4:13
	103	Hebrews 11:1
	151	I John 5:4
	256	I Peter 5:9
Faithless	119	John 20:27
Fault	203	Matthew 18:!5
Fear	56	II Timothy 1:7
Fellowship	181	I John 1:6
	200	I John 1:3
Filled	214	Ephesians 5:18
	215	Acts 2:4
Flesh	218	Galatians 5:19

Foolish	69	Titus 3:3
	73	Galatians 3:1
	197	Psalm 73:3
Foolishness	102	I Corinthians 1:18
Forgive	260	II Corinthians 2:7
Forgiveness	27	Ephesians 1:7
Fornicators	101	I Corinthians 6:9
Fruit of the Spirit	162	Galatians 5:22
Fulfilled	139	Romans 8:4
Fulness	50	Ephesians 1:23
	254	Colossians 2:9

G

Gifts	47	Ephesians 2:8
	163	Romans 12:6
	163	Ephesians 4:7
Glorious	65	Philippians 3:21
	65	Ephesians 5:27
Glory	64	I Peter 1:7
	64	I Thessalonians 2:12
	64	II Peter 1:3
Godliness	184	I Timothy 4:8
Gospel	90	Ephesians 1:13
	169	I Peter 1:25

Index

Grace	25	John 1:17
	45	Ephesians 2:5
	53	I Peter 4:10
	53	James 4:6
	54	Acts 20:32
	54	II Peter 3:18
	83	Romans 5:20
	185	II Timothy 2:1
	233	Titus 2:11
	246	Romans 5:20
	246	Romans 6:1
	258	II Corinthians 12:9
Griefs	105	Isaiah 53:4
Grieve	35	Ephesians 4:30
Groaning	179	Romans 8:26
Guides	183	Acts 8:31

⇛ H ⇚

Healed	105	Isaiah 53:5
Healing	177	Acts 10:38
	216	Acts 4:22
Hear	159	Acts 2:22
	159	Acts 2:33
	175	John 5:24
Heart	61	Acts 15:9
	61	Colossians 3:15
	106	Romans 10:10
Heed	167	Psalm 119:9

Heirs	19	Romans 8:17
Help	121	Acts 26:22
Helper	145	John 14:16
Hiding Place	180	Psalm 32:7
Holiness	6	II Corinthians 7:1
Holy	49	Ephesians 1:4
	64	I Peter 1:15
Holy Ghost	156	John 7:39
	157	John 20:22
	158	Acts 1:8
	158	Acts 2:4
Holy Spirit	51	Luke 11:13
Honour	143	John 5:23
Hope	17	I John 3:3
	88	Titus 2:13
	179	Romans 8:24
	186	Ephesians 1:18
	213	I John 3:3
Humble	207	James 4:10
	256	I Peter 5:6
Humbled	29	Philippians 2:8
Hypocrisy	184	I Timothy 4:2

Index

I

Ignorance	14	Acts 17:30
	34	Ephesians 4:18
	41	I Peter 1:14
Ignorant	106	Romans 10:3
Image	3	Genesis 1:26-28
	11	II Corinthians 3:17-18
	11	Romans 8:29
	11	Colossians 3:9-10
Imagination	100	Romans 1:21
Immortality	42	II Timothy 1:10
Impossible	26	Luke 1:37
Imputes	44	Romans 4:6
Infirmities	108	Hebrews 4:15
	128	Romans 8:26
Inherit	68	Galatians 5:21
	68	I Corinthians 6:9
Inheritance	28	Ephesians 1:11
	276	I Peter 1:4
Iniquities	167	Psalm 51:9
Intercession	44	Isaiah 53:12
	87	Romans 8:26

J

Jesus	136	Titus 3:6
	137	Acts 4:10
	143	John 10:9
	147	I John 3:23
Joy	40	Psalm 16:11
Joyful	38	Isaiah 61:10
Judge	14	Acts 17:31
Justification	48	Romans 5:16
Justified	15	Romans 3:24
	59	Romans 5:1
	69	Titus 3:7
	150	I Corinthians 6:11
	229	Romans 3:20
Justify	105	Isaiah 53:11

K

King	40	Jeremiah 23:5
Kingdom	230	Luke 18:16
	277	II Peter 1:11
	277	Romans 14:17
Know	220	John 17:3
Knowledge	131	Psalm 139:6
	182	Proverbs 22:17
	255	II Corinthians 4:6

L

Lacked	137	Acts 4:34
Lacketh	95	II Peter 1:9
Lamb	168	I Peter 1:19
Law	178	Romans 8:2
Learn	268	Deuteronomy 31:12
Liberty	59	Galatians 5:13
Licentiousness	92	Jude 4
Lie	101	Romans 1:25
Life	176	John 6:33
Light	25	John 1:9
	255	II Corinthians 4:6
Longsuffering	61	Colossians 3:12
	231	II Peter 3:9
Looked	135	Acts 1:10
Looking	113	Titus 2:13
Love	59	Romans 13:8
	59	Romans 5:5
	222	I John 3:14
Loved	221	John 17:23
Lust	235	I John 2:16

M

Manifestation	129	I Corinthians 12:7
Mediator	132	Hebrews 9:15
	231	I Timothy 2:5
Meditate	107	Psalm 1:2
	265	Joshua 1:8
Mercy	33	Ephesians 2:4
	114	Titus 3:5
	180	Psalm 103:11
	194	Psalm 51:1
Mind	34	Ephesians 4:17
	142	Romans 8:27
	148	Hebrews 10:16
Minister	93	Colossians 1:25
	144	Hebrews 8:2
Mocked	218	Galatians 6:7
Mockers	80	Jude 18
Mortal	32	Romans 6:12
Mouth	106	Romans 10:8
Mystery	74	Ephesians 3:9
	93	Colossians 1:26
	141	Ephesians 1:9

N

Name	50	Ephesians 1:21
	50	Ephesians 3:15
	53	I Peter 4:14
	62	Colossians 3:17
Needed	14	Acts 17:25
Neighbor	39	Psalm 15:3
	59	Romans 13:9
New	31	II Corinthians 5:17
Newness	247	Romans 6:4
Night	60	Romans 13:12
	131	Psalm 139:11

O

Obedient	41	I Peter 1:14
	272	Isaiah 1:19
Obeying	169	I Peter 1:22
Obtained	132	Hebrews 9:12
Offense	46	Romans 4:25
	48	Romans 5:15
	122	Acts 24:16
Offer	144	Hebrews 9:25
Offering	148	Hebrews 10:14
	297	

Offspring	228	Acts 17:28
Oppressed	180	Psalm 103:6
Overcome	151	I John 5:4
	248	I John 4:4

⇛ P ⇚

Painful	198	Psalm 73:16
Partaker	58	Hebrews 12:10
	62	Hebrews 3:14
	171	II Peter 1:4
Patience	142	Romans 8:25
Peace	46	Romans 5:1
	60	Philippians 4:7
	198	Psalm 37:37
Pentecost	158	Acts 2:1
Perfect	221	John 17:23
Perish	102	I Corinthians 1:18
Persecutest	121	Acts 26:14
Persecution	22	II Timothy 3:11
Please	175	John 8:29
Power	42	II Timothy 1:7
	115	Luke 10:19
	116	Colossians 2:15
	136	Acts 4:7

	137	Acts 4:33
	171	II Peter 1:3
	204	II Corinthians 13:4
Powerful	7	Hebrews 4:12
Practice	243	Romans 7:19
	243	Romans 7:15
	244	Galatians 5:21
Praise	38	Isaiah 61:11
Preached	183	Acts 8:35
Predestinate	27	Ephesians 1:5
	91	Romans 8:29
Priest	108	Hebrews 4:14
	144	Hebrews 8:1
Profession	108	Hebrews 4:14
Profitable	22	II Timothy 3:16
	114	Titus 3:8
Progress	185	I Timothy 4:15
Promise	94	II Peter 1:4
	104	Romans 4:13
	140	Titus 1:2
	157	Acts 1:4
	278	I John 2:25
Proof	157	Acts 1:3
Prophesied	64	I Peter 1:10
Prophesy	163	Romans 12:6
Prosper	40	Jeremiah 23:5

Prosperity	197	Psalm 73:3
Prosperous	265	Joshua 1:8
Purge	27 95	Hebrews 9:14 II Peter 1:9
Purgeth	173	John 15:2
Purified	144 169	Hebrews 9:23 I Peter 1:22
Purifying	27	Hebrews 9:13
Purpose	21 27 42	II Timothy 3:10 Ephesians 1:9 II Timothy 1:9

Q

Quarrel	61	Colossians 3:13

R

Rage	216	Acts 4:25
Reap	218	Galatians 6:9
Rebel	272	Isaiah 1:20
Reconcile	31 81 85	II Corinthians 5:18 Colossians 1:20 Romans 5:10
Redeem	24	Galatians 4:5

Index

Redemption	76	Hebrews 9:12
	193	Romans 3:24
Refuse	272	Isaiah 1:20
Regenerating	126	John 16:10
Regeneration	114	Titus 3:5
Reign	40	Jeremiah 23:5
	83	Romans 5:21
	84	Romans 6:12
Rejoice	60	Philippians 4:4
Remembrance	165	John 14:26
	176	Acts 10:31
Remission	15	Romans 3:25
Renewed	102	Ephesians 4:23
	103	II Corinthians 4:16
Repent	14	Acts 17:30
	117	Acts 2:38
Repentance	52	Acts 11:18
	52	II Peter 3:9
	99	Acts 20:21
	194	II Corinthians 7:10
Rest	62	Hebrews 3:18
	62	Hebrews 4:1
	63	Hebrews 4:9
Restore	195	Psalm 51:12
Restoreth	75	Psalm 23:3

Restraining	116	John 16:11
Resurrection	160	Romans 6:5
Revealed	71	I Corinthians 2:10
Revelation	186	Ephesians 1:17
Reward	240	II John 8
Righteousness	40	Jeremiah 23:6
	133	Matthew 3:15
	133	Isaiah 11:4
	153	Romans 10:3
	160	II Corinthians 5:21
	228	Acts 17:31
	229	Romans 3:21
	244	Romans 8:10
Robe	38	Isaiah 61:10

S

Safely	271	Proverbs 1:33
Salvation	194	II Corinthians 7:10
	233	Titus 2:11
Sanctified	86	Hebrews 2:11
	162	Romans 15:16
	221	John 17:19
Sanctification	162	II Thessalonians 2:13
Sanctify	221	John 17:17
Satan	253	Revelation 12:9
	260	II Corinthians 2:11

Index

Saved	47	Romans 5:9
Savior	185	I Timothy 4:10
Sealed	141	Ephesians 1:13
	201	Ephesians 4:30
Seed	16	Galatians 3:29
Seek	14	Acts 17:27
Self-Control	257	I Corinthians 7:5
Sensual	80	Jude 19
Shortsighted	171	II Peter 1:9
Sinned	192	II Samuel 12:13
	193	Romans 3:23
	193	Psalm 51:4
	195	I John 1:10
Slaves	24	Galatians 4:7
	274	Romans 6:17
Slothfulness	271	Proverbs 19:15
Sorrow	194	II Corinthians 7:10
Soul	10	III John 2-4
	147	Mark 14:34
	272	Psalm 103:1
Sower	251	Mark 4:3
Spirit	51	Luke 11:13
	177	Romans 8:1
	263	Romans 8:26
Stand	259	Ephesians 6:14
Steadfastness	54	II Peter 3:17

Strength	199	Psalm 73:26
	199	Psalm 37:39
Strife	51	James 3:16
	73	I Corinthians 3:3
Submit	207	James 4:7
Substance	103	Hebrews 11:1
Success	265	Joshua 1:8
Sufficient	72	II Corinthians 3:5

T

Teach	118	John 14:26
	184	I Timothy 1:3
Teaching	113	Titus 2:12
Temple	70	I Corinthians 3:16
	137	I Corinthians 6:19
Tempt	257	I Corinthians 7:5
Temptation	242	Mark 14:38
Testify	124	Acts 10:42
Tongue	229	James 3:8
Tongues	215	Acts 2:3
	222	I John 3:18
	229	James 3:5
Tormented	254	Revelation 20:10
Transformed	67	Romans 12:2

Transgressor	198	Psalm 37:38
Treasure	269	Exodus 19:5
Trial	95	I Peter 4:12
Tribulation	55	II Corinthians 1:4
Triumphing	116	Colossians 2:15
True	212	I John 5:20
Trust	182	Proverbs 22:19
	199	Psalm 37:40
Truth	10	III John 2-4
	38	Isaiah 61:8
	175	John 8:32
	177	Acts 10:34
	181	I John 1:6
	181	I John 2:4
	182	Proverbs 22:21
	221	John 17:17
	222	I John 3:18
	227	Malachi 2:6
	231	I Timothy 2:4

U

Unbelief	62	Hebrews 3:12
Unblameable	210	Colossians 1:22
Unclean	27	Hebrews 9:13
Uncleanness	34	Ephesians 4:19
	66	Romans 6:19

Undefiled	79	I Peter 1:4
Understanding	60	Philippians 4:7
	152	Psalm 119:99
	152	Psalm 119:130
	212	I John 5:20
Understood	198	Psalm 73:17
Unfruitful	155	Ephesians 5:11
Ungodly	80	Jude 18
	198	Psalm 73:12
Unity	77	Ephesians 4:13
	127	Ephesians 4:3
Unjust	122	Acts 24:15
Unrighteous	101	I Corinthians 6:9
Unrighteousness	100	Romans 1:18
Unstable	51	James 1:8
Utterance	54	I Corinthians 1:5
	188	Ephesians 6:19
	215	Acts 2:4
Unworthy	201	I Corinthians 11:27

Vain	53	James 4:5
Valley	75	Psalm 23:4

Vengeance	111	II Thessalonians 1:8
Victory	276	I John 5:4
Virgin	26	Isaiah 7:14
Vision	121	Acts 26:19
	130	Acts 16:9
Voice	85	John 5:25
	133	Matthew 3:17
	216	Acts 4:24
	222	John 10:27
	269	Exodus 19:5

W

Wait	110	Galatians 5:5
Waiting	178	Romans 8:23
Walk	178	Romans 8:4
Watch	53	I Peter 4:7
	242	Mark 14:38
Wavering	148	Hebrews 10:23
Wicked	197	Psalm 73:3
Wickedness	52	Acts 8:22
Will	148	Mark 14:36
Willing	272	Isaiah 1:19
Wisdom	50	James 1:5
	307	

	51	James 3:13
	74	Ephesians 3:10
	91	Ephesians 1:17
	141	Ephesians 1:8
Witness	146	Romans 8:16
	262	Acts 26:16
Word	24	John 1:1
	221	John 17:20
	271	John 8:51
World	154	I John 2:16
	154	I John 5:4
	235	I John 2:15
Worthy	64	I Thessalonians 2:12
	82	Colossians 1:10
	111	II Thessalonians 1:5
	242	Luke 21:36
Wrath	35	Colossians 3:6
Wretched	5	Romans 7:24

Yield	247	Romans 6:13
	251	Mark 4:8
Yieldeth	59	Hebrews 12:11
Yoke	61	Acts 15:10

Z

Zeal	23	Isaiah 9:7
	153	Romans 10:2
Zealous	113	Titus 2:14

www.ingramcontent.com/pod-product-compliance
Lightning Source LLC
Chambersburg PA
CBHW060148050426
42446CB00013B/2723